2025

Abitur

Original-Prüfungsaufgaben
mit Lösungen

Hamburg

Englisch

STARK

Inhalt

Aufgaben zum Prüfungsteil Hörverstehen

Aufgaben zum Prüfungsteil Sprachmittlung

Abitur 2024 . . . . **www.stark-verlag.de/mystark**
Sobald die Original-Prüfungsaufgaben 2024 freigegeben sind, können sie als PDF auf der Plattform MySTARK heruntergeladen werden (Zugangscode vgl. Umschlaginnenseite).

MP3-Dateien

Abitur 2021: GA

Abitur 2021: EA

Abitur 2022: GA

Abitur 2022: EA

Abitur 2023: GA

Abitur 2023: EA

Abitur 2024: GA

Abitur 2024: EA

Auch auf die Audio-Dateien können Sie über die Plattform MySTARK zugreifen.

Autorinnen und Autoren

Hinweise und Tipps zum Zentralabitur Hamburg: R. Neumeier
Basiswissen: R. Jacob
Übungsaufgaben mit Videoanleitung: Redaktion
Lösungen der Original-Prüfungsaufgaben:
S. Redmer (GA 2015: Textaufgabe),
R. Jacob (EA 2016: Textaufgabe, GA 2021 und EA 2021: Sprachmittlung und
Textaufgaben),
Redaktion (GA und EA 2021: Hörverstehen, GA 2023: Hörverstehen),
C. Rieske (GA 2022: Sprachmittlung, Hörverstehen),
D. Just (EA 2022 und 2023: Hörverstehen),
R. Klimmt (EA 2022 und 2023: Sprachmittlung),
K. Nussdorf (GA 2023: Sprachmittlung)

Vorwort

Liebe Schülerinnen, liebe Schüler,

bald werden Sie Ihre zentrale Abiturprüfung im Fach Englisch ablegen. Wir begleiten Sie auf Ihrem Weg zu einem guten Abschluss und helfen Ihnen, sich mit den Anforderungen des zentralen Abiturs in Hamburg vertraut zu machen.

Sie sollten nicht nur die Rahmenbedingungen und Hauptschwierigkeiten der Abiturprüfung in Hamburg kennen, sondern auch lernen, wie Sie die Aufgaben am geschicktesten und zeitsparendsten angehen, wobei Ihnen das Kapitel mit **Hinweisen und Tipps** helfen kann. Der Band umfasst zudem ein **Basiswissen** zu den Themen *Politics, Culture and Society – between Tradition and Change: USA, Crime and Punishment in Literature and Film* und *Social Media – Boon or Bane in the 21st Century?*, das Ihnen bei der inhaltlichen Vorbereitung auf Ihre Prüfung nützlich sein wird.

Der zweite Teil des Buches enthält eine Sammlung von **Original-Abituraufgaben** bzw. eigens im Abiturformat erstellter **Übungsaufgaben**, mit denen Sie sich auf die drei in Ihrer Prüfung abgefragten Kompetenzbereiche **Schreiben**, **Hörverstehen** und **Sprachmittlung** vorbereiten können. Zu zwei der Schreibaufgaben liefern Ihnen **Lernvideos** hilfreiche **Bearbeitungstipps**, während die anderen Aufgaben mit abgedruckten **Musterlösungen** Ihre Vorbereitung unterstützen. Die Lernvideos, die aktuellen Original-Aufgaben aus dem Jahr 2024 sowie sämtliche Hörtexte stehen Ihnen **online** auf der Plattform MySTARK zur Verfügung. Diese und weitere **digitale Inhalte**, die Ihnen dieser Band bietet, werden auf den folgenden Seiten näher erläutert.

Sollten nach Erscheinen dieses Bandes noch **wichtige Änderungen** im Zentralabitur 2025 von der Hamburger Behörde für Schule und Berufsbildung bekannt gegeben werden, finden Sie aktuelle Informationen dazu ebenfalls auf der Plattform MySTARK.

Schon jetzt wünschen wir Ihnen viel Erfolg bei Ihrem Zentralabitur!

Ihr STARK Verlag

Hinweise zu den digitalen Inhalten

Auf alle digitalen Inhalte können Sie online über die Plattform **MySTARK** zugreifen. Ihren persönlichen Zugangscode finden Sie auf der Umschlaginnenseite.

PDF der Original-Prüfungsaufgaben 2024

Um Ihnen die Prüfung 2024 schnellstmöglich zur Verfügung stellen zu können, bringen wir sie in digitaler Form heraus.
Sobald die Original-Prüfungsaufgaben 2024 freigegeben sind, können sie als PDF auf der Plattform MySTARK heruntergeladen werden.

Kurzgrammatik

Mit der Kurzgrammatik können Sie sich eine knappe und verständliche Übersicht über die wichtigsten Themenfelder der englischen Grammatik herunterladen. Schlagen Sie hier die Grammatikregeln zu Fehlern nach, die Sie noch häufig machen.

Lernvideos

Textaufgaben sind Teil vieler Prüfungen und Klausuren – und machen oft einen Großteil der Prüfungsleistung aus. Mithilfe der **Lernvideos zum richtigen Umgang mit Textaufgaben** können Sie sich optimal auf die Anforderungen in diesem Bereich vorbereiten. Am Beispiel von zwei Texten mit je drei Aufgabenstellungen wird gezeigt, wie man an eine Textaufgabe herangeht und sie erfolgreich löst.

Die Lernvideos beinhalten:

- **Schritt-für-Schritt-Anleitungen** zum richtigen Vorgehen in der Prüfung
- **Sachtext** und **literarischer Text** als Grundlage
- nützliche Hinweise zu **häufigen Operatoren** und **Zieltextsorten**

Die in den Videos behandelten Texte und Aufgaben sind im Kapitel „**Aufgaben zum Prüfungsteil Schreiben**" (S. 1 bis 5) abgedruckt. Hier können Sie sich schon einmal einen Eindruck verschaffen, worum es in den Videos geht.

MP3-Dateien

Über die Plattform MySTARK können Sie sich außerdem die Hörverste-henstexte der Abiturprüfungen 2021 bis 2024 anhören.

Interaktives Training

Im **Online-Training "Basic Language Skills"** erhalten Sie Zugriff auf zahlreiche **interaktive Aufgaben** zu Grundlagen wie **Hörverstehen, Lese-verstehen** und **Sprachverwendung im Kontext**. Dies sind ganz wichtige "Basics", die Sie für eine gute Sprachbeherrschung brauchen.

Das interaktive Training bietet Ihnen:

- **"Listening"** – authentische Audiodateien mit vielfältigen Aufgaben, die Ihr Hör-verstehen testen
- **"Reading"** – abwechslungsreiche Lesetexte und dazugehörige Aufgaben
- **"English in Use"** mit gemischten Aufgaben rund um den Gebrauch der englischen Sprache
- Alle Aufgaben können Sie direkt am PC oder Tablet bearbeiten und erhalten so-fort eine Rückmeldung zu Ihren Antworten.

Web-App "MindCards"

Mit der Web-App **"MindCards"** können Sie am Smartphone Vokabeln lernen. Auf diesen interaktiven Karteikarten finden Sie hilfreiche Wendun-gen, die Sie beim Schreiben von Texten oder im mündlichen Sprach-gebrauch einsetzen können.
Scannen Sie einfach die QR-Codes oder verwenden Sie folgende Links, um zu den "MindCards" zu gelangen:
https://www.stark-verlag.de/mindcards/writing-2
https://www.stark-verlag.de/mindcards/speaking-2

Writing

Speaking

Hinweise und Tipps zum Zentralabitur Englisch in Hamburg

Allgemeiner Aufbau der Abiturprüfung

Die schriftliche Abiturprüfung besteht sowohl im grundlegenden als auch im erhöhten Anforderungsniveau aus drei Teilen. Sie setzt sich zusammen aus dem **Hörverstehensteil**, der **Sprachmittlung** und der **Schreibaufgabe**, auf deren Bearbeitung der Schwerpunkt der Abituraufgabe liegt. Das Hörverstehen dauert 30 Minuten, für die Sprachmittlungsaufgabe werden 60 Minuten veranschlagt. Es besteht keine Wahlmöglichkeit. Beide Prüfungsteile werden nach Ablauf der Bearbeitungszeit eingesammelt, bevor der Prüfungsteil „Schreiben" beginnt. Erst dann erhalten Sie die beiden Textaufgabenvorschläge, von denen einer auszuwählen ist. Für die Bearbeitung der Schreibaufgabe haben Sie 225 Minuten Zeit (auf erhöhtem Anforderungsniveau) bzw. 195 Minuten (auf grundlegendem Anforderungsniveau). Eine Lese- und Auswahlzeit ist in diesem Zeitrahmen inbegriffen. Oft basiert ein Vorschlag auf einem **literarischen Text**, der andere auf einem **nicht-fiktionalen Text**. Als **Hilfsmittel** werden Ihnen sowohl ein einsprachiges als auch ein zweisprachiges Wörterbuch sowie ein Wörterbuch der deutschen Rechtschreibung für alle Prüfungsteile zur Verfügung gestellt.

Die einzelnen Prüfungsteile

Hörverstehen

Es ist sehr wahrscheinlich, dass das **Hörverstehen** aus mehreren Teilen besteht. Textgrundlage für diesen Aufgabentyp können Radiobeiträge, Reden, Interviews, Ausschnitte aus Diskussionen oder Gesprächen etc. sein. Die Hörtexte sind maximal fünf Minuten lang. Die gesamte Bearbeitungszeit beträgt 30 Minuten. In diesem Kompetenzbereich können **geschlossene** bzw. **halboffene Aufgabenformate** vorkommen, z. B. *multiple choice,* Zuordnung *(multiple matching), short answer questions, table completion, sentence completion.* Dabei steht das reine Hörverstehen im Vordergrund, deshalb werden Sie – wenn überhaupt – nur kurze Phrasen oder Sätze schreiben müssen. Sprachliche Fehler werden nur dann gewertet, wenn sie das Verständnis beeinträchtigen.

I

Konkretes Vorgehen beim Hörverstehen

Sie werden jeden Hörtext zweimal hören. Nutzen Sie die Zeit vor dem ersten Durchgang, um sich mit den Aufgaben auseinanderzusetzen, und verschaffen Sie sich einen Eindruck von dem Kontext, in den sie eingebettet sind. Dann wird die Audiodatei **ein erstes Mal** vorgespielt. Versuchen Sie, sofort alle Lösungen festzuhalten, von deren Richtigkeit Sie überzeugt sind. Halten Sie sich nicht lange mit einer Aufgabe auf, sondern gehen Sie direkt zur nächsten über, auch wenn Sie sich nicht sicher sind, damit Sie nicht die nächste Antwort verpassen. In der Regel sind die Aufgaben in der Reihenfolge angeordnet, in der auch die Lösungen vorkommen. Nach dem ersten Durchlauf gibt es eine kurze Pause, während der Sie Ihre Aufzeichnungen weiter ergänzen können; dann hören Sie den Text **ein zweites Mal**. Nach dem zweiten Hören haben Sie wieder Zeit, um Ihre Lösungen zu vervollständigen und zu überprüfen.

Hier ein paar praktische Tipps:

- Achten Sie auf Schlüsselwörter *(key words)* oder Formulierungen, die Teile der Aufgabenstellung in anderen Worten wieder aufgreifen (z. B. „global warming" statt „climate change"), so finden Sie schneller relevante Stellen im Hörtext.
- Markieren Sie sich Lücken, die Sie im ersten Durchgang nicht füllen konnten, mit Bleistift, damit Sie dort beim zweiten Durchgang ganz genau hinhören.

Damit Sie sich optimal auf die Prüfungssituation einstellen können, finden Sie im Online-Angebot zu diesem Buch (auf MySTARK) MP3-Dateien zu den vergangenen Abiturjahrgängen: Sie beinhalten jeweils mehrere Hörtexte, die Sie zweimal hören werden, inklusive Ansagen und Pausen.

Sprachmittlung

Die Sprachmittlung basiert auf einem oder mehreren deutschen Ausgangstext(en), aus denen von Ihnen **die wichtigsten Informationen** vom Deutschen **ins Englische übertragen** werden sollen. Ziel ist es, einer bisher uninformierten Leserschaft die wesentlichen Inhalte eines längeren Textes nahezubringen. Hier sehen Sie zwei Beispiele für mögliche Aufgabenstellungen: „Verfassen Sie auf der Basis des *Zeit*-Artikels über die Todesstrafe eine E-Mail an den Gouverneur von Texas, in der Sie sich für die Abschaffung der Todesstrafe aussprechen" oder „Schreiben Sie einen Artikel für die Schülerzeitung Ihrer englischen Partnerschule, der sich mit der Situation von Migrantinnen und Migranten auseinandersetzt, deren Familien nun schon in der zweiten Generation in Deutschland leben". Üben Sie das Abfassen einer Sprachmittlung anhand von Artikeln aus deutschen Zeitschriften, die Sie für (imaginäre) englischsprachige Bekannte ins Englische übertragen.

Obwohl bisher die Textsorte des Artikels bzw. der E-Mail in den Aufgabenstellungen dominierte, bietet es sich an, auch die typischen Merkmale anderer **Textsorten** zu wiederholen. Gebräuchlich sind *blog entry, comment, formal letter, letter to the editor, personal letter, report, review, speech* und *summary.*

Konkretes Vorgehen bei der Sprachmittlung

Gehen Sie wie folgt an die Aufgabenstellung heran:

- Bestimmen Sie zuerst die zentrale Aussage des Textes.
- Formulieren Sie einen *umbrella sentence*, der diese Kernaussage enthält sowie ggf. Informationen zu Autor*in, Titel, Quelle und situativem Rahmen des Textes.
- Sie haben durch die Aufgabenstellung einen konkreten Schreibanlass genannt bekommen. Beachten Sie diesen Kontext, insbesondere den Adressaten bzw. die Adressatin und die Umstände, unter denen der Zieltext verfasst werden soll (z. B. keine Umgangssprache in einer E-Mail an den Gouverneur von Texas).
- Wählen Sie nun Informationen aus dem Ausgangstext, die für die Bearbeitung der Aufgabenstellung wesentlich sind.
- Verwenden Sie Konnektoren, um logische und zeitliche Bezüge herzustellen.
- Umschreiben Sie Ausdrücke, die nicht übersetzt werden können, in Ihren eigenen Worten, wenn deren Verständnis wesentlich für die Aufgabenstellung ist. Erklären Sie kulturspezifische Begriffe, die Ihre Zielgruppe sonst nicht verstehen würde (z. B. „ARD" = *German broadcasting corporation, similar to BBC*).
- Denken Sie daran, dass Ihre *mediation* nur etwa ein Drittel des Ausgangstextes umfassen sollte.

Beachten Sie, dass sowohl Inhalt als auch Sprache bewertet werden.

Folgende Kriterien sind ausschlaggebend für die Benotung:

- Beachtung der Aufgabenstellung (Nennen der wesentlichen Aspekte)
- Adressaten- und Situationsbezug
- Inhaltliche und sprachliche Korrektheit

Schreibaufgabe

Ob erhöhtes oder grundlegendes Niveau, Sie werden im Abitur in jedem Fall mit einer **Schreibaufgabe** konfrontiert sein. Im Mittelpunkt der Bearbeitung steht ein authentischer englischsprachiger Text zu einem der Schwerpunktthemen. Sie müssen das **Verständnis des Textinhalts** nachweisen *(Comprehension)* und den **Text analysieren** – im Hinblick auf die Argumentation des Autors/der Autorin, Gestaltungsmerkmale des Textes oder Ähnliches *(Analysis)*. Im letzten Teil haben Sie die Wahl, entweder wesentliche Aspekte oder Thesen des Textes **persönlich zu bewerten** *(Comment)* oder in einer kreativen Schreibaufgabe **in eine neue Textsorte zu übertragen** *(Creative Writing)*. Lassen Sie hier Ihr Hintergrundwissen (z. B. zum Thema *Politics, Culture and Society – between Tradition and Change: USA*) einfließen. Es ist generell möglich, dass in die Schreibaufgabe auch Bildmaterial in Form von Fotos, Cartoons oder Diagrammen integriert ist.

Sie werden **zwei Vorschläge** zur Schreibaufgabe bekommen, die sich auf je eines der beiden Schwerpunktthemen beziehen. Entscheiden Sie sich zügig für eine der beiden Aufgaben. Wenn Sie sich entschieden haben, vergessen Sie die andere Aufgabe und wenden Sie sich Ihrem Thema zu.

Nun beginnt die eigentliche Arbeitszeit. Machen Sie zuerst eine **grobe Zeitplanung**. Rechnen Sie am Ende etwa eine halbe Stunde für das **Korrekturlesen** Ihrer Arbeit ein. Verweilen Sie nicht zu lange bei der ersten Teilaufgabe. Oft verlangen die analytischen und Transferaufgaben mehr Arbeit im Detail.

Lesen Sie den Text zunächst gründlich. Schlagen Sie in den relevanten Textpassagen alle Ihnen **unbekannten Wörter** nach, damit Sie nicht einen für die Aufgabe wichtigen Begriff übersehen. In weniger wichtigen Passagen können Sie unbekannte Wörter oft aus dem Zusammenhang erschließen. Bei der Produktion Ihres eigenen Textes sollten Sie sich zunächst auf den für die Prüfung gelernten Wortschatz verlassen und nicht zu häufig im Wörterbuch nachschlagen; das braucht viel Zeit und unterbricht ständig Ihren Gedankengang. Markieren Sie Wörter oder Kollokationen, bei denen Sie sich nicht sicher sind, mit Bleistift und überprüfen Sie sie beim Korrekturlesen.

Gehen Sie systematisch vor, damit Ihr Text eine **klare Struktur** erhält. Achten Sie **genau auf die Aufgabenstellung** und verwenden Sie nur das, was tatsächlich für die Bearbeitung des Arbeitsauftrags gebraucht wird. Zu viele Informationen, die mit der Fragestellung nichts zu tun haben, können nämlich auch zu Punktabzug führen.

In der längerfristigen Vorbereitung auf das Abitur sollten Sie sich vor allem auf die Entwicklung Ihrer **textanalytischen und produktiven Fertigkeiten** konzentrieren, denn diese können und müssen Sie in der Prüfung mit Sicherheit einsetzen – schließlich macht die **sprachliche Seite** 60 % der Gesamtbewertung der Textaufgabe aus.

Bearbeitung der einzelnen Aufgabenbereiche der Schreibaufgabe

In der ersten Aufgabe müssen Sie immer den Inhalt oder wesentliche Aspekte des Inhalts zusammenfassen. Sie müssen hier also die Textsorte *summary* beherrschen, die ganz bestimmte Merkmale hat: Ihr Text ist deutlich kürzer als der Ausgangstext, beschränkt sich auf das Wesentliche und enthält Abstraktionen, die Details zusammenfassen. Er ist im Präsens *(simple present)* abgefasst und enthält weder wörtliche Rede noch Zitate aus dem Ausgangstext. Er enthält außerdem keine eigenen Wertungen.

Die vorherrschende Textsorte im zweiten Teil ist der **analytische Essay**. Wichtig ist hier, dass Sie sich klarmachen, was genau Sie analysieren sollen. Lesen Sie den Text immer mindestens einmal und markieren Sie farblich, welche Textstellen für die Bearbeitung der Aufgabe relevant sind.

Notieren Sie sich anschließend die Punkte, die Sie erwähnen wollen, in Stichworten und ordnen Sie sie in der Reihenfolge, in der sie später in Ihrem Text vorkommen sollen. Oft gibt die Formulierung der Aufgabe Ihnen bereits eine Struktur vor.

Streben Sie eine klare, transparente Darstellung an. Die erreichen Sie z. B. dadurch, dass Sie mit einer allgemeinen Aussage beginnen, die Sie dann in mehreren Absätzen erläutern. Jeder Absatz sollte dabei einen Gedanken, eine Idee im Mittelpunkt haben. Verknüpfen Sie zudem Ihre Sätze und Absätze nachvollziehbar miteinander. Benutzen Sie aber nicht nur die gängigen Wörter *but* und *because*, sondern stellen Sie bewusst präzise Zusammenhänge her, um es Ihrer Leserschaft zu erleichtern, Ihren Gedankengang bzw. Ihre Argumentation nachzuvollziehen.

Eine Auswahl hilfreicher Wendungen finden Sie in der folgenden Tabelle sowie auf den digitalen „MindCards" (vgl. „Hinweise zu den digitalen Inhalten"):

Function	Connectives	Examples
to list/add points, arguments, aspects, pieces of evidence	• firstly, secondly, finally • on top of that • too, also • additionally, in addition • similarly, in the same way, likewise • furthermore, moreover	**Firstly,** she's bright; **secondly,** she's beautiful; and **on top of that** she's rich. He is too weak to do physical labour; **in addition,** his memory is failing him. His comedies still appeal to modern audiences. **In the same way,** his tragedies are still incredibly moving.
to illustrate points made	• such as • for example, for instance, e. g.	Cities (**such as** Mexico City) have grown globally, (**for instance/for example/e. g.** Mexico City).
to summarise your findings, a longer argument, etc.	• to conclude, in short, in conclusion • to sum up, to summarise • in other words	**To conclude,/In conclusion,/In short,** Shakespeare is still relevant to modern audiences.
to indicate a direct result	• therefore, thus, that is why • consequently, as a result	He went out dancing every night; **therefore,/consequently,/as a result,** he failed his English class.
to contrast two elements of your text	• but, however, yet • on the one hand/on the other hand • on the contrary • unlike, in contrast to, contrary to • despite, in spite of	This is quite a run-down hotel; **yet,** it is located in a beautiful place. Shakespeare has not been forgotten. **On the contrary,** he is still popular all over the world. **Unlike/in contrast to/contrary to** Scotland, England is quite densely populated. **Despite/In spite of** some progress, Black people have not yet achieved equality.
to concede *(zugestehen)* something	• even though • it is true that (…), but	**Even though (It is true that)** France has a lot to offer, **(but)** I prefer Italy for my summer holidays.
to state something that is clear or likely to be true	• evidently, apparently, obviously • doubtless, undoubtedly	**Evidently,/Apparently,/Obviously,** the painters have finished and gone home for the day. **Doubtless,/Undoubtedly,** there's a lot of work left for them to do tomorrow.

Schließen Sie Ihren analytischen Essay mit einer zusammenfassenden Bemerkung ab, sodass am Schluss klar wird, zu welchem Ergebnis Sie gelangt sind. Üben Sie diese Art der Textstruktur intensiv in der Vorbereitung und bitten Sie Ihren Lehrer oder Ihre Lehrerin um Rückmeldung zu Ihren Texten. So stehen Ihnen eigene Modelltexte als Orientierung für die Abitur-Klausur zur Verfügung.

Dies gilt ebenso für die beiden Textsorten, die im dritten Teil der Schreibaufgabe gefordert sind. Dies ist einmal der Kommentar mit einer relativ klaren Struktur, zum anderen die kreative Aufgabe, die viele verschiedene Textsorten ansteuern kann.

Im *comment* geht es darum, persönlich Stellung zu nehmen. Machen Sie sich vor Beginn des Kommentierens klar, welche Position Sie zu der aufgeworfenen Problematik einnehmen wollen. Sammeln Sie Argumente, die Ihre Meinung stützen; denken Sie auch an mögliche Gegenargumente, die Sie im Verlauf Ihres Kommentars entkräften wollen. Gehen Sie von Gedanken aus, die im Ausgangstext geäußert werden, beschränken Sie sich aber nicht darauf. Hier können Sie häufig viele gelernte Inhalte einbringen, natürlich immer bezogen auf die Aufgabe. Nehmen Sie klar Stellung und ändern Sie nicht im Laufe des Schreibens Ihre Meinung.

In der **kreativen Aufgabe** sollen Sie sich oft in eine Person hineinversetzen und aus deren Sicht schreiben. Nehmen Sie alle Hinweise, die der Ausgangstext bietet, auf und verarbeiten Sie sie in Ihrem kreativen Text (z. B. Hinweise auf die Persönlichkeit dieses Menschen, seinen sozialen Hintergrund, seine Meinung zu bestimmten Fragen). Vielleicht enthält der Text Andeutungen dazu, wie die Person spricht. Auf jeden Fall müssen Sie darauf achten, auf welcher Sprachebene Ihr Text laut Aufgabenstellung angesiedelt sein soll (eher formell wie in einem *letter to the editor* oder informell wie in einer E-Mail an einen Freund/eine Freundin; eher an gesprochener Sprache orientiert wie in einem mündlichen Dialog oder in einem auffordernden Modus wie in einem Werbetext). Hier können Sie zeigen, wie gut Sie sich auf verschiedenen Sprachebenen ausdrücken können.

Für die drei verschiedenen Anforderungsbereiche *(Comprehension, Analysis, Comment/Creative Writing)* gibt es typische Formulierungen der Aufgabenstellung (Operatoren), die im Folgenden erläutert werden:

Operator	Erklärung	Beispiel
Anforderungsbereich I		
outline (skizzieren, umreißen, kurz darstellen)	Dieser Operator verlangt, dass Sie die Hauptgedanken, die Struktur oder allgemeine Prinzipien eines Textes wiedergeben. Details sollen dabei weggelassen werden.	*Outline the author's views on equality.*
point out, state (angeben, knapp darlegen)	Hier sollen Sie bestimmte Textaspekte knapp und klar darlegen.	*Point out why the Black perspective is so important to the author.* *State briefly the major developments apparent in the first chapter.*

summarise, sum up (den Inhalt zusammenfassen)	Sie sind aufgefordert, die wichtigsten Punkte knapp wiederzugeben – den Konventionen einer *summary* entsprechend.	*Summarise the information given in the text about racial profiling in the USA.*

Anforderungsbereich I und II

describe (beschreiben)	Hier sollen Sie etwas detailliert darstellen. Die Komplexität des Darzustellenden lässt die Aufgabe dem Anforderungsbereich I oder II angehören.	*I: Describe the protagonist's outward appearance.* *II: Describe the way the author creates tension.*

Anforderungsbereich II

analyse, examine (analysieren, eingehend untersuchen)	Hier werden Sie aufgefordert, bestimmte Aspekte oder Merkmale des Textes detailliert zu beschreiben, d. h. ihre Funktion, Wirkung etc. zu erklären.	*Analyse the way the author tries to win his readers over to his position.* *Examine the playwright's use of language.*
explain (erklären)	Aspekte aus dem Text sollen u. a. mithilfe von Begründungen und Beispielen verständlich gemacht werden.	*Explain the protagonist's obsession with money.*
illustrate (erläutern, veranschaulichen)	Etwas soll anhand von Beispielen erläutert werden.	*Illustrate the poet's use of imagery.*
give/write a characterisation of	Dieser Operator fordert Sie auf, eine stichhaltige Charakterisierung einer Figur zu schreiben.	*Give a characterisation of the protagonist in the excerpt at hand.*

Anforderungsbereich II und III

compare (vergleichen)	Hier sind Sie aufgefordert, Gemeinsamkeiten und Unterschiede zwischen zwei oder mehreren Dingen herauszuarbeiten und gegenüberzustellen.	*Compare the authors' views on the question whether capital punishment should be abolished.*
interpret (interpretieren, deuten)	Hier sollen Sie die Bedeutung (von Aspekten) eines Textes herausarbeiten und ggf. Ihre Position dazu beschreiben.	*Interpret the message the author wishes to convey.*

Anforderungsbereich III

assess (abschätzen, beurteilen, bewerten)	Dieser Operator verlangt die ausgewogene Betrachtung und Einschätzung eines Sachverhalts, eines Problems oder einer These.	*Assess the relevance of discipline in today's schools.*
comment (kommentieren, Stellung nehmen)	In diesem Fall sollen Sie Ihre eigene Meinung zu einem Thema formulieren und diese sorgfältig begründen.	*Comment on the protagonist's behaviour in the first chapter of the book.*

discuss (diskutieren, erörtern)	Hier sollen Sie im Sinne einer Pro-/Kontra-Diskussion die Gründe für und gegen eine These oder verschiedene Aspekte einer Problematik gegenüberstellen und persönlich gewichten.	*Discuss ways of dealing with youth crime.*
evaluate (auswerten, beurteilen)	Bei dieser Aufgabe müssen Sie einen Sachverhalt beurteilen (vgl. *assess*).	*Evaluate the effectiveness of the measures against the massive income inequality.*

Mithilfe der Lernvideos zu diesem Band (Zugang über MySTARK, vgl. Umschlaginnenseite) können Sie das optimale Vorgehen in einer Schreibaufgabe Schritt für Schritt nachvollziehen. Sie erfahren darin, worauf Sie unbedingt achten sollten, wenn Sie eine Aufgabe bearbeiten, und bekommen einen Einblick, was von Ihnen erwartet wird. Nicht nur auf die Schreibaufgabe, auch auf die anderen in Ihrer Prüfung geforderten Kompetenzen können Sie sich außerdem mit dem Band *Abitur-Training Englisch* (Best.-Nr. 94460D) gut vorbereiten.

Inhaltliche Vorbereitung

Die Beschreibung der Schwerpunktthemen durch die Behörde für Schule und Berufsbildung enthält recht detaillierte Angaben dazu, was von Ihnen inhaltlich im Abitur erwartet wird. Gemeinhin werden (z. B. geografische, soziologische, historische) Grundkenntnisse zu der vorliegenden Thematik verlangt. Dieses Wissen soll Ihnen ermöglichen, den Abiturtext in größere Zusammenhänge einzuordnen, was für Analyse und Kommentierung wichtig ist.

Ein **Basiswissen** in englischer Sprache zur Vorbereitung auf die Schwerpunktthemen *Politics, Culture and Society – between Tradition and Change: USA, Crime and Punishment in Literature and Film* bzw. *Social Media – Boon or Bane in the 21st Century?* finden Sie in diesem Band. Darüber hinaus bietet sich für die inhaltliche Vorbereitung unser *AbiturSkript Englisch* (Best.-Nr. 10546S2) an. In diesem werden die wichtigsten Themen des Oberstufenlehrplans kurz und prägnant zusammengefasst. Bitte beachten Sie, dass die Inhalte der **Hörverstehenstexte** und der **Sprachmittlung** auch im Abitur meistens nicht auf die Hamburger Schwerpunktsetzung abgestimmt sind.

Schwerpunktthemen für das Zentralabitur 2025

Thema I (allgemeinbildende/berufliche Gymnasien): *Politics, Culture and Society – between Tradition and Change: USA*
Als wirtschaftliche, politische und militärische Weltmacht üben die Vereinigten Staaten von Amerika großen globalen Einfluss aus. Parallel dazu wächst auch die kulturelle Anziehungskraft des Landes. Ideale wie der *American Dream* und Grundwerte, wie sie in der *Declaration of Independence* formuliert sind, tragen viel zum Selbst-

verständnis sowie zur Fremdwahrnehmung der USA bei. Dennoch werden auch kritische Stimmen lauter: Nicht nur außenpolitisch wird das Land mit seiner *manifest destiny*, seinem bisweilen explizit erklärten Ziel, Demokratie und Freiheit, gleichzeitig aber auch Kapitalismus und Marktwirtschaft, weiterzuverbreiten, oftmals als imperialistisch eingeschätzt. Gerade auch innenpolitisch ist die vielbeschworene *equality* der äußerst diversen Bevölkerungsgruppen eher Mythos als Realität. Politische Spannungen zeugen von dieser Position zwischen Ideal und Wirklichkeit. Mithilfe von historischen Betrachtungen, aber auch unter Einbeziehung aktueller Ereignisse soll ein differenziertes Bild des *global player* USA entstehen.

Folgende Bereiche sind sowohl im GA als auch im EA relevant:
- Von der Vergangenheit bis heute: Amerikanische Ideale und ihre Verwirklichung
  – *freedom, equality and the pursuit of happiness*
- Aktuelle Themen und Ereignisse: Identitätsfragen, politische, kulturelle und soziale Entwicklungen

Thema II (allgemeinbildende Gymnasien): *Crime and Punishment in Literature and Film*

„Crime sells" – das gilt nicht nur für das sogenannte *„Golden Age of Crime Fiction"*, als bekannte Größen des Kriminalromans wie Agatha Christie ihre Bücher schrieben. Auch heute noch bestimmt das Thema Verbrechen viele beliebte Erzeugnisse in Literatur, Film und Fernsehen. Im digitalen Zeitalter gibt es darüber hinaus neue Erscheinungen wie True-Crime-Podcasts oder Internetforen für die gemeinsame Detektivarbeit.

Im Unterricht sollen diese medialen Darstellungsformen von Verbrechen nicht nur eingehend untersucht werden, sondern sie sollen auch als Aufhänger dienen für weiterführende Diskussionen zu den Themen Moral, Recht und Gerechtigkeit. Dabei spielen sowohl der sozial-gesellschaftliche Kontext von Verbrechen und Verbrechensbekämpfung als auch deren individuelle, psychologische Auswirkungen eine wichtige Rolle.

Folgende Fragestellungen sind sowohl im GA als auch im EA relevant:
- Täter*innen und Opfer: Veranlagung oder Umwelt – was bringt Menschen dazu, Verbrechen zu begehen?, Mit welchen Folgen haben Verbrechensopfer zu kämpfen?
- Wie definieren verschiedene (anglophone) Gesellschaften Verbrechen und welcher Umgang mit Verbrechen und Bestrafung herrscht in diesen Gesellschaften vor?
- Welche unterschiedlichen Herangehensweisen an „gerechte" Strafen gibt es? Nulltoleranzstrategien und *Stand your ground laws* vs. Rehabilitation, Täter-Opfer-Ausgleich, *Truth and Reconciliation Commission* o. Ä.
- Gibt es Situationen, in denen Verbrechen gerechtfertigt sind?
- Was macht die ungebrochene Faszination von Verbrechen aus?

Sowohl im GA als auch im EA soll die Beschäftigung mit Sachtexten sowie fiktionalen Texten bei der Beantwortung dieser und ähnlicher Fragen helfen. Auf dem **erhöhten Anforderungsniveau** kommt literarischen Texten eine besondere Bedeutung zu. Hier wird mindestens eine Langschrift gelesen und ein Film vertiefend behandelt.

Dabei soll auch der Umgang mit Grundbegriffen der Literaturanalyse wie *narrative perspective, atmosphere, setting, stylistic devices*, etc. eingeübt werden.

Thema II (berufliche Gymnasien): *Social Media – Boon or Bane in the 21st Century?*
Die flächendeckende Internetnutzung und speziell der Dauergebrauch sozialer Medien wird trotz vieler begrüßenswerter Entwicklungen auch immer öfter Gegenstand kritischer Diskussionen. Dabei geht es vor allem um Gefahren im gesellschaftlich-politischen Bereich, wie eine drohende Spaltung der Gesellschaft, aber auch um die mit z. T. fragwürdigen Mitteln erreichte Wirtschaftsmacht von Medienkonzernen. Eine kritischere Nutzung sozialer Netzwerke ist ein Ziel des Unterrichts.
Folgende Bereiche sind relevant (EA und GA):
– Grundwissen zu sozialen Netzwerken und ihrer utopischen sowie dystopischen Aspekte
– politische Folgen und Gefahren sozialer Netzwerke (Algorithmen, Verschwörungstheorien, Polarisierung der Gesellschaft, Wahlmanipulationen etc.)
– das fragwürdige Wirtschaftsmodell der sozialen Netzwerke (*"If you are not paying for the product, you are the product."*)
– Konsequenzen von übermäßigem Medienkonsum auf die körperliche und mentale Gesundheit
– Lösungsvorschläge für bessere Regulierung und Schutzmechanismen
Auf **erhöhtem Anforderungsniveau** sollen mindestens eine literarische Langschrift oder ein Sachbuch und ein Film zum Schwerpunktthema behandelt werden.

Sprachliche Vorbereitung

Wortschatz

Sowohl für das **Hörverstehen** als auch für die **Sprachmittlung** ist ein großer Wortschatz in der Fremdsprache die zentrale Voraussetzung für ein gutes Abschneiden. Ob Sie Ihr Sprachvermögen am liebsten mit englischsprachigen Filmen, (Hör-)Büchern, Zeitschriften oder Songtexten trainieren, bleibt Ihnen überlassen, wobei Filme, Hörbücher und Podcasts natürlich den Vorteil haben, dass Sie hier neben allgemeiner Wortschatzarbeit auch gleich das Hör(seh)verstehen konkret trainieren können. Als Vorbereitung auf die Sprachmittlung können Sie beispielsweise auch Informationen über Sachverhalte bzw. bestimmte Charaktere deutscher Filme und Romane oder deren Entwicklung im Laufe der Handlung auf Englisch zusammenfassen. Wenn Sie Themen auswählen, die Sie auch privat interessieren, steigert das Ihre Motivation und das Lernen kann richtig Spaß machen.

Damit Sie sich möglichst differenziert und komplex zu den Inhalten der **Schreibaufgabe** äußern können, benötigen Sie einen sowohl themenbezogenen als auch analytischen Wortschatz (z. B. *evidence, description, portray, suggest, consequently*). In beiden Bereichen sollten Sie auf jeden Fall den im Unterricht erarbeiteten Wortschatz lernen und üben. Falls nicht bereits geschehen, sollten Sie sich Listen zu bestimmten Funktionen anlegen (z. B. Textbezug: *refer to, imply, ll. 6–8*; Konnektoren: *as a re-*

sult, therefore, finally; Charakterisierung: *shy, assertive, modest, boastful, ...*). Nutzen Sie Texte, die Sie im Unterricht lesen, als Fundus, aus dem Sie sich gezielt bedienen. Eine detaillierte Analyse sprachlicher Gestaltungsmittel wird nur für das erhöhte Niveau erwartet.

Beim Wortschatz-Lernen ist es zur Vermeidung von Fehlern sehr zu empfehlen, dass Sie Wörter in Kollokationen lernen (im Zusammenhang mit anderen Wörtern, mit denen sie einen festen idiomatischen Verband bilden). Statt nur zu lernen „*play* = Theaterstück", lernen Sie „*to perform a play* = ein Theaterstück aufführen"; oder statt „*talk* = Vortrag", lernen Sie „*to give a talk* = einen Vortrag halten". Solche Ausdrücke lassen sich hervorragend in eigene Texte einsetzen, sie erhöhen die Präzision Ihrer Aussagen und helfen Ihnen zu vermeiden, dass Ihr Text deutsch klingt.

Zur Erweiterung und Vertiefung Ihres thematischen Wortschatzes können Sie z. B. mit dem Band *Abitur-Training Englisch: Themenwortschatz* (STARK Verlag, Best.-Nr. 82457D) arbeiten. Insbesondere zum Training Ihres analytischen Wortschatzes bietet sich auch der Einsatz der digitalen MindCards (vgl. „Hinweise zu den digitalen Inhalten") an.

Grammatik

Zwar gibt es keinen separat bewerteten „Fehlerindex", aber die Sicherheit, mit der Sie formulieren, ist dennoch ein wesentlicher Aspekt bei der Ermittlung Ihrer sprachlichen Note für die Abiturklausur. Um herauszufinden, in welchen Bereichen der englischen Sprache Sie noch Schwierigkeiten haben, empfiehlt es sich, dass Sie Ihre von Ihrer Lehrkraft korrigierten Texte auf Fehlerschwerpunkte hin untersuchen (z. B. Verwendung von Adjektiven statt Adverbien, Verwechslung von bestimmten Zeitformen, falsche Präpositionen nach bestimmten Nomen oder Verben). Wenn Sie solche Problemfelder identifiziert haben, gehen Sie die relevanten Regeln mithilfe einer englischen Grammatik (z. B. der Kurzgrammatik im Online-Angebot auf MySTARK) noch einmal durch.

Die Erfahrung zeigt, dass es oft ganz bestimmte Strukturen sind, die vielen Schülerinnen und Schülern Schwierigkeiten machen. Dazu gehören vor allem *simple past vs. present perfect, adjectives vs. adverbs* sowie *conditional clauses*. Zur Übung dieser und weiterer grammatischer Strukturen können Sie z. B. mit dem *Abitur-Training Englisch: Grammatikübungen* (Best.-Nr. 82452D) des STARK Verlags arbeiten. Zusätzlich bietet Ihnen das interaktive Training zum vorliegenden Band (auf My-STARK) die Möglichkeit, den Bereich „English in Use" mit vielfältigen Aufgaben zu trainieren.

XI

Basiswissen zu den Schwerpunktthemen

From past to present: American ideals and realities

Even in colonial times, i. e. before the Declaration of Independence in 1776, but especially since the 19th century, the "New World" was and has been a promising destination for people from around the globe. The USA remains a **land of promise** to this day because of the economic opportunities, cultural diversity and personal freedoms and individual rights it guarantees. Millions who live in poverty, under repressive political regimes or in situations of war and unrest perceive America as their dreamland, where they can find refuge and security. Additionally, people whose livelihoods are not at stake are lured by the limitless possibilities for self-improvement the country seems to offer. Many people even take risks or resort to illegal means to escape their homelands and start afresh in North America. Today, the United States is among the largest countries in the world according to both population and size. Arguably, it is also the wealthiest and most powerful nation on earth. Because of its **economic and military power**, the USA's fascination and attraction remain unbroken.

The influence the country enjoys today is the result of a development that began in the 18th century with the passing of the **Declaration of Independence** in 1776. For the first time in history, the authors of the Declaration, among them men like Thomas Jefferson, John Adams and Benjamin Franklin, put the philosophical theories of the European **Age of Enlightenment** into practice. Based on the assumption "that **all men are created equal**", they abolished the despotic structures of the European absolute monarchies and replaced them with a **social contract** between the government and the governed. This contract stated that a government could only be legitimate if it received the consent of the governed, i. e. the people. It is the government's responsibility to secure its citizens' natural human rights, such as the "unalienable Rights [to] **Life, Liberty and the pursuit of Happiness**". If the government fails in its duties, it is people's right to rebel and choose a new government. The ideals in the Declaration of Independence represent the guiding principles for the American nation – at least in theory. However, reality often fails to meet these values.

The ideal of liberty

The United States national anthem, "The Star-Spangled Banner", ends with the lines "the star-spangled banner in triumph shall wave/O'er the land of the free and the home of the brave!" The belief in **individual freedom and personal autonomy** is a central American ideal. The **First Amendment** to the Constitution protects the freedom of religion, speech, press and assembly. Americans value the ability to pursue their goals, make choices and enjoy the rights mentioned above with limited interference from Congress or the government. Referring to the social contract expressed in the Declaration of Independence and the Constitution, Republican President Ronald Reagan (1981–1989) stated the basic conviction, "We are a nation that has a government – not the other way around".

Sometimes the American focus on personal freedom, independence, self-confidence and individualism is seen as a **legacy of the "frontier spirit"**. During the westward expansion, which mainly took place in the 19th century, settlers were often left to their own devices and could only rely on their own abilities, initiative and perseverance. They were spurred on by the myth of **Manifest Destiny**, which claims that the expansion of the American ideals and values is a God-given right. This idea fits well to the belief that America is "**God's own country**". It goes back to the early years of colonisation, when many settlers fled religious persecution in their homelands and saw the "New World" as their "New Canaan". Since then, the idea of **American exceptionalism** has often been evoked when it comes to the country's character of a role model and its self-declared mission to spread freedom and democracy.

Freedom in reality

Unrestricted freedom and individualism often come at a price, particularly if they result in a "survival of the fittest" logic and are combined with valuing one mindset and culture above all others. The pioneers' belief in their absolute freedom to settle in new territories, for instance, resulted in the **near-extermination of the Indigenous peoples of America**. The land the settlers took for themselves was not uninhabited – it had been the home of Native Americans for thousands of years. During the frontier movement, however, settlers killed large numbers of Native Americans or drove them relentlessly off the lands of their ancestors into reservations, usually barren, infertile grounds. All of this was justified by the belief in Manifest Destiny, which claimed that it was the Godly mission of the Europeans to conquer the wilderness and civilise the "Indian savages".

It is not only the USA's legacy of **dispossession and slavery** (regarding slavery, see the chapters on (in)equality) that is seen in an increasingly critical light. According to some, unrestrained freedom and a free-for-all attitude have also created a **capitalist society** characterised by selfishness, competition, ruthlessness and self-interest. Social norms and considerations for others often take second place in a worldview which is so focused on individual development and progress. In 2010, for example, President Barack Obama of the Democratic Party signed a law to provide affordable healthcare coverage for millions of impoverished and uninsured Americans. The Republican Party heavily campaigned against the law, commonly known as **Obamacare**, and tried to repeal it. They argued that by making health insurance obligatory, the law violated individual freedoms and represented an undue intrusion by the government into personal responsibilities. Because of this common belief in as little government interference as possible, many social welfare programmes have a difficult stance in American politics. The view that every decision should be left in the hands of the individual is also responsible for the widespread resistance to **gun control** (see "Current issues: Gun control" below).

The ideal of equality

In the Age of Enlightenment, philosophers and thinkers propagated the idea that all people were equal and all individuals should enjoy the same rights. This principle was taken up by the Founding Fathers of the United States in the **Declaration of Independence:** "We hold these truths to be self-evident that **all men are created equal**". It is one of the fundamental convictions that Americans are proud of and cherish today. The idea of equality is generally held in high esteem in nations that observe **human rights** and oppose all types of discrimination based on gender, race, ethnic origin, religion, political convictions, disability, age or sexual orientation, etc. Organisations such as the United Nations or the European Union are also committed to the protection of human rights (cf. the United Nations' Universal Declaration of Human Rights of 1948, for example). Both in the USA and other countries, however, reality is often far removed from the lofty ideal of equality.

Social inequality

The ideal of a society of equals has not become reality in the USA. According to its **gross national product** (GNP) – the volume of goods and services produced by the workforce of a country – the USA is the wealthiest country in the world. However, the statistics often do not show the **uneven distribution of wealth**. In 2023, nearly 70 per cent of the total wealth in the United States was owned by the top 10 per cent of earners. The lowest 50 per cent of earners owned less than three per cent of the total wealth. Multibillionaires like Jeff Bezos, the founder of Amazon, Elon Musk, the CEO or shareholder of some of the most successful business ventures, Bill Gates, the co-founder of Microsoft, and investor Warren Buffett top the list of the richest people in the USA and the whole world. At the bottom of the table, on the other hand, there are millions of people, many of them from ethnic minorities, who live in poverty and face significant challenges when it comes to making a living. The **racial wealth gap** between White and Black[1] Americans in particular has been a long-standing issue.

Racial inequality

The wealth gap between Black and White Americans is only one of several examples of racial inequality in the USA. Such inequality has a long tradition in the country, particularly when it comes to **African Americans** and **Native Americans** (for Native Americans and their dispossession and extermination, also see the section entitled "Freedom in reality"). Not even back in the days of adopting the Declaration of Inde-

---

1 The words "Black" and "White" are capitalised to signal that they are not natural categories but social ones (for more background information on this topic see, for example https://www.theatlantic.com/ideas/archive/2020/06/time-to-capitalize-blackand-white/613159/).

pendence and the Constitution did the right to equality apply to the above-mentioned groups, because their members were not regarded as "men" or "people", nor were they citizens of the United States. Many of the Founding Fathers – White males of European descent and wealthy property holders – owned slaves, and **slavery** was practised in all of the 13 original colonies, which was not regarded as a contradiction to the equality demanded by the Declaration of Independence. Enslaved people were often treated with brutality, degradation and inhumanity. Furthermore, they were usually denied educational opportunities, such as learning how to read or write, and were ruthlessly exploited.

The **agricultural South** in particular depended on enslaved Africans working on the plantations, while in the **industrial northern states**, slavery gradually came under heavy criticism. Anti-slavery societies were formed, which raised moral questions about slavery and advocated the abolition of this inhuman form of exploitation. In **1807**, President Thomas Jefferson signed legislation that officially ended the African slave trade. However, this act did not end slavery; in fact, it increased the slave trade in the United States. The abolition of slavery was one of the reasons for the **American Civil War**. As a result of the war and the **Union's victory** over the **Confederate Army from the South**, slavery was officially abolished with the passing of the **13th Amendment to the Constitution in 1865**. During the years after the Civil War, known as the **Reconstruction era**, legal rights for Black people were introduced with the **14th and 15th Amendments**, including citizenship and suffrage. However, particularly in the South, slavery was replaced by **segregation**, and many of the newly won rights for Black people were restricted by **Black Codes** and later by **Jim Crow laws**. In a landmark decision in **1896**, the Supreme Court of the United States legitimised the practice of "**separate but equal**" facilities for the races. This meant that businesses and public accommodation could be segregated according to race. In buses, trains, restaurants, hotels, schools, theatres and jails, there were special sections reserved for White people and others for Black people, with the facilities for the latter often being in worse shape than those for the former.

All in all, the Jim Crow laws maintained the unfair treatment of the Black section of the population from before the Civil War and also hindered Black people from exercising the rights guaranteed by the Reconstruction Amendments, such as their right to vote. One significant step towards equality for Black Americans was the **1954 landmark decision of the Supreme Court** which overthrew the ruling of 1896 and concluded that segregation was against the US Constitution. Further progress in the fight for racial equality was made by the non-violent **Civil Rights Movement**, which had its heyday in the 1950s and 1960s and was led by Martin Luther King. In his famous "I Have a Dream" speech in 1963, King reminded the American nation that the promises of the Declaration of Independence had not been fulfilled for America's Black people. The **Civil Rights Act of 1964** and the **Voting Rights Act of 1965** were important milestones in that direction.

One step to promote equal opportunities for Black Americans and other minorities in employment, business and education not only on paper, but also in reality is the **affirmative action** strategy. This aims to create a more diverse and inclusive society where everyone has the chance to succeed regardless of their background. America's universities, for example, used to give preference to Black, Hispanic and Native American students in order to expand their numbers in higher education, despite their potentially more limited access in the first place. However, affirmative action has **never** been **free from controversy** and a Supreme Court ruling of 2023 declared race-based affirmative action in college admissions as unconstitutional. While some arguments against affirmative action need to be taken seriously, such as its perpetuating racist bias or benefiting the most privileged members of a minority in comparison to the least privileged of the majority, decisions like this could further widen the educational gap that exists between Black and Hispanic students on the one hand and White and Asian students on the other.

Other fields of daily life where Black Americans and other people of colour are still denied equality and experience racism include housing, healthcare access, the criminal justice system and voting. The disadvantages with regard to the criminal justice sector in particular have been widely publicised in recent years: in 2013, after Trayvon Martin, an African American teenager, was killed by a White police officer, the "**Black Lives Matter**" movement was formed and has since organised nationwide marches to protest against police brutality and unfair treatment of Black people. There is statistical evidence of disproportionate amounts of **police brutality** against African Americans and of **racial profiling**, which means that Black people are stopped and searched more often than White people. In courts, judges tend to pronounce harsher sentences for Black defendants than for White defendants who have committed similar crimes. As a result, Black Americans are incarcerated at a much higher rate than White Americans.

Gender inequality

It is not only ethnic minorities for whom the promise of equality has not been fulfilled in the USA. Women are another group who were not included in the equality definition of the Declaration of Independence. Neither have they achieved full equality today. While the percentage of women in the labour force has increased significantly and they play a crucial role in the American economy, politics and society at large, gender inequality is persistent. Women remain **underrepresented** in top positions in both politics and the working world, for example. As of 2023, women held less than 30 per cent of positions in the House of Representatives and the Senate. Similarly, they were still underrepresented in managerial positions. The main reasons for this inequality include **gender stereotypes** and **bias**. One example of this is what is known as the similarity bias. According to this psychological phenomenon, people tend to prefer the company of others who are similar to themselves. Therefore, if bosses of big companies are predominantly male, this can lead them to promote other men instead of women, for instance. In other words, it often remains hard for women to advance beyond a certain level and occupy leading positions. This invisible barrier is known as the **glass ceiling effect**, limiting women's upward mobility.

Even in cases when they do have similar qualifications and job responsibilities, women often receive less pay than their male colleagues. Although progress has been made towards closing this **gender pay gap**, male annual earnings continue to outpace those of female workers. This is in spite of the **Equal Pay Act (1963)**, which prohibits wage discrimination based on sex. In recent years, efforts have been made to narrow the gulf between men's and women's earnings, but progress is slow. Concerted actions, such as wage transparency and awareness-raising activities, are needed to remove barriers to female employment opportunities and achieve true equality.

The ideal of the pursuit of happiness
The unalienable right to the pursuit of happiness allows any human being to decide freely about their individual aspirations in life and choose their path to happiness. The pursuit of happiness is often primarily associated with **material well-being**, although it can also include other free and unlimited choices for an individual's contentment. The promise that **every person can rise to success through hard work** – no matter where they come from – has been one of the main pull factors for millions to cross the Atlantic and make a new start in America. The hope of rising "from rags to riches, from dishwasher to millionaire" is what is quintessentially meant by the term "**American Dream**". The term was coined by historian James Truslow Adams in 1931, who was convinced that in a free and open society, individual commitment would lead to a better and richer life for each generation. The trust in personal achievement through private initiative and hard work has remained one of the most cherished American myths.

The reality: The deferred or unfulfilled American Dream
Originally, the American Dream was viewed as achievable for anyone. However, the USA is no longer – and arguably never has been – the land of open opportunities for everyone and many people find it hard or impossible to fulfil their dreams. Although there are success stories of individuals who have made it to the top thanks to their economic spirit, vision and genius, millions of Americans struggle with self-realisation. In a society that values success above all else and presents it as something that only depends on a person's own stamina and ambition, failure can be catastrophic because it is likely to impact people's self-esteem negatively, and they will not have many networks to support them.

In *Death of a Salesman* (1949), for example, Arthur Miller shows the darker side of the American Dream. The protagonist of the play, Willy Loman, clings to the values connected to it. He finally commits suicide when he is unable to live up to his ambitions.

For minorities, it can be especially difficult to fulfil the promises of the American Dream. It often remains an illusion and an unattainable goal. Lorraine Hansberry's drama *A Raisin in the Sun* (1959) illustrates an African American family's difficult living conditions in racist Chicago. The play's title refers to a line from a poem by Langston Hughes, who described the unfulfilled American Dream for African Americans by asking, "What happens to a dream deferred?/Does it dry up/Like a raisin in the sun?"

B 6

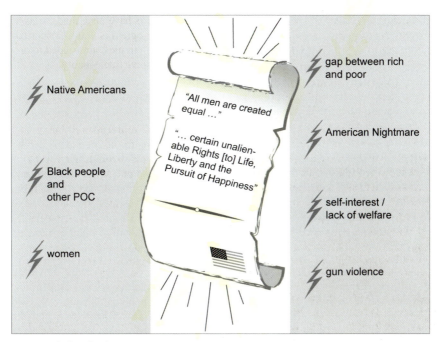

American ideals and realities

Current issues: Questions of identity, political, cultural and social developments

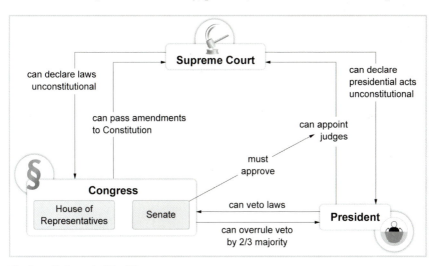

Checks and balances in US politics

Polarisation

The United States has a **two-party system:** the **Republican Party** ("Grand Old Party", founded in 1854) and the **Democratic Party** (founded in 1828). This system has the advantage that a clear-cut majority usually enables a strong government. However, a two-party system can lead to **polarisation**, which means the rivals may become ideologically rigid, pushing away from the centre. Another difficulty arises from the division of power between the different branches of US politics (cf. "Checks and balances in US politics" graphic on the previous page): in a system of **checks and balances**, each branch's power is limited by the others. It may happen that if the president is a Democrat, the people vote for a Republican majority in the **House of Representatives**, the **Senate** or both, which means that a president will have to contend with a majority from the opposition in one or both of the two chambers of **Congress**. In this case, **bipartisanship** and cooperation between the competing parties are challenging tasks. Opposition to an initiative of one party may then be more rooted in ideology than facts, which may lead to a **gridlock** or **deadlock** in Congress and hinder effective governance.

Observers agree that the country's division along party lines has become more entrenched in recent years. This is especially evident when it comes to what are known as **culture war issues**. These include topics subject to moral dispute and controversy. Positions on these topics are exaggerated and defended uncompromisingly by each party, so that people who think differently can easily be marked as enemies and any attempt at diplomacy fails. During the 2016 presidential campaign, Republican **Donald Trump** used the slogan "Make America Great Again" to win over voters among the electorate who believed that the USA had once been great but had lost its status. It was the start of the MAGA movement, whose supporters hold the failed policies of Democrat governments responsible for America's downfall. As their criticism often focuses on the fields of **immigration, multiculturalism, globalisation** and a certain ideology around **gender norms**, "Make America Great Again" can be read as a homophobic, sexist or racist slogan, or even as inciting violence.

In January 2021, after losing re-election, Donald Trump urged a crowd to **march on Congress**, where politicians had met to certify Democrat Joe Biden's win. In his State of the Union Speech of 2024, President Biden called 6 January 2021 "the darkest of days", adding that the insurrectionists who stormed the Capitol had "placed a dagger to the throat of American democracy".

Foreign policy

Since its foundation, the USA's foreign policy has vacillated between the two poles of **isolationism** on the one hand and **interventionism** on the other. In phases of isolationism, the country tends to keep out of foreign conflicts and focus on its own internal affairs. Interventionism is quite the opposite, meaning that the USA takes an active stance in foreign conflicts because it sees its own interests impacted or enhanced by them. That a successful American foreign policy is not clear-cut can also be seen from global reactions to the USA's decisions: sometimes the country is criticised for playing the "**policeman of the world**" and mingling in foreign affairs with a kind of missionary zeal reminiscent of Manifest Destiny. On the other hand, as arguably the strongest military power on earth, the USA is also relied upon by other countries in times of conflict.

One particularly influential event for the USA's self-image was the **terrorist attack of 9/11**, when, on 11 September 2001, Islamist terrorists hijacked four planes and flew them into the World Trade Center in New York, the Pentagon in Arlington County in Virginia and into a field in Pennsylvania (on the way to Washington, D.C.). The attack killed almost 3,000 people and injured thousands more. It was the single deadliest terrorist attack in recent history and deeply traumatised the American nation, as it was carried out on American soil and was seen as an attack on America's standing in the world. 9/11 impacted both domestic and foreign policies: Homeland Security laws were tightened so much that some critics even spoke of unconstitutional encroachments on people's personal rights and freedoms. Globally, the USA launched several campaigns of its so-called **War on Terrorism** – in Afghanistan or Iraq, for instance. With terrorism making a direct enemy quite difficult to identify, these military operations garnered international support but also came under heavy criticism and tarnished the USA's reputation. Not only was the USA accused of exacerbating tensions in the Middle East, but the lawfulness of some of the attacks and particularly the treatment of "enemy combatants" in the infamous detention camp **Guantanamo**, for example, were called into question and created a public outcry.

Poverty – Health coverage and food stamps
One of the most pressing worries for millions of Americans today is how to pay for medical treatment. Health services in surgeries or hospitals are costly. Unlike the United Kingdom and Germany, the US does not have a **centralised healthcare system**. This means that individuals, including employees and the self-employed, normally have to pay for their insurance policies on the market. As a result, covering the high cost of proper health insurance has become challenging or even impossible for the lower income brackets. The insurance policies people can afford differ in price and extent of coverage. As healthcare is so expensive, some companies offer health insurance plans as part of their benefits package to attract employees. However, healthcare costs are still a significant burden and too costly for millions of Americans. As the socio-economic status of individuals and families often strongly correlates with **ethnicity**, African American, Native American or Hispanic people are at a **disproportionate risk** of being uninsured or lacking sufficient healthcare.

The number of Americans without healthcare coverage has dropped considerably since the 1960s, mainly due to legislation initiated by Democratic president Lyndon B. Johnson. In 1965, Congress adopted two social plans, **Medicaid** and **Medicare**, to help people pay for hospital stays, doctor's visits, preventive care and prescription drugs. Medicare primarily supports people of 65 or older and individuals under 65 with certain disabilities or specific conditions. The other programme, Medicaid, provides health coverage to people on a low income or none at all, who could otherwise not pay for their treatment. These programmes remain essential pillars of social security in the United States today despite vigorous demands from some quarters – particularly Republicans – for support to be reduced.

In order for health insurance to spread to all Americans, President Barack Obama managed to get his Affordable Care Act (usually referred to as **Obamacare**) through Congress in 2010. Republicans have fought that law from the start, and Obamacare remains one of the main disputes between the two parties. Many Republicans seek to repeal the law, arguing that it is too expensive, hurts the economy and is an example of undue government interference in the citizens' self-determined lives (cf. sections on "Liberty"). Consequently, during his election campaign, Republican Donald Trump vowed to take back the Affordable Care Act, a plan which was not completely successful, however.

In 2021, the Democratic Joe Biden-Kamala Harris Administration made healthcare reform a priority again and the national uninsured rate reached an all-time low. However, the Republicans adhere to their resistance against the Affordable Care Act and further healthcare reforms.

Another problem in one of the wealthiest countries in the world concerns millions of American citizens who still cannot afford a decent living and struggle to survive every day. The **Supplemental Nutrition Assistance Program** (**SNAP**), formerly known as the **Food Stamp Program**, helps people on a low income or none at all to buy food for themselves and their families in order to maintain adequate nutrition and overall health. Generally, Republicans aim to cut welfare programmes whereas Democrats are more inclined to provide support for underprivileged citizens.

Immigration
The United States has been called "**a nation of immigrants**" because of its great ethnic diversity. However, this term does not include Native Americans, the original inhabitants of the continent, nor the slaves who were brought there against their will. Still, millions arrived searching for a better life or to flee from persecution or famine. In the **19th century**, immigrants were mostly welcomed with open arms to help build the United States of America. However, the tables soon turned. Earlier immigrants opposed further influx from abroad and US governments introduced restrictions such as the **Chinese Exclusion Act** (**1882**) and the **Immigration Act** (**1924**), which reflected the changing policies and attitudes towards newcomers, particularly those from ethnic backgrounds that were not yet represented in the US population.

Today, the United States has more immigrants than any other country and still prides itself on being a haven for refugees and asylum seekers. However, immigration remains an intensely **polarising issue** for US citizens. In some opinion polls it is even ranked as the country's most significant problem, surpassing inflation and the economy. Of great concern is the number of **illegal** crossings, particularly at the border to Mexico. In 2021, undocumented immigrants made up over one-fifth of the total foreign-born US population.

Over the years, Republicans and Democrats have been trying to find solutions to this problem, but they are still in a deadlock. Republicans tend to take a stricter stance, but both parties struggle to strike the right balance between protecting the rights of refugees, supporting the economy and ensuring border security. What constitutes proper **integration of migrants** is also a constant subject of debate: from the 18th century onwards, the USA was often called a **melting pot**, where people of different origins were fused into one common American identity. This metaphor of **assimilation** has more recently been substituted by other images, such as that of a **salad bowl** or **mosaic**. The latter two stress the fact that despite various sections of the population retaining their unique cultural features, there can be a harmonious whole.

In connection with illegal immigration, there is also a large group of undocumented immigrants who did not enter the US of their own free will but were brought to the country by their parents as children. These are known as "**Dreamers**". One immigration policy implemented in 2012, the **Deferred Action for Childhood Arrivals (DACA)**, is intended to protect them from deportation and allow them to work or study in the USA.

For a time, undocumented migrants even hoped for a pathway to citizenship. However, the DACA act is another highly contested piece of legislation. The issue has not been resolved conclusively, and the fate of the Dreamers remains uncertain.

Abortion
Abortion, the deliberate termination of a pregnancy, is another issue which continues to cause controversy. Opinions are divided on whether it is **legally and ethically acceptable** to terminate a pregnancy deliberately. Advocates argue that the right to have an abortion is rooted in the proposition of the Founding Fathers that every citizen has the right to freedom and the pursuit of happiness. Consequently, all individuals must have the right to **self-determination over their bodies** and sexuality. By contrast, conservative, often religiously motivated groups, especially in the southern states known as the **Bible Belt** states, argue that the foetus is a human being from conception and, therefore, has a **right to life** from that time on.

While abortion was neither criminalised nor legalised nationally before the 1970s, in the landmark Supreme Court ruling **Roe v. Wade** of 1973, the judges decided that states may not ban abortions in the first three months of pregnancy and may only ban them in the first six months of pregnancy under certain conditions. As a result, many states liberalised their laws, but opponents continued to press vigorously for prohibition. The **pro-life** movement campaigned to reverse Roe v. Wade, whereas their opponents, known as the **pro-choice** movement, stressed the importance of the ruling with regard to women's control over their own bodies.

After nearly 50 years of heavy campaigning on both sides, the Supreme Court **overturned Roe v. Wade** in 2022 on the grounds that "the Constitution of the United States does not confer a right to abortion". This landmark decision changed abortion laws in the United States significantly. The right to abortion was no longer protected, and the states were allowed to ban the procedure. Since the ruling, some states have made the termination of pregnancy outright illegal, others with antiabortion laws allow abortion in some very restricted instances, and many are undecided, still deliberating on how to act. This means that legislation varies from state to state, leaving the future of abortion in limbo. It has happened more than once that women have had to leave their home states and cross the border to have their pregnancies terminated.

**LGBTQI+ (lesbian, gay, bisexual, transgender, queer, intersexual and others')
rights**
For a long time, the freedom of choice and right to have self-determination over their
bodies and sexuality has been denied to people who either have a non-heteronorma-
tive **sexual orientation** or a **gender identity** that does not correspond with their as-
signed sex at birth. In the first half of the 20th century, **same-sex relations**, particularly between men, were **outlawed** in the USA. Female homosexuality tended to be
largely ignored in legal frameworks.

Since the 1960s and 1970s, public opinion and laws concerning homosexuality
have changed considerably. However, it was only in **2003** that the US Supreme Court
declared all remaining laws against same-sex sexual activity unconstitutional. Another landmark decision of 2015 made **same-sex marriage** legal across all 50 states.

When it comes to non-discrimination laws regarding both homosexuality and people's **gender recognition**, there is no universal court ruling in the USA that guarantees these and laws vary by state. While it has certainly become easier to live a non-
heteronormative life and / or to identify as transgender, LGBTQI+ people suffer widespread prejudice or even violence to this day, in some areas more so than in others.

The film *Boy Erased*, for instance, is set in a conservative milieu in Arkansas. It
shows the dilemma of a young homosexual boy who is forced to hide his sexual orientation. He is even sent to a centre where a pseudoscientific practice, Conversion
Therapy, is applied. While this practice has been widely criticised and banned in several states, there are also some that still allow it to happen.

Gun control
Gun control has been among the most fiercely debated issues in the United States.
Pro-gun activists on the one hand and **gun control advocates** on the other are deeply entrenched in their beliefs. There is statistical evidence to show that gun-related
crimes and deaths are substantially higher in the US than in any other country of
similar economic development. Gun-related deaths occur as homicides, suicides, accidents or in **mass shootings** that often draw substantial media attention. Mass shootings are by definition firearm-related incidents with four or more casualties. After
every such tragedy, politicians express their heartfelt sympathy and call for renewed
efforts to reduce violence and improve gun safety.

The heated exchange between the pro-gun lobby, including the **National Rifle Association (NRA)** and **Gun Owners of America (GOA)**, and anti-gun violence
movements, such as Everytown or Brady, revolves around the **Second Amendment
to the Constitution** (1791). This includes the passage "… the right of the people to
keep and bear Arms shall not be infringed". Pro-gun lobby groups have always used
these words of America's Founding Fathers for their campaigns against any stricter
gun legislation. Some states have even passed "permitless (concealed) carry" laws,
which allow a person to carry a handgun either openly or covertly without requiring a
licence or training. To support their view, the National Rifle Association (NRA) ar-
gues that having more armed civilians will help boost public safety, making it more
likely that "good guys" with guns will intercept "bad guys" with guns. Furthermore,
stricter gun laws will not prevent the acquisition of firearms because they can always

be obtained on the black market. The "unalienable right of freedom", the ideal formulated in the Constitution, may have contributed to the development of a violence-prone society. Firearms are regarded as **symbols of freedom and power** – a view that has created a culture of weaponry.

Anti-gun violence groups deplore the continued needless loss of life and demand **stricter gun laws**. They maintain that the easy availability of firearms and lax licensing rules account for the large number of suicides and accidents with guns. It is too easy to acquire weapons in gun shops, on the Internet and at gun shows, where people buy and sell firearms, firearm accessories and ammunition. Furthermore, research shows that guns do not help to prevent crime – on the contrary, more guns are linked to more crimes: murders, rapes and others. Consequently, gun access should be made more difficult. Another aspect connected with the issue of gun control is the question of **racism**: Several fatal shootings of Black people by White deputies have occurred. The police officers assumed (or claimed) the people they had stopped and searched were trying to pull a gun, which was not the case. These incidents frequently trigger protests or in some cases even riots and rekindle the vigorous debate about the racial prejudice of law enforcement officers against African Americans. If there were fewer firearms around, some of these tragedies might be avoided.

However, there are some hopeful developments as well. In 2022, for the first time in many years, Democrats and Republicans managed to overcome their long-standing dispute about gun control. Together, they worked out the **Bipartisan Safer Communities Act**. The law imposes stricter background checks for buyers under the age of 21 and encourages states to implement "red flag" laws. These give a court the power to temporarily remove firearms from people believed to be at high risk of harming themselves or others. Despite this remarkable progress, gun control and violence remain an issue which seriously puts the ideal of freedom to the test.

The fascination of crime

Why are we so intrigued by crime and crime stories? Crime-related content is extremely popular in all kinds of media. People find great **pleasure, excitement, thrill and suspense** when they enter a fictional world full of mysteries, frightening events and strange characters. The experience of diving into a crime novel or watching a detective film or series provides an escape from ordinary life and a glimpse into the darker side of humanity. People are curious and eager to know the perpetrator of a crime and can hardly wait for the culprit to be found out and brought to justice and for order to be re-established. Psychologists explain that much of the action (and the fear) occurs in people's minds and imagination. Therefore, readers or viewers of thrillers **experience frightening emotions in a controlled manner**, which is very often coupled with the satisfying sense of closure that a happy ending provides or the reassurance that their own life is good and peaceful in comparison. The enormous popularity of crime content is reflected in the extensive output of crime literature and crime series on TV and in digital formats like streaming services and podcasts.

Crime in literature
The theme of crime has a long tradition. **Edgar Allan Poe** (1809–1849) is sometimes credited with inventing the literary form and narrative technique of the detective story. He created the character of C. Auguste Dupin, who became the model for many detectives in literature, such as Sherlock Holmes (Arthur Conan Doyle, 1859–1930), Hercule Poirot and Miss Marple (Agatha Christie, 1890–1976). These detectives solve their cases by gathering evidence, watching closely and thinking logically. The typical narrative structure of the early crime stories has earned them the title of "**whodunits**" (= Who has done it?). They begin with a murder or other violent crime, which is solved during the course of the story. Whodunits are still very popular because many readers like to speculate along with the characters from the story and find satisfaction in being on the right track, maybe even before the detectives in the stories are. American writers Raymond Chandler (1888–1956), Dashiell Hammett (1894–1961) and James M. Cain (1892–1977) represent the so-called "**hardboiled**" **school of detective fiction** because of their tough, realistic and unsentimental style of writing. Among today's most successful crime writers are James Patterson (*1947), Val McDermid (*1955), Mark Billingham (*1961), Stephen King (*1974) and Karin Slaughter (*1971).

Crime in TV and digital formats
The crime drama television series *The Sopranos*, centring around a New Jersey mafioso and produced by the American pay TV network HBO, is generally regarded as the start of the "Second Golden Age of TV" (the first was in the 1950s). It ran for six seasons from 1999 until 2007 and combined criminal elements with a psychologically constructed plot and family story. With the **rise of online streaming services**, traditional series like *The Sopranos* or *The Wire*, an American police drama series from

B 14

the early 2000s, have gained new popularity. Additionally, a flood of new detective series specifically designed for the streaming platforms prove the ongoing fascination for the genre. Moreover, a variety of true crime series and podcasts (e. g. *Serial, Casefile*), many of which cover cold cases, are attracting an increasing number of regular listeners. Hobby detectives can also join forces in various **online communities** to try and solve fictional crimes or find new evidence or clues for real-life cold cases.

The definition of crime

By definition, crimes are **activities that involve breaking the law**, ranging from **property crimes**, such as theft, to **violent crimes** when people are harmed or even killed, such as rape, robbery or murder (homicide).

Property crime

Property crime is one of the most frequent forms of crime. Typical property crimes include larceny or theft, especially vehicle theft, shoplifting, arson, vandalism, burglary or robbery, with the last offence transgressing the boundary to violent crime.

Two of the most spectacular property crimes in the UK were the Great Train Robbery of 1963 and the Hatton Garden safe deposit burglary of 2015. In both cases, the thieves hatched a clever plan to steal cash and valuable items worth millions of pounds. In 1963, a gang stopped and robbed a Royal Mail train en route from Glasgow to London, bringing £2.3 million into their possession (which would be more than £30 million today). In 2015, six experienced thieves drilled a hole through the 50-cm-thick vault walls of an underground safe depository, removing valuables estimated at £14 million. Categorising the Great Train Robbery or the Hatton Garden heist, criminologists would use the term **blue-collar crime** to denote that the offence was committed by individuals in a more or less hands-on fashion.

In contrast, **white-collar crimes** are often committed by government or business professionals and typically do not involve manual work or even the physical presence of criminals on a crime scene. Instead of force or violence, white-collar criminals use deceit and concealment in order to gain money or property. Today, property thefts which involve hard physical work are regarded as "old school" and are becoming less frequent. Thus, bank robberies are being replaced by **a new type of crime** which is much more lucrative and can often harm a great number of people simultaneously. The most frequent white-collar crimes are **fraud, blackmail** and **forgery**. With the advances in computer technology and the worldwide extension of the web, they are mostly committed online these days. New words such as **cybercrime** or **wire fraud** have been coined to cover these offences.

Fraud is under-reported to the police and not included in many crime statistics. However, the financial industry, including the UK's Payments Association, for example, records high financial losses resulting from this type of crime. Criminals use scam phone calls, text messages and emails as well as fake websites and social media posts to trick people into disclosing personal details and passwords. This information is then used to target victims and convince them to authorise payments. More and more cases of illegal access to data stored online (**identity theft**) are being discovered. This is why Internet security has become a topic of the highest priority. Warnings are issued to users of social network sites not to reveal too much personal data on their accounts.

A particular type of fraud is **tax evasion**. In recent years, a global network of several hundred investigative journalists has uncovered the illegal activities of wealthy individuals and public officials. Millions of confidential electronic documents (the **Panama**, **Paradise** and **Pandora Papers**) revealed that many politicians, business tycoons and celebrities had established offshore letterbox companies with the aim of hiding money from public scrutiny. One of America's most infamous gangsters was Al Capone, who continuously avoided arrest for the multiple crimes he was responsible for. However, he was finally imprisoned for not paying his taxes: Capone was indicted for **income-tax evasion** in 1931 and sentenced to 11 years in prison.

Criminals are also using the web to perpetrate what has been called **ransomware** attacks, a particular kind of **blackmail**. Hackers gain unauthorised access to systems or networks of private individuals or firms and block them with a safe password. They then send a ransom note instructing the victim not to contact the police but to pay a certain amount of money to receive the password to unlock their network or files. Due to the international and anonymous nature of the crime, police find it almost impossible to trace the person or gang behind the blackmail threat. Additionally, blackmailing individuals and local businesses can also be a source of terrorist financing.

Forgery means copying or imitating a document, signature, banknote or work of art. For instance, forged paintings are offered on the market or forged banknotes are brought into circulation. Special cases of forgery include imitations of clothing, software, pharmaceuticals, watches, electronics, and company logos and brands. Criminologists talk about **product piracy**. A recent and extremely dangerous trick of cyber criminals is known as Cross-Site Request Forgery (CSRF), which allows access to a user's trusted website and the performance of actions in their name.

Organised crime

The British government passed the Economic Crime (Transparency and Enforcement) Act in 2022, which was designed to tackle the growing problem of illicit financial activities such as the laundering of dirty money to be used for financing organised crime. A criminal syndicate that emerged in Sicily in the mid-nineteenth century became notorious in the US in the 1920s. During the years of Prohibition (1920–1933) the **Mafia** greatly profited from **bootlegging** (= illegal trafficking in alcoholic beverages), but also made money from gambling, loansharking (= lending money at huge rates of interest) and **drug dealing**. The illegal activities of members and associates of the Mafia, particularly in New York City and Chicago, have been depicted in numerous novels and films, such as *The Godfather* (1972) based on a story by Mario Puzo. Conflicts between rivalling gangs in Chicago resulted in killings such as the St Valentine's Day Massacre of 1929. In recent years, the Mafia has undergone major changes and has also faced increased government opposition in its homeland of Italy. In 2023, Italy's most wanted fugitive, one of the last leaders of the Sicilian mob, was arrested at a hospital after eluding capture for 30 years. The word "Mafia" is still used as a general term for any underworld criminal organisation – the Russian, Mexican-American, Chinese (= Triad) and Japanese (= Yakuza) Mafia, for example.

Violent crime
Violence spans a wide range of offences from minor assaults, such as pushing and shoving, to serious assault and murder. **Knives and sharp instruments** continue to be among the most common offensive weapons in the **UK**. The British Parliament passed the **Offensive Weapons Act** in 2019, which made it illegal to possess certain dangerous weapons even in private settings. Further measures, such as restrictions on the online sale of knives and enhanced age verification checks, were also part of the attempt to prevent knife crime. At some school gates airport-style metal detectors have been installed to tackle the problem.

In the **USA**, **gun crime** is even more widespread than knife crime. This is probably due to the rather lax laws on individual gun possession (at least in some states), which can be traced back to the **Second Amendment** to the US Constitution. This states "the right of the people to keep and bear Arms". Despite the **safety concerns** that are regularly raised by proponents of stricter gun laws and despite **statistical evidence** backing these claims, such as more gun-related deaths in the USA on one day than in the UK in a year, the **NRA** (National Rifle Association) and its supporters continue to see individual gun possession and the **right to self-defence** as a sign of personal **freedom** and **democratisation**.

Among the different types of violent crime, incidents of **sexual assault, rape and domestic abuse** have concerned not only police officials but also politicians. **Domestic abuse** is a worldwide problem which cuts across social, economic and class barriers. It is sometimes – although not exclusively – labelled **gender-based violence**, because women and girls are the victims to a disproportionate degree. According to World Health Organisation data from over 150 countries, more than one woman in four will be beaten or sexually abused by a partner in her lifetime. In many countries, domestic violence is seen as a private matter that should not be interfered with. The COVID-19 pandemic exacerbated domestic abuse because many victims were locked down in their homes with their abusers, isolated from support networks and services.

In connection with sexual crime in particular, the number of cases of domestic violence is estimated to be much higher than officially recorded. Many **offences remain undetected** because the victims – usually partners, wives or girlfriends – are unwilling and/or afraid to report the perpetrator to the police. To reduce violence against women, it is not only necessary to provide stricter laws but it is also essential to raise awareness of the issue and **change cultural attitudes**.

The propagation of crime

Particularly cruel criminal acts like mass shootings or bomb attacks always make the headlines and are covered extensively by the media worldwide. In 2022, a gunman armed with a semi-automatic rifle entered Robb Elementary School in Uvalde, Texas, and opened fire, killing nineteen students and two teachers. It was one of the deadliest **school shootings** in the United States. In his State of the Union address of 2023, President Joe Biden made a strong appeal for a **ban on assault weapons**, mentioning the recent Monterey Park shooting in California which had happened only one month earlier. There, a gunman had killed eleven people and injured nine others.

These incidents as well as the above-mentioned omnipresence of crime on various media outlets could give the impression that crime is on the rise today and that we are living in a world of ever-increasing violence. However, statistics tell a different story. Despite the constant media images of cruel and spectacular murders, crime rates – especially those regarding violent crime – **have generally been falling** since the Second World War in nearly all industrialised countries, though with slight fluctuations and to differing degrees. The homicide rate in the USA is usually much higher than in Europe, for instance, probably due to the country's different approach to gun laws.

Investigation and detection

Methods of **investigation** and **detection** have improved greatly since the times of literary detectives like Sherlock Holmes or Hercule Poirot. While they solved their mystery cases by applying logical reasoning, adopting clever disguises or using very basic scientific skills, it is impossible to imagine modern policing methods and detective work without ample **DNA testing** or the elaborate investigations of pathology experts. Nowadays, teams of forensic scientists and profilers can solve murder cases even if they were committed years ago. To date, several hundred people in the United States have been exonerated by DNA testing, including some who served time on death row. In one famous example from Canada, a man was wrongfully convicted of the rape and murder of a nursing student and imprisoned for life. After 23 years in prison, he was eventually released and exonerated after a laboratory was able to prove his innocence through DNA analysis.

Another modern technology which helps the police to detect crimes is the installation of surveillance cameras. The system of **CCTV** (= **closed circuit television**) is used to monitor public places in city centres, buildings and shops to protect people from crime such as assault, mugging or shoplifting. Studies have shown that video surveillance can reduce certain types of crime, such as drug dealing, unruly behaviour, and vehicle and property crime. Although the presence of cameras does not affect the level of violent crime, video footage can help identify suspects after a crime has been committed. On the other hand, the installation of cameras in public places is not undisputed. People fear that their **right to privacy** will be interfered with and do not want to hand over too much power to a domineering **surveillance state**.

This **balance between security and the protection of human rights**, even those of potential criminals, has been even harder to strike in other cases: in their efforts to detect crime and convict offenders, police officers and investigators have occasionally resorted to **debatable and even illegal methods** of interrogation. During the so-called War on Terrorism, for instance, the American Central Intelligence Agency (CIA) and US Armed Forces used programmes of torture which they euphemistically termed "enhanced interrogation techniques" or "enhanced interrogation" at remote sites around the world. After the methods were disclosed, a Senate committee investigated the matter and published a report condemning those methods. In the EU, the European Court of Human Rights investigates violations of human rights. It is generally agreed that "**the end does not justify the means**" and that information obtained under questionable circumstances cannot be used in legal proceedings.

Nature versus nurture – what makes a criminal?

The question of why people turn bad and can become vicious murderers has been at the centre of a long-standing debate. Are a person's character and behaviour determined by **nature** (innate biological factors; a person's genes) or formed by **nurture** (someone's upbringing and experiences)? Are criminals made or born? As it has been the case for years that men have been much more likely to be the perpetrators of violent crime at least, masculinity has often been linked to more aggression or even brutality. However, more modern scientists stress that genetics and a person's social environment are never independent of each other. That is to say that nature and nurture interact, which means that criminal behaviour is caused by a combination of biological predisposition and social circumstances.

Delinquency is also **closely linked to social problems** such as poverty and unemployment, lack of opportunities, frustration and boredom, coupled with alcohol and drug addiction. As the gulf between rich and poor becomes wider and wider, those who are excluded from prosperity may resort to illegal means. An exposure to violence and having been victimised themselves are also seen as factors that could make people prone to commit crime. However, this does not mean that unfavourable circumstances inevitably lead to crime and make criminals of anyone.

The reasons why individuals or groups commit crimes are manifold. The **most frequent motivations** include greed, hatred, revenge, peer group pressure, boredom and desperation.

Is there such a thing as a "just crime"?

Many highly publicised crimes are also committed for **political or religious reasons**. One of the best known religiously motivated attacks occurred on **September 11, 2001**, as four planes were hijacked by Al-Qaeda terrorists to be flown into several important buildings including the Pentagon, the US Department of Defense, and the Twin Towers of the World Trade Center in New York City. Extremists in different parts of the world also name **political reasons** for their attacks on civilians. In Ireland, members of the IRA, for instance, saw themselves as freedom fighters against British occupation.

In the political sphere in particular, the question might arise as to whether there are **cases in which crime could be justified**. Does the killing of a radical dictator, for instance, amount to a crime or is it justified because it could **prevent further suffering**? In a similar vein, it is sometimes discussed whether **self-preservation** or the **defence of others** legalise violence. Should a plane hijacked by terrorists, for example, be shot down because not doing so might exacerbate the violence? These are both **moral and legal** questions that also need to be taken into account when deciding on punishments.

Punishment

Towards a just punishment

Generally speaking, most people would agree that a punishment should be fair considering the facts of each case and the severity of the crime. The defendant's past and their personal circumstances, such as family, upbringing, education, social conditions and so on, may be taken into account in an effort to find a just punishment. In US courts, a judge decides whether to admit past convictions of the defendant depending on whether they are regarded as helpful to the jury or unfair to the accused.

The function of punishment

When it comes to the question of how severe a sanction should be, opinions vary because people might see the main function of punishment as lying in **retribution** and **deterrence** or **rehabilitation**. Furthermore, various attitudes towards law and order and human nature play a role. The pessimistic view that people are basically bad was first expressed by philosopher Thomas Hobbes (1588–1679), who believed that human life in its natural state would be "solitary, poor, nasty, brutish, and short". To keep everyone from exercising too much power and to guarantee the safety and well-being of all, a strong political authority was necessary, which, in Hobbes' view, was an absolute monarch. People who see humans as inherently bad, self-centred, ruthless and greedy often advocate grave punishments to keep bad instincts in check.

The traditional approach – the full force of the law

After especially atrocious and tragic crimes (e. g. the bombing of civilian targets, kidnappings, mass shootings, gang rapes or violence against children), politicians and sections of the public often demand stricter measures to be imposed upon offenders. They believe that perpetrators should feel the full force of the law and pay for violating social rules. They should experience some of the horrors their victims or their loved ones endured, which is sometimes circumscribed by the biblical saying "**an eye for an eye**". Stiffer penalties can mean **longer prison sentences**, for example. In the USA, it is common to accumulate prison terms, so verdicts of several life sentences or hundreds or even thousands of years in prison are not unheard of. In some legislatures, what is called a "**three-strikes law**" is practised: this means that repeat offenders are automatically given a life sentence after their third felony even if the actual crime they have committed would not necessarily warrant such a harsh verdict.

Arguably, the severest form of punishment which can be applied today is the **death penalty** and it is also one of the most controversial penalties. Today, the death penalty is legal in 27 states in the United States as well as on a federal level and in the military. Although support for the death penalty has declined, a slight majority of Americans still endorsed it for people convicted of murder in 2022. Opponents of capital punishment argue that it is **morally wrong to kill someone**, even for justice. "Thou shalt not kill" is one of the Ten Commandments in the Bible. Moreover, it is feared that innocent people could be executed – a **miscarriage of justice** that could never be corrected. Furthermore, a state endorsing murder could be seen as promoting a **culture of violence**. Defenders of the death penalty insist that it is a more effective **deterrent** to murderers than long-term imprisonment and the only real safeguard against repeat offenders. However, neither the deterrent argument nor the often cited financial benefits of the death penalty compared to life imprisonment have ever been proven conclusively.

In confrontations it is not only police officers who are permitted to use force which may cause serious injury or death, but this right is also extended to civilians. In more than 30 US states the "**stand-your-ground law**" permits citizens to defend themselves, even with deadly force, if they fear for their lives or fear great bodily harm. While a right to **self-defence** is common practice in many countries around the world, its too easy application is criticised as a return to the "shoot first" ethic of the Old West, especially in states with very relaxed gun laws.

The alternative approach – restorative justice

Proponents of **zero tolerance policies** argue that offenders should always feel the full force of the law and that the police and other authorities should not be able to judge individual cases subjectively, take extenuating circumstances into account or exercise discretion if justified. On the other hand, people with a more optimistic view of human nature often explain lawless behaviour by citing unfair and unjust social conditions which should consequently be taken into consideration when judging crimes. So, while sanctions should be severe enough to make the perpetrator realise their wrongdoing, all penalties should also offer a chance of **rehabilitation**. In other words, justice's ultimate aim should be to reintegrate wrongdoers into society again. During their time in prison, offenders should be able to reflect on their actions and try to put right the damage done. They might also be required to do work that is in the public interest.

One specific way of trying to achieve justice and repair harm – not only for individuals but also for larger groups or society as a whole – is called **restorative justice**. The basic idea behind this principle is that perpetrators and victims of crimes should be brought together. Instead of a punitive approach based on vengeance and a negative retrospective, justice systems should find constructive paths of reconciliation for people to be able to move forward. One example of this approach is the **Truth and Reconciliation Commission** (TRC) of South Africa, which was established in 1996 after the end of the apartheid regime. The Commission examined the causes, nature and extent of serious violations of human rights committed between 1960 and 1994. While giving victims a platform to address the injustices done to them and ideally heal from the experience, perpetrators could also confess to their crimes publicly and be granted amnesty in certain cases. Other countries, like Australia, Canada and Sierra Leone, followed South Africa's example and set up Reconciliation Commissions to redress grave injustice, such as the displacement or killing of First Nations people. In 2000, South Africa established the Institute for Justice and Reconciliation as the successor organisation of the original TRC.

Victim-offender mediation

In many cases where crime has traditionally been dealt with, the perpetrators take centre stage but the victims are frequently neglected. Although the **consequences of being a victim of a crime** vary widely depending on the severity of the incident and the individual's circumstances, an offence can be life-changing for those affected by it. Victims suffer **emotionally, mentally, physically** and also **financially**, for example, when they are unable to continue with their job. Many victims of violence withdraw into themselves, struggling hard to cope with **depression, PTSD** (post-traumatic stress disorder) and **sleeplessness**.

Over the past few years, more and more victims have decided to meet the person responsible for the harm done to them **face to face**. They wish to confront the offender in a safe and victim-sensitive setting and inform them of the consequences they have suffered and had to cope with. Talking about their situation after a crime can help victims overcome the trauma. The process of victim-offender mediation can also help find answers to many issues that have not yet been addressed and open the door to a new start.

Social Media – Boon or Bane in the 21st Century?[2]

The global extension of the Internet has made our world a smaller place and has opened up a variety of opportunities. Among the most popular features of the Internet are social networking sites, which have experienced an enormous growth in recent years. Users can stay in touch, exchange messages about private or work-related affairs, post views on topical issues, send photos or consume videos, films or music. Logging on to their accounts has become daily routine for millions all over the world. Not only private individuals, but also businesses, banks, governments and agencies in the public sector use networking sites. They are now a mainstream **communications technology**. The most important social media companies are Facebook (renamed Meta in 2021), Snapchat, Twitter (acquired by Elon Musk in 2022 and renamed X in 2023), Instagram, YouTube, Google, Pinterest, reddit and LinkedIn, all of which were founded in the United States and have their headquarters in California. TikTok, which focuses on videos, is owned by a Chinese company.

People's increasing interest in remaining anonymous online has given rise to platforms like Telegram although it is unclear whether it really offers more **data security** than "conventional" messenger services. Signal, on the other hand, is rated as quite safe by most data security experts. Still, there is an ongoing controversy about how much data a messenger service should be obliged to share with justice enforcement or government agencies.

Considering the variety of social networking sites and the myriad of messages posted online, observers ask how we – i.e. the human brain – can cope with the information overflow. Too much input (**"information overload"**) makes it impossible for people to process all the information and think independently. It may thus prevent them from taking good decisions. In this way, it is sometimes argued that the age of information has turned into an **age of disinformation**. Consequently, the question must be asked whether social networking sites are a bane or a boon.

Political consequences of social media

Before the arrival of the Internet and social networking sites, most people relied on newspapers and television news programmes as their primary sources of information about governments, current political events and elections. Barack Obama was one of the first politicians who recognised the potential of networking sites for addressing younger voters in particular. After his re-election in 2012, he proclaimed his success to the nation via his Twitter account. His tweet, "four more years", became the most popular tweet at the time. Republican President Donald Trump was also a frequent user of both his personal and official Twitter accounts, regularly posting his opinion of people and all kinds of topics. The question arises whether the widespread use of social media plays a positive or negative role in the political arena.

---

2 Schwerpunktthema ist nur relevant für das berufliche Gymnasium.

The media and elections
At the start of an important election, campaigners use the Internet to raise funds, or-ganise action groups, muster volunteers and mobilise voters. Candidates use social media and a personal website as cheap and effective methods to reach a large part of the electorate. In 2018, a scandal revealed the **illegal harvesting of social media user profiles** for political advertising. Social networking providers use special tech-niques, so-called **algorithms**, to analyse and collect information about their users, their posts, their likes and dislikes to establish a complete personal profile. In 2016, **Cambridge Analytica**, a now defunct political consultancy, used the detailed data of about 50 million Facebook profiles without permission to target American voters for the presidential campaign of Donald Trump and allegedly the Brexit referendum in Britain. The company filed for bankruptcy, and Facebook was accused of and fined for careless privacy practices. The scandal made people more aware of the necessity to protect their personal data online. Analysts believe that there are still companies like Cambridge Analytica which use social media to influence politics.

Political polarisation through social media
In addition, data consultants warn that algorithms are causing **political polarisation** in society. This can be explained by the fragmentation of news media and the spread of misinformation on the net. More often than not, news on the Internet is not objec-tive but opinionated, facts are distorted, untruths circulate and people are "nudged" toward certain behaviours. When social media first appeared, most people believed they would promote democracy because users could freely exchange views and, for example, voice their protests against dictatorial regimes. However, in the meantime, many observers have come to regard social media as a threat to democratic societies as many **users tend to spread rumours**, judgements and opinions rather than facts. Equally damaging is the fact that social media users become caught in so-called "**fil-ter bubbles**". As service providers employ algorithms to filter the mass of informa-tion and personalise it according to their users' preferences, on social media people receive news which mirrors and reinforces their own opinions and beliefs. Very rare-ly, or not at all, are they presented with divergent points of view or alternative ideas.

The spreading of fake news for political purposes
Another serious problem is the fact that social media platforms are used to publish inaccurate information and **fake news** in order to massively and often surreptitiously influence the views of a considerable number of people. A study found that false news online is 70 per cent more likely to be spread than the truth. In the political arena, leaders and officials frequently ignore or deliberately distort facts. What they sell as "alternative facts" is in reality a set of lies. After losing the US election in 2020, Donald Trump kept publishing his unfounded assertion, "The election is rigged!", meaning he only lost because of massive amounts of voter fraud nationwide. Interest-ed parties do not refrain from attacking and insulting opponents personally if it seems to support their aims. For instance, President Barack Obama was discredited by so-cial networking users who spread the news that Obama was born outside America. During the US election campaign of 2016, a conspiracy theory, termed "**Pizzagate**", went viral to disgrace Trump's opponent in the race, Democrat Hillary Clinton.

Faked emails linked Clinton to a child sex-trafficking ring in a pizzeria in Washington. While this was later exposed as sheer fabulation, it remains unclear how much damage to the candidate's reputation the rumour had already caused.

Propaganda and cyber censorship

Extremists from all sides of the political spectrum use social networking accounts to publicise **radical propaganda** and recruit supporters for their activities. It is not surprising, therefore, that government officials want to increase surveillance of social networking sites. On the other hand, this must also be done with caution in order not to constitute an abuse of power too. In some South Asian countries, social networking sites are in the hands of **authoritarian regimes** which use them to consolidate power and advance their political goals, both domestically and internationally. In Myanmar, for example, the military rulers wiped out years of fragile democratic gains. After a landslide victory in the general election of 2015 the country's liberal National League for Democracy (NLD) could form a government but it was overthrown in a military coup in early 2021. In 2018, a UN report confirmed that Facebook had played a huge role in the violence inflicted on Rohingya Muslims by marauding Buddhists. The platform admitted that it had not done enough to prevent its services from being abused. Other rulers use the Internet to exert control over and spy on citizens. Political observers warn of the spread of "**digital authoritarianism**", especially as Artificial Intelligence is about to play a greater role in enhancing and enabling authoritarian governance and surveillance. The idealised vision of the Internet and social media as the platform of free speech and exchange of information has become obscured as governments like China use techniques to censor, suppress or block critical content. The Great Wall of China has now become the **Great Firewall**, a term for the Communist party's massive Internet censorship system.

Economic consequences of social networking sites

The business model of social media sites

In the documentary *The Social Dilemma* (2020), former Google worker Tristan Harris analyses the techniques and strategies of social media platforms. In his view, the business model of the companies focuses mainly on three elements: engagement/attention by the users, growth of the platform advertisement and the revenue generated. Users of social networks may believe that the service is free of cost. However, Harris reveals the truth behind the complimentary usage: "**If you are not paying for the product, you are the product.**" This is to say, Facebook, Google, X, Instagram and other sites make use of the data and information which people willingly supply once they join a service. The platforms register all the activities of their users, for example the sites they visited, the searches they executed and what and how much they "liked" or "disliked". Analysing these user profiles, the services know a great deal about a person's emotions, relationships, interests and spending habits. The data is then used to make money. So, you and your data become the products which are sold to advertisers, publishers, insurance companies or political parties – in fact, anybody who thinks they can use the information and is willing to pay for it. For example,

Google offers a special service, Google Ads, to marketers, retailers, advertisers and publishers for a certain fee. In return, Google delivers adverts to users which are tailored to their preferences. Once you have googled an article online, you are bound to receive an advert sitting next to an article you are about to read on the net. "Social networking sites sell attention to advertisers", an analyst summed up. Google's ad technology is based on cookies and apart from allowing the display of adverts on websites, it can also control how often and for how long an ad is shown. Any click on the advert will increase Google's ad revenues.

Surveillance capitalism
The American social psychologist Shoshana Zuboff coined the phrase "surveillance capitalism" to explain the methods applied in today's digital economy. Social media services gather more and more information on ever larger portions of people's daily existence – how they shop, exercise or socialise – and then use that information to **both predict and shape their buying habits.** Users believe they are enjoying a service at no cost and willingly agree to the company's terms, which allow a practically unrestricted collection and assigning of data. As a result, phones track people's whereabouts so that firms can geotag them for advertisements. Location-based marketing displays ads to users in a relevant geographic area. Similarly, so-called loyalty cards or shopper club cards which big stores provide for their customers store shoppers' buying habits. Retailers can turn their knowledge into profit, since they know the preferences of their customers. They inundate patrons with individualised ads and other selling messages based on the information of the recorded buying habits. Critics of the system maintain that "Big Brother" is omnipresent on the Internet. They draw links to the totalitarian state in George Orwell's dystopian novel *1984* in which "Big Brother" constantly monitors people's movements to maintain absolute control. Like "Big Brother", social networking sites surveil their users, collect private data without their knowledge and use it for profit-making. As Shoshana Zuboff writes, "[s]urveillance capitalists know everything *about us*, whereas their operations are designed to be unknowable *to us*. They accumulate vast domains of new knowledge *from us*, but not *for us*. They predict our futures for the sake of others' gain, not ours."[3] To illustrate the extent of intrusion into customers' lives, newspapers reported that data analysts had found a link between the negativity of a community's social media posts and the higher risk of heart diseases in that community. Furthermore, your social media activities could be used as an indication of how likely you are to repay a loan.

Big Data to forecast developments and shape people's actions
IT specialists use analytics techniques, such as machine learning or artificial intelligence, to process the enormous amount of data. Besides being used to influence people's actions and behaviour, the gained information can also forecast developments. On the positive side, **predictive analytics** can help businesses and organisations to **work effectively**. For instance, raw material deliveries could be based on projected

---

3 Shoshana Zuboff, *The Age of Surveillance Capitalism. The Fight for a Human Future at the New Frontier of Power*, Profile Books, 2019.

future demands or Big Data can assist police in New York and other big cities to fight crime. With the help of data, the NYPD can analyse arrest patterns and geolocate crime hotspots. The results are used to take measures to strengthen public safety in dangerous areas.

However, worrying for many people is the risk of an Orwellian nightmare if the collected information comes into **the wrong hands**. More precisely, when arguing with Shoshana Zuboff, it already is in the wrong hands because it is used to **manipulate** us: In a commercial view, it is not the individual who ultimately decides independently where or what to buy, but the social networking sites influence and nudge them towards the decision.

Artificial Intelligence is neither objective nor failproof
When AI is used to collect and analyse big data, it is important to remember that the results the AI technologies come to can easily be misleading, and decisions taken with the help of machines need not be better than those taken by humans. The American mathematician and data scientist Cathy O'Neill found that algorithms are not objective, but "opinion[s] embedded in maths", because they ultimately rely on **previous data** as well as on **individual definitions of success** and are therefore **biased**. So, the blind trust in AI's objectivity will often lead to inaccurate or flawed results. For example, when algorithms were used to supposedly make hiring more objective, it transpired that women as well as ethnic minorities were discriminated against simply because the data the algorithm had been fed was also biased against them. Consequently, decisions taken on the basis of algorithms may be false. Today's economy requires steadily improved and more refined artificial intelligence technologies – especially considering the importance and scope of big data.

In light of the constant progress that is being made with AI technologies, worries that people might soon be surpassed and replaced by machines are increasing. That is why skills that are unique to human beings become all the more important. Four of these so-called **21st-century skills**, collaboration, creativity, critical thinking and communication, are summarised as the **4Cs**. Furthermore, heated discussions as to rules and regulations, laws and control systems centre around the use of AI.

"Data is the new oil"
Economists have coined the phrase "data economy" to describe the influence and prominence of big data in today's society. Industrialists agree that in the 21st century, data has taken the role which oil played for industrialisation and economic growth in the 18th and 19th centuries. It has become the world's most valuable resource today, opening up opportunities for governments, local authorities and businesses. However, just like oil, raw data is not valuable in itself, it needs to be processed and refined. This means, the mass of information must be gathered completely and accurately, connected to other relevant data and used efficiently. Another valid point of comparison with oil is that the negative side effects of big data compilation and the reliance upon it must not be overlooked.

Psychological consequences of social networking

Social media and addiction
Social networking sites' primary aim is to grab their users' attention. To achieve this, the companies apply the same methods as gambling firms and the video games industry. This is why social media tools have been compared with slot machines, which create **psychological dependencies**. The computer specialist Edward Tufte aptly described the addiction in the following words: "There are only two industries that call their customers 'users': illegal drugs and software." In other words, many users become addicted and cannot refrain from constantly checking and scrolling through their accounts and networking sites.

For actively participating in social networks, the users receive symbolic rewards ("likes" or "hearts"). This produces **dopamine** in their brains, which is then released into their systems. Recent neurological studies suggest that the constant stream of reposts, likes and shares triggers the same kind of chemical reaction as if the users were injected with a dose of cocaine. Young people in particular cannot resist the lure of their smartphones. Like addicts, they seem to be craving another dose of dopamine. Pleasure is usually followed by a feeling of hangover or comedown, which would disappear after some time. However, there is a natural tendency to immediately counteract the negative emotion by going back to the source of pleasure for another dose. Neuroscientists, psychologists and general practitioners warn of the excessive and compulsive use of social media because it may have the same negative effects as any other substance abuse. Some people just cannot leave their cell phones alone and other areas of life tend to get too little attention, which is socially and physically harmful. Not only are **meaningful real-life interactions substituted** with somehow artificial online encounters, but also people's **physical health** obviously **suffers** from them constantly staring at a computer or smartphone screen and neglecting sports, fresh air and movement. Furthermore, smartphones present an even greater risk when used in traffic. Consequently, laws have been passed banning handheld cell phone use or text messaging while operating a motor vehicle.

Information overload (infobesity)
The **global 24-hour availability** of news, posts and stories on the net creates an overwhelming load of information which few people can keep up with. The processing power of computers is steadily increasing, whereas that of the human brain is not. Consequently, it is getting harder to tell what is important or irrelevant, what is true and what is false. The term "information overload" describes the situation when the amount of input to a system exceeds its processing capacity. The excess of information, sometimes referred to as **infoxication** (an allusion to intoxication) or **infobesity** (a combination of info and obesity), is considered the disease of the digital society. It becomes time-consuming and difficult to sort through the confusing mass of information, understand an issue and then make an effective decision. Information overload is regarded as **the enemy of good decisions**. As the volume of information is steadily growing on the Internet, it is essential to **learn how to search the web effectively** and filter useful bits of news from less useful ones.

The vulnerability of young people

In February 2022, the Kids Online Safety Act was introduced in Congress to try and mitigate the harmful effects social media could have on younger users in particular. The photo and video sharing app Instagram – owned by Facebook (now Meta) – is often regarded as particularly damaging to a significant portion of young users, above all teenage girls. Its negative influence on teenagers' self-esteem comes from young users comparing themselves with beautiful and often ultra-thin models online. What complicates matters is the fact that Instagram posts are not necessarily realistic and balanced depictions, but photos can be easily manipulated and the people who are posting on the app tend to exaggerate positive aspects of their lives while glossing over more negative ones. **Feelings of personal failure, self-loathing and mental distress** as well as the inability to deal with difficult emotions can eventually lead to self-harm. Statistics have found connections between social media usage and **eating disorders, depression and even suicide**.

In addition, educators and parents worry about the addictive nature of social media through which **young people lose contact with reality**. They neglect their social contacts and daily duties when they spend hours in virtual worlds. Reducing phone use is extremely difficult because at first, it causes the brain's pleasure-pain balance to tilt to the side of pain, making people feel restless and miserable. The time-consuming and negative impact of social networking sites has made many users, including some of Silicon Valley's biggest tech managers, decide to curb their time on social media. Some have even installed apps to control their usage.

Social networking can also become dangerous because today youngsters are at greater **risk of abuse** while sitting in their bedroom in front of a computer screen than outside on the street. Social networks are often used to be offensive or nasty towards other people. Repetitive and persistent personal attacks, insults and threats affect the victims of **cyberbullying** tremendously. It is also necessary to protect young users from being bombarded with sexual messages over the Internet. Although it is rather difficult to investigate computer crimes because of the **anonymity of the net**, the police are increasing their efforts to trace the producers and traffickers of child pornography and similar forms of sexual abuse on the Internet.

The lure of "influencers"

Apart from sending out messages on television, radio or in the print media, companies spend millions on **social-media advertisements**, many of which are targeted at adolescents. Many bloggers or "online influencers" collaborate with firms to market their products or services to an enormous number of potential customers. More often than not, the posts and links referring to manufacturers are not disclosed as paid advertisements. **Concealed advertising** is hard to detect and can create needs in young people, who are persuaded to buy the things "influencers" show in their clips. So, social-media marketing is a lucrative and rapidly growing business and has become a continually growing pillar of the advertising industry.

Possible solutions to the social dilemma

The documentary *The Social Dilemma* deals with the problem that social media, which were originally supposed to be or could be a force for good, have deteriorated into a destructive element in many individuals' lives and society at large. As the trailer of the film puts it, "the technology that connects us also divides us, manipulates us, distracts us, controls us, polarises us, monetises us". Step by step, researchers have discovered that there is a link between social media and mental health, that users get addicted to their electronic devices, they are often isolated in filter bubbles and cyber-attacks and fake news can have serious political consequences. So, social media might have transformed the information age into the disinformation age, thus eroding democracy and the social fabric.

Can companies regulate themselves?

In 2021 in the aftermath of the violent riots of Trump supporters, who even stormed the Capitol and had apparently largely organised themselves through social media, the leaders of the biggest tech firms, such as Twitter, Facebook and Google, had to appear before a panel of the US Congress and explain how they took responsibility for the problems connected with their platforms and what they intended to do about them in the future. All managers said they were willing to improve the safety, privacy and wellbeing of their users as well as the networks' influence on society at large and made various suggestions. For instance, they promised to **crack down on misinformation or incitements to violence**. However, there remains the general conflict of how much freedom of speech the platforms should allow and the decision about what constitutes more than a mere expression of opinion and is rather harmful.

Furthermore, what is so **destructive is the very business model** on which the social media sites are operating, namely that algorithms are used to filter the content which is being shown to users. This content aims at catching their attention, binding them to the platform and making them receptive for personalised advertisements. The advertisements are what the tech companies profit from because they are paid by the advertisers. On the other hand, the algorithms are also responsible for the filter bubbles that are accused of causing polarisation and a division of society. Other points of discussion are **youth protection laws** and the ever-recurring theme of **how safe the users' data** are on the social networks.

Government measures to protect users from the big tech giants

As became apparent during the above-mentioned Congress panel with tech giants, social media legislation in the USA is incomplete and rather lax. For instance, **Section 230 of the Communications Decency Act** even explicitly frees tech platforms from being held responsible for content posted by users. However, demands for some sort of supervision and regulation have become louder and even the revocation of Section 230 has been suggested.

Another topic that has been at the forefront of attention for quite some time (and especially since scandals like the one surrounding Cambridge Analytica came to light) is **data protection** and how much data tech companies are allowed to collect and process. While the companies still do collect billions of bits of information, they are at least partly obliged to disclose their usage of them, and passing on unknowing users' data has been fined in several sensational lawsuits. Particularly during the Covid-19 pandemic, when even more activities moved online so that tech giants, in contrast to "real-life" companies, profited immensely, a **tax on the collection of data** has been suggested. If "data is the new oil", it should also be treated thus and seen as something valuable, which it undoubtedly is. So far, however, there has been no comprehensive suggestion on how to go about introducing a digital data collection tax.

In Europe, governments have taken a firmer stand against America's tech giants. The European Union has been at the forefront of regulating the digital economy, leveraging its **antitrust laws** against big tech companies such as Google. For example, in 2017 the European Commission levied a € 2.4 billion fine on Google for abusing its monopoly on online shopping. Considering the vast power and worrying impact on people's behaviour, politics and freedom of speech, governments have passed specific laws or established agencies to govern and control social networking sites. In 2021, the 27-nation community confirmed Europe's role as a pacesetter for regulating the tech industry. The ambitious plan is to update the EU's regulations for digital companies and adopt measures to rein in Big Tech and protect users on their platforms. The **Digital Services Act** (DSA) and **Digital Markets Act** (DMA) require social media companies like Google and Facebook to treat rivals fairly, scan their platforms for illegal content or hate speech and delete them if necessary. "We are now democratically reclaiming our online environment," a EU Parliament member said. "The DSA is bringing EU tech regulation into the 21st century, and it is about time." When it comes to Artificial Intelligence and its regulation and control, the EU has acted as a trailblazer once more: The **EU Artificial Intelligence Act (2024)** is the world's first extensive legal framework attempting to rein in the technology's risks and guarantee its safe and ethical usage.

What users can do

Users of social media networking sites must realise that the business model of the companies is to "rake in money" by grabbing the users' attention and selling it to advertisers. The awareness of how algorithms work in this process should make social media users **consciously search for alternative opinions** in order not to stay trapped in their own filter bubbles. Furthermore, **time limits** for online usage are an important step against addiction. Jaron Lanier, an American computer scientist and author of the non-fiction book *Ten Arguments for Deleting Your Social Media Accounts Right Now*, goes even further. According to him, it is not only true that users become the product of social media sites, but "[i]t's the gradual, slight, imperceptible change in your own behaviour and perception that is the product." This means, social media changes what you do, how you think, what you are. So, Lanier's advice is rather radical in postulating: "You, you, you have the affirmative responsibility to invent and demonstrate ways to live without the crap that is destroying society. Quitting is the only way, for now, to learn what can replace our grand mistake."[4]

---

4 Lanier, Jaron. *Ten Arguments for Deleting Your Social Media Accounts Right Now*. Henry Holt and Co., 2018.

Sachtext   Video-Set 1

Assignments

1. **Outline** the author's view on social media. *(Video 1)*

2. **Analyse** the means he uses to convey his attitude and the effect they have on the reader. *(Video 2)*

3. **Write a letter to the editor/blog entry/speech** expressing your own opinion on the chances and dangers of social media. *(Video 3)*

I Used to Think Social Media Was a Force for Good. Now the Evidence Says I Was Wrong
by Matt Haig
More and more, it's clear these platforms create divisions, exploit our insecurities and risk our health. They're as bad as the tobacco industry.

1 I used to think social media was essentially a force for good, whether it was to initiate the Arab spring of 2011, or simply as a useful tool for bringing together like-minded people to share videos of ninja cats. Having spent a lot of time thinking about mental health, I even saw social media's much-maligned potential for anonymity as a good
5 thing, helping people to open up about problems when they might not feel able to do so in that physical space we still quaintly call real life. [...]

Yes, I would occasionally feel that maybe staring at my Twitter feed near-continuously for seven hours wasn't that healthy [...]. Yes, I'd see articles warning of the dangers of excessive internet use, but I dismissed these as traditional, reactionary
10 takes. I saw social media naysayers as the first reviewers of Technicolor movies, who felt the colour distracted from the story, or were like the people who walked out on Bob Dylan at Newport folk festival for playing an electric guitar, or like those who warned that radio or TV or video games or miniskirts, or hip-hop or selfies or fidget spinners or whatever, would lead to the end of civilisation. [...]
15 Then I started the research for a book I am writing on how the external world affects our mental health. I wanted to acknowledge the downsides of social media, but to argue that far from being a force for ill, it offers a safe place where the insanities of life elsewhere can be processed and articulated.

But the deeper into the research I went, the harder it was to sustain this argument.
20 Even the internet activist and former Google employee Wael Ghonim – one of the initiators of the Arab spring and one-time poster boy for internet-inspired revolution – who once saw social media as a social cure – now saw it as a negative force. [...]: "The same tool that united us to topple dictators eventually tore us apart." Ghonim saw social

1

media polarising people into angry opposing camps – army supporters and Islamists –
25 leaving centrists such as himself stuck in the middle, powerless.
And this isn't just politics. It's health too. A survey conducted by the Royal Society of Public Health asked 1,500 young people to keep track of their moods while
on the five most popular social media sites. Instagram and Snapchat came out worst,
often inspiring feelings of inadequacy, anxiety and self-loathing. [...]
30 Kurt Vonnegut said: "We are what we pretend to be, so we must be careful who
we pretend to be." This seems especially true now we have reached a new stage of marketing where we are not just consumers, but also the thing consumed. If you have
friends you only ever talk to on Facebook, your entire relationship with them is framed
by commerce. When we willingly choose to become unpaid content providers, we
35 commercialise ourselves. And we are encouraged to be obsessed with numbers (of
followers, messages, comments, retweets, favourites), as if operating in a kind of
friend economy, an emotional stock market where the stock is ourselves and where
we are encouraged to weigh our worth against others.
Of course, humans comparing themselves to others isn't new. But when the oth-
40 ers are every human on the internet, people end up comparing themselves – their
looks, their relationships, their wealth, their lives – to the carefully filtered lives of
people they would never meet in the real world – and feeling inadequate.
Reading first-hand accounts by people with bulimia and anorexia who are convinced that social media exacerbated or even triggered their illnesses, I began to real-
45 ise something: this situation is not the equivalent of Bob Dylan's electric guitar. It is
closer to the tobacco or fast-food industries, where vested interests deny the existence
of blatant problems that were not there before. [...]
We are traditionally far better at realising risks to physical health than to mental
health, even when they are interrelated. If we can accept that our physical health can
50 be shaped by society – by secondhand smoke or a bad diet – then we must accept that
our mental health can be too. And as our social spaces increasingly become digital
spaces, we need to look seriously and urgently at how these new, business-owned societies are affecting our minds. We must try to see how the rising mental health crisis
may be related to the way people are living and interacting.
55 Facebook's Mark Zuckerberg says that "by giving people the power to share,
we're making the world more transparent". But what we really need to do is make
social media transparent.
Of course, we won't stop using it – I certainly won't – but precisely for that reason
we need to know more about what it is doing to us. To our politics, to our health, to
60 the future generation, and to the world around us. We need to ensure we are still the
ones using the technology – and that the technology isn't using us. *(842 words)*

*Matt Haig: "I Used to Think Social Media Was a Force for Good. Now the Evidence Says I Was
Wrong", https://www.theguardian.com/commentisfree/2017/sep/06/social-media-good-evidence-
platforms-insecurities-health, 06 September 2017, Copyright Guardian News & Media Ltd 2020*

Annotations
l. 2   *Arab spring:* series of protests and rebellions against authoritarian regimes, e. g. in Tu-
            nisia, Egypt and Libya
ll. 13/14   *fidget spinner:* a popular toy
l. 30   *Kurt Vonnegut:* famous American writer (1922–2007)

Literarischer Text   **Video-Set 2**

Assignments

1. **Describe** the night of the shooting as it is presented in the interview and as Starr remembers it. *(Video 1)*

2. **Characterise** the police officer as he is presented in this extract. Take the narrative perspective into account. *(Video 2)*

3. " 'His life always matters more!' [...] 'That's the problem!' " (ll. 82/83) **Discuss** the statement referring to the general situation of African Americans in the US. *(Video 3)*

The Hate U Give
by Angie Thomas
Starr, who lives in the fictional, Black neighborhood of Garden Heights, is the only witness of a police shooting in which her childhood friend Khalil got killed. She goes to a school in a different district, which is mainly attended by White kids. For fear of being singled out she does not talk to her school-friends about her life in Garden Heights, not even about the shooting.

1 "Back up, back up," I tell Maya. She flicks through the channels, and when he ap-pears again, I say, "Right there!"

I've pictured his face so much. Actually seeing it again is different. My memory is pretty spot-on – a thin, jagged scar above his lip, bursts of freckles that cover his
5 face and neck.

My stomach churns and my skin crawls, and I wanna get away from <u>One-Fifteen</u>. My instinct doesn't care that it's a photograph being shown on TV. A silver cross pendant hangs from his neck, like he's saying Jesus endorses what he did. We must believe in a different Jesus.
10 What looks like an older version of him appears on the screen [...].

"My son was afraid for his life," he says. "He only wanted to get home to his wife and kids."

Pictures flash on the screen. One-Fifteen smiles with his arms draped around a blurred-out woman. He's on a fishing trip with two small, blurred-out children. They
15 show him with a smiley golden retriever, with his pastor and some fellow deacons who are all blurred out, and then in his police uniform.

"Officer Brian Cruise Jr. has been on the force for sixteen years," the voice-over says, and more pics of him as a cop are shown. He's been a cop for as long as Khalil

3

was alive, and I wonder if in some sick twist of fate Khalil was only born for this
20 man to kill.

"A majority of those years have been spent serving in Garden Heights," the
voice-over continues, "a neighborhood notorious for gang and drug dealers."

I tense as footage of my neighborhood, my home, is shown. It's like they picked
the worst parts – the drug addicts roaming the streets, the broken-down Cedar Grove
25 projects, gangbangers flashing signs, bodies on the sidewalks with white sheets over
them. What about Mrs. Rooks and her cakes? Or Mr. Lewis and his haircuts? Mr. Reu-
ben? The clinic? My family?

Me?

I feel Hailey's and Maya's eyes on me. I can't look at them.

30 "My son loved working in the neighborhood," One-Fifteen's father claims. "He
always wanted to make a difference in the lives there."

Funny. Slave masters thought they were making a difference in black people's
lives too. Saving them from their "wild African ways." Same shit, different century. I
wish people like them would stop thinking that people like me need saving.

35 One-Fifteen Sr. talks about his son's life before the shooting. How he was a
good kid who never got into trouble, always wanted to help others. […]

The interviewer asks about that night.

"Apparently, Brian pulled the kid over 'cause he had a broken taillight and was
speeding."

40 Khalil wasn't speeding.

"He told me, 'Pop, soon as I pulled him over, I had a bad feeling,'" says One-
Fifteen Sr.

"Why is that?" the interviewer asks.

"He said the kid and his friend immediately started cursing him out –"
45 We never cursed.

"And they kept glancing at each other, like they were up to something. Brian says
that's when he got scared, 'cause they could've taken him down if they teamed up."

I couldn't have taken anyone down. I was too afraid. He makes us sound like
we're superhumans. We're kids.

50 "No matter how afraid he is, my son's still gonna do his job," he says. "And
that's all he set out to do that night."

"There have been reports that Khalil Harris was unarmed when the incident took
place," the interviewer says. "Has your son told you why he made the decision to
shoot?"

55 "Brian says he had his back to the kid, and he heard the kid say, 'I'm gon' show
your ass today.'"

No, no, no. Khalil asked if I was okay.

"Brian turned around and saw something in the car door. He thought it was a gun –"
It was a hairbrush. […]

60 "Brian's a good boy," he says, in tears. "He only wanted to get home to his family, and people are making him out to be a monster."

That's all Khalil and I wanted, and you're making us out to be monsters. […]

"How has your son's life changed since this happened?" the interviewer asks.

"All our lives have been hell, honestly," his father claims. "Brian's a people per-
65 son, but now he's afraid to go out in public, even for something simple as getting a
gallon of milk. There have been threats on his life, our family's lives. His wife had to
quit her job. He's even been attacked by fellow officers." […]
"This is awful," Hailey says. "That poor family."
She's looking at One-Fifteen Sr. with sympathy that belongs to Brenda and Ms.
70 Rosalie.
I blink several times. "What?"
"His son lost everything because he was trying to do his job and protect himself.
His life matters too, you know?"
I cannot right now. I can't. I stand up or otherwise I will say or do something re-
75 ally stupid. Like punch her.
"I need to … yeah." I say all that I can and start for the door, but Maya grabs the
tail of my cardigan. […]
"Maya," I say, as calmly as possible. "Please let me go. I cannot talk to her. Did
you not hear what she said?"
80 "Are you serious right now?" Hailey asks. "What's wrong with saying his life
matters too?"
"His life always matters more!" My voice is gruff, and my throat is tight. "That's
the problem!" *(970 words)*

Thomas, Angie: The Hate U Give. *London: Walker Books Ltd, 2017. pp. 243–247*

Annotations
l. 6   *One-Fifteen:* One-Fifteen is the badge number of the police officer who shot Khalil.
ll. 69/70   *Brenda and Ms. Rosalie:* Khalil's mother and grandmother

5

Politics, Culture and Society – between Tradition and Change: USA

Die nachfolgende Abituraufgabe behandelt das Thema African American Experiences. *Dieses stellt einen Teilbereich des Themas* Politics, Culture and Society – between Tradition and Change: USA *dar.*

Assignments

Comprehension

1. Summarize how people react to the decision of websites not to promote plantation weddings anymore.

Analysis

2. Analyze the author's view on plantation weddings.

Comment/Creative Writing (Choose one.)

3.1 Comment on plantation weddings in today's America. Refer both to the article and your coursework.

or

3.2 Imagine your American friend has told you of his/her idea of getting married on a plantation. You write an email to him/her in which you give your opinion about this idea, considering African American experiences today.
Write that email.

Plantation Weddings Are Wrong. Why Is It so Hard for White Americans to Admit that?
by Malaika Jabali, *The Guardian*, 11 December 2019

Last Thursday, BuzzFeed News reported that online platforms, including Pinterest and the <u>Knot Worldwide</u>, would restrict content that features or romanticizes weddings held on former slave plantations. These changes were the result of a campaign by the social justice organization *Color of Change*. In a letter, *Color of Change* wrote that
5 "plantations are physical reminders of one of the most horrific human rights abuses the world has ever seen. The wedding industry routinely denies the violent conditions Black people faced under <u>chattel slavery</u> by promoting plantations as romantic places to marry."
   Color of Change posted the news on Facebook, where it was, of course, received
10 with appropriate empathy and contemplation. The 600 comments included lots of gems such as "Proud of our civil war plantation wedding! Eat shit color of change [sic]!!" because one exclamation point wasn't enough. There was the old-faithful

6

"slavery was too long ago" argument, with one commenter adding, "So stupid. That was hundreds of years ago. Why not call them beautiful homes or restored homes.
15 Are they canceling castle weddings too?" And the unheard-of sentiment: "There were slaves of every color."

The basic themes were echoed by the wedding vendors quoted in news reports: that slavery was in the past, that it wasn't that bad, that the splendor of plantations has outlived whatever negativity they might represent. While these pronouncements
20 can be easily countered with reason, logic unfortunately doesn't matter.

Slavery was indeed "in the past" – a shocker to readers, I'm sure. Yet this hasn't prevented America from fervently preserving the history it does deem worthwhile, no matter how far back or inconsequential. Many Americans zealously defend their right to praise the Confederate flag, defend inanimate buildings from demolition or resto-
25 ration (have you seen the passion among landmark preservationists?), and, yes, scroll endlessly through plantation-inspo, with none of the icky historical context.

Historical texts, news articles and academic research are all available for anyone genuinely interested in examining slavery's brutality, which was often most severe in the deep south states where slave-owners built plantation mansions. If anything, the
30 cruelty of the institution has been underestimated. Southern school districts are known to issue textbooks reducing enslaved black men, women and children to mere "workers" – rather than what they were: forced laborers who often lived in perpetual terror and were sold as property with no human rights.

There's also the persistent trope that black people were happy slaves. But most
35 African Americans don't find much joy in seeing plantations glorified and their human histories deemed a niggling inconvenience.

For people committed to this narrative, however, facts don't matter. That their feelings are regularly given such credence reveals one end of America's white supremacist spectrum. While we tend to associate white supremacy with reactionary vio-
40 lence and alt-right trolls, it also lives in more subtler spaces. It's not just about the maintenance of white power structures, but the prioritization of white Americans' feelings and experiences.

These are the same feelings that have discounted black oppression in every era of black American life. In 1964, just a few months after the Civil Rights Act was
45 passed and its effects were yet to be seen, a majority of white New Yorkers polled by the *New York Times* felt that the civil rights movement had gone too far. While the Voting Rights Act and Fair Housing Act had yet to be passed, claims of "reverse discrimination" already abounded.

Today, plenty of people still claim that the Confederacy had nothing to do with
50 hatred, and was a movement founded for personal freedom and "states' rights". Similarly, discrimination against black consumers and homeowners wasn't about subjugation, but asserting one's private rights without government interference.

The same logic guides the people who apparently believe that wedding websites restricting plantation content is an affront to the abstract rights of white Americans.
55 White people being told what to do, even in theory, is a problem.

Many white Americans insist that they had no role in slavery and that it was "so long ago". Yet they seem quite adamant about defending it. Of course, denying black

7

Americans' pain – and preserving and normalizing the symbols of black subjugation – is just as American as slavery itself.   *(695 words)*

Malaika Jabali: "Plantation Weddings Are Wrong. Why Is It so Hard for White Americans to Admit that?", The Guardian, 11 December 2019, https://www.theguardian.com/commentisfree/2019/dec/11/ plantation-weddings-are-wrong-why-is-it-so-hard-for-white-americans-to-admit-that © Guardian News & Media Ltd 2021

Annotations

l. 2   *Knot Worldwide:* an online company which organizes big family events, especially weddings

l. 7   *chattel slavery:* a type of slavery where the slaves are regarded as the personal property (chattel) of the owner

l. 12   *[sic]:* used to indicate that a quote was reproduced exactly like in the original – including possible mistakes

l. 26   *plantation-inspo:* material advertising events at plantations / *inspo:* abbreviation for inspiration

l. 34   *trope:* stylistic device that creates a mental image; *here:* a common or overused theme or device

l. 37   *narrative:* description of events

l. 40   *alt-right:* a group of people with extreme right-wing views, including supremacist views on race, who use the internet rather than traditional politics to organize and share opinions

l. 40   *troll:* a writer of intentionally annoying or offensive messages on the internet, in order to get attention or cause trouble

Lösungsvorschläge

1. *The assignment tells you to summarise, that is give the basic ideas of the text in your own words. In this case, you should limit your answer to people's reactions to the idea of not promoting plantation weddings anymore. In other words, you have to present different attitudes as to plantation weddings. The task talks of "people" quite generally. So, you can mention reactions in social media, the wedding vendors, but also the journalist herself and the civil rights group* Color of Change *she mentions. When it comes to structuring your answer, you should start with an introductory paragraph, in which you give the main information about your source, and then group together reactions critical of the decision (Facebook users, vendors) on the one hand and approval (Jabali,* Color of Change*) on the other.*
You could structure your answer like this:
   – *introductory paragraph*
   – *approval of platforms' decision:*
     • Color of Change's *campaign (cf. ll. 3–8)*
     • *author of the article agrees with* Color of Change *(cf. for example headline)*
   – *criticism of platforms' decision:*
     • *Facebook users' anger and argument that the past should not have such an impact on the present (cf. ll. 9–16)*
     • *vendors' similar attempts to downplay the horrors of slavery (cf. ll. 17–19)*
     • *assault on personal freedom of White Americans to do as they please (cf. ll. 53–55)*

In her article "Plantation Weddings Are Wrong. Why Is It so Hard for White Americans to Admit That?", published in *The Guardian* in December 2019, Malaika Jabali talks about the decision of several online platforms to no longer promote former slave plantations as wedding venues. This move was received controversially and caused a multitude of reactions. introduction

A campaign of *Color of Change* initiated the new advertising policy. So, the civil rights organisation and their supporters certainly see the platforms' attitude against plantation weddings as positive and a step in the right direction. So does the author of the article herself, who repeats *Color of Change's* argument that arranging weddings in places which are reminders of African Americans' misery, suffering and deaths is disrespectful. approval of platforms' decision

Many people, however, also reacted in a less supportive manner and greeted the decision with anger and incomprehension. A common way to try and justify keeping plantations as wedding venues is to disconnect the enormity of past slavery from the present. According to these views, times have changed and the plantation mansions should only be seen as beautiful buildings. Some Americans even see the online platforms' decision not to criticism of platforms' decision

9

show certain content as a limitation of people's personal freedom to choose to marry wherever they want. The wedding industry echoes those views and also tries to downplay the insult and hurt connected with these historical monuments. *(229 words)*

2. *The author's view on plantation weddings is very obvious: She is opposed to them and therefore applauds the platforms' decision to no longer promote them. Yet, for an assignment like this, it is not enough to state this, you also need to find proof and explain how she shows her opinion. You should argue both with the content from Jabali's article and with the language she uses to express herself. The following aspects could come up in your solution:*
   - *Jabali's clear rejection of plantation weddings:*
     - *headline of the article*
     - *argumentation of* Color of Change *(cf. ll. 5–8)*
   - *discrediting of opponents' views:*
     - *sarcasm with regard to aggressive and insensitive Facebook posts (cf. ll. 9–16)*
     - *opponents' views presented as illogical and unconvincing (cf. ll. 19/20, 27, 37)*
       - *past arbitrarily either glossed over or remembered (cf. ll. 12/13, 13/14, 18 vs. 21–26)*
       - *playing down slavery (cf. ll. 29–36)*
   - *wider context of White supremacy:*
     - *historical example of Civil Rights Movement which triggered claims of "reverse discrimination" (cf. ll. 43–48)*
     - *preference given to White opinions and experiences (cf. ll. 40–42, 53–55)*
     - *damning assessment that "denying black Americans' pain [...] is just as American as slavery itself" (cf. ll. 57–59)*

That Malaika Jabali rejects plantation weddings is apparent throughout her article. The headline explicitly says, "Plantation Weddings Are Wrong. Why Is It so Hard for White Americans to Admit that?". Thus, she not only expresses her disapproval, but also points to the resistance of Americans to accept this. To justify her own stance, she quotes the argumentation of *Color of Change* that plantations were places where slaves were treated with brutality and that hosting celebrations there is completely disrespectful (cf. ll. 5–8). | Jabali's clear rejection of plantation weddings

Having thus established her own negative view, the rest of the article focuses on presenting and discrediting opposing views. In the paragraph from line 9 to line 16, she sarcastically calls Facebook users' aggressive and insensitive posts "gems" (l. 11) that were written "with appropriate empathy and contemplation" (l. 10). In fact, the opposite is true and the commentators just | discrediting of opponents' views: sarcasm

10

bleat out their stupidity and ignorance unthinkingly and vulgar-
ly, but full of conviction (cf. ll. 11/12).

Jabali mocks this stupidity and postulates that many arguments
in favour of advertising plantation weddings "can be easily
countered with reason" (l. 20). In other words, she denies the
critics of the advertising ban a convincing and logical argumentation. "Historical texts, news articles and academic research"
(l. 27) would present opportunities to truly understand the controversy, but in Jabali's opinion neither "logic" nor "facts" matter to those who just do not want to see the moral wrongness of
plantation weddings (cf. ll. 20, 37).

opponents' views presented as il-logical and un-convincing

One proof of this lack of logic is the argument that the past
should no longer impact the present (cf. ll. 12/13, 13/14, 18),
which is repeatedly brought forward by exactly the same people
who "fervently preserv[e] the history [they] deem worthwhile"
(l. 22). Jabali goes on to corroborate this criticism with the further accusation that slavery is often downplayed, for instance
when enslaved people are called "mere 'workers'" (ll. 31/32) or
even the blatant lie of the "happy slaves" (l. 34) is perpetuated.
In other words, the arguments that are given in favour of plantation weddings are depicted as hypocritical.

arbitrary dealing with the past

According to Jabali, all that is part of a wider movement with
the aim to hold up current power structures and to give White
Americans' opinions and experiences preference over Black
Americans' (cf. ll. 40–42). This is shown by a historical example, namely that even the Civil Rights Movement, which is
nowadays seen as more than necessary and even too incomplete
in its achievements, triggered "claims of 'reverse racism'" (cf.
ll. 44–48).

wider context of White supremacy

To put it in a larger context, Jabali ends her article with the
damning assessment that many White Americans are quick to
feel endangered in their own liberties (cf. ll. 53–55) whereas
they are very slow to admit "black Americans' pain" (ll. 57/58).
Her last sentence that glossing over the cruel reality of Black
people's suffering "is just as American as slavery itself" (l. 59)
essentially accuses the practice of plantation weddings, this
clear evidence of a denial of history, as a perpetuation of injustices.   *(508 words)*

preference given to White opinions and experiences

3.1 *The assignment asks you to comment on plantation weddings. This means that
you should give your own opinion for or against the practice and justify it with
some convincing arguments. You do not need to take into account pros und cons,
although you can of course mention aspects, about which you are not entirely
sure. As the article is against plantation weddings, it is probably easier to take*

11

this position too. The current state of race relations, which you learnt about in your coursework, should also be taken into consideration.

The sample solution mentions the following points:
- *introduction: importance of wedding day and venue for many couples*
- *main part: criticism of plantation weddings*
  - *argument 1: weddings are celebratory occasions, so there will be a tendency to gloss over and downplay the horrors of the past*
  - *argument 2: legacy of slavery still alive, African Americans still disadvantaged*
- *conclusion: plantation weddings as a symbol of ignorance and a lack of respect for African American history*

Most people who plan to get married want to make this day a very special and memorable experience. So, the place where the ceremony and reception are to be held are of great importance for them. Wedding planners come to the couple's help, offering various locations for the event, such as not only hotels or restaurants, but also historic buildings, like country houses, ancient castles or other spectacular sites, for instance plantations in the south of the United States.

introduction

At a superficial glance, the mansions on these plantations are just grand, columned houses that have been perfectly restored to serve as solemn backdrops for such an important occasion. However, a campaign of *Color of Change*, an organisation advocating racial justice and campaigning for the civil rights of African Americans, has brought plantation weddings into disrepute. The activists describe the plantations as sites of violence and brutality. In their view, places that existed only because of the inhuman and cruel exploitation of Black slaves can in no way be accepted as suitable for a happy celebration.

main part: criticism of plantation weddings

I agree with this view. Wedding planners and plantation museums may argue that they offer visitors information about the history of the grand buildings and are therefore not shunning the past. This could be an important argument for preserving the historical sites and opening them to the public. They are not, however, places for staging happy get-togethers there. Wedding guests do not usually want to hear about the sufferings and deaths of enslaved Africans, on whose backs the wealth of their White owners was built. So, holding a wedding in one of these spots is disrespectful, as it will almost automatically downplay the suffering that these places have seen.

argument 1: celebrating on plantations downplays horrors of the past

Of course, in a way the same could be said about every single potential wedding venue: Who knows what happened there way back in the past and whose experiences might be disrespected by people happily celebrating in a place where others suffered?

transition to argument 2

12

Yet, the problem with slavery is that it is not enough to say that it has long been abolished, that we live in different times and the situation for African Americans has changed completely. African Americans' position in society has certainly improved since the days of the Civil Rights Movement but racism is still alive. Racial disparities have been reduced and people of colour have achieved equality in many areas. However, often this is only theoretically and legally speaking. Reality looks different: Black Americans still experience injustice and discrimination in almost all spheres of life. They are more often out of work and live below the poverty line than White Americans, they are discriminated against in employment, politics and the justice system. Furthermore, Black Americans are much more likely to be shot during an encounter with the police than White Americans. So, true equality is still a long way off. Taking all this into consideration, it is simply not true to claim that slavery is over and done with because its legacy is very much felt today.

argument 2: legacy of slavery still alive

In conclusion, I would agree with *Color Of Change's* campaign and the social media sites' reaction to it. Slavery and its repercussions are still too harmful to just ignore. One of these repercussions of slavery is exactly the tendency to deny or downplay its horrors. This tendency should not be supported by turning places of brutality and oppression into party venues, but the past should rather be faced honestly in order to achieve reconciliation and pave the way for a better future.   *(585 words)*

conclusion

3.2 *This is a creative task because you have to write an email to a fictional American friend, who is thinking about getting married on a plantation and asks you for your opinion. That you are writing to a friend should be reflected in the format of your text, which should include greetings typical for a personal email, the style of language you use as well as in the way you address him/her. Of course, in essence, this is an argumentative text because you should write about reasons why you approve or disapprove of a plantation wedding. Yet, even when you disapprove, which you will probably decide to do because it is easier to find arguments (from the text and your coursework) that bolster that position, make sure that you talk to your friend in an appropriate, that is friendly and empathetic, manner.*
The following points come up in the sample solution:
- *introduction: address and reference to friend's idea to marry on a plantation*
- *main part: personal opinion against plantation weddings*
  - *argument 1: horrors of the past in contrast to a celebratory occasion*
  - *argument 2: plantation weddings a further strain on race relations*
- *conclusion: empathy towards your friend, but advice to marry in another place*

Hi Janet, introduction

In your last email you wrote that you had come across an offer on a wedding planner site for a "dream wedding" on a beautiful plantation in Georgia. You said you were playing with the idea of surprising Dave with this plan but wanted to know what I thought about plantation weddings first – especially after you had heard criticism against this practice.

Well, let me start by telling you what happened to another American couple, friends of mine whom I met on their tour of Europe in Hamburg. We got chatting and they told me how they had met and eventually planned to get married. They had a "classic Southern" wedding in mind, which was being offered by a website. The location was absolutely terrific, a grand, columned mansion on a plantation in Georgia! Luckily, they decided to take a tour of the estate before the actual booking to learn a bit more about the history of the plantation. They expected to simply gain some interesting background knowledge about their wedding venue, but it turned out quite differently. The tour led them around the grounds, they saw the impressive mansion, but also the shabby huts and sheds where the slaves had lived under miserable conditions. So, they became very much aware of the dreadful history of the place and, in the end, they chose not to celebrate there. Of course, one could argue that if the people working at the mansion had known about their plans to book it as wedding venue and had not given them the historical tour, they could have just celebrated there without worrying about anything much. Yet, I still think that wouldn't have been right. I mean, simply keeping quiet about it doesn't make the past go away. Plantations are and should be reminders of a dark period of American history, of a time of violence and brutality and are therefore, in my view, simply not suitable for celebrations.

main part: argument 1 against plantation weddings: horrors of the past in contrast to a celebratory occasion

In addition, we all know – you perhaps better than me – that at present, race relations in the US are rather strained. Remember for instance the killings of Black people by members of the police force that happen with shocking regularity! In combination with other disadvantages and discriminatory practices that Black people face on an almost daily basis, it is not surprising that these acts of violence arouse anger and trigger civil rights protests. Consequently, many Black Americans would understandably see plantation weddings as just another sign of how much disrespect many White Americans show to the plight of their ancestors and how ignorant they are of the still-existent inequalities today. In short, I think the choice of a plantation as

argument 2 against plantation weddings: current race relations are strained enough

14

the place to arrange your nuptials, could be seen to have a political aspect.

I know that this might not be easy to accept, Janet, because in conclusion the end, your wedding is your very personal day and its planning your individual decision. So, what is most important to me, as your friend, is that you feel good about the day. Yet, as you are apparently already insecure yourself and started to wonder what the right thing to do would be, I am totally convinced that you and Dave will find a better place for your big day.

Please tell me what you decide. I'm looking forward to hearing from you.

Hanna   *(557 words)*

Politics, Culture and Society – between Tradition and Change: USA

Die nachfolgende Abituraufgabe behandelt das Thema African American Experiences. *Dieses stellt einen Teilbereich des Themas* Politics, Culture and Society – between Tradition and Change: USA *dar.*

Assignments

Comprehension

1. Summarize Barack Obama's experiences at college.

Analysis

2. Analyze the different attitudes to black identity at college and the stylistic means used to illustrate them.

Comment / Creative Writing (Choose one.)

3.1 Discuss to what extent different ways to overcome racism in the US have proved successful so far. In your answer refer to the excerpt as well as to your coursework.

or

3.2 Imagine you are an exchange student at an American high school who has joined the debating society of this school. In a competition with another school you have to debate the current state of race-relations in the US. The excerpts from Barack Obama's memoir below have inspired you.
Write the opening speech for your team.

Dreams from My Father
by Barack Obama
In this excerpt from his memoirs, Barack Obama revisits his college days, starting with what his old mentor Frank had warned him about beforehand.

1 What had Frank called college? *An advanced degree in compromise.* I thought back to the last time I had seen the old poet, a few days before I left Hawaii. […] Finally he had asked me what it was that I expected to get out of college. I told him I didn't know. He shook his big, hoary head. "Well," he said, "that's the problem, isn't it?
5 You don't know. You're just like the rest of these young cats out here. All you know is that college is the next thing you're supposed to do. And the people who are old enough to know better, who fought all those years for your right to go to college – they're just so happy to see you in there that they won't tell you the truth. The real price of admission."

16

"And what's that?"

"Leaving your race at the door," he said. "Leaving your people behind." He studied me over the top of his reading glasses. "Understand something, boy. You're not going to college to get educated. You're going there to get trained. […] They'll train you so good, you'll start believing what they tell you about equal opportunity and the American way and all that shit. They'll give you a corner office and invite you to fancy dinners, and tell you you're a credit to your race. Until you want to actually start running things, and then they'll yank on your chain and let you know that you may be a well-trained, well-paid nigger, but you're a nigger just the same." "So what is it you're telling me – that I shouldn't be going to college?" Frank's shoulders slumped, and he fell back in his chair with a sigh. "No. I didn't say that. You've got to go. I'm just telling you to keep your eyes open. Stay awake." […]

Anyway, most of the other black students at Oxy didn't seem all that worried about compromise. There were enough of us on campus to constitute a tribe, and when it came to hanging out many of us chose to function like a tribe, staying close together, traveling in packs. […]

Our worries seemed indistinguishable from those of the white kids around us. Surviving classes. Finding a well-paying gig after graduation. Trying to get laid. I had stumbled upon one of the well-kept secrets about black people: that most of us weren't interested in revolt; that most of us were tired of thinking about race all the time; that if we preferred to keep to ourselves it was mainly because that was the easiest way to stop thinking about it, easier than spending all your time mad or trying to guess whatever it was that white folks were thinking about you.

So why couldn't I let it go? I don't know. I didn't have the luxury, I suppose, the certainty of the tribe. Grow up in Compton and survival becomes a revolutionary act. You get to college and your family is still back there rooting for you. They're happy to see you escape; there's no question of betrayal.

But I hadn't grown up in Compton, or Watts. I had nothing to escape from except my own inner doubt. I was more like the black students who had grown up in the suburbs, kids whose parents had already paid the price of escape. You could spot them right away by the way they talked, the people they sat with in the cafeteria. When pressed, they would sputter and explain that they refused to be categorized. They weren't defined by the color of their skin, they would tell you. They were individuals. […]

One day I asked [my college friend Joyce] if she was going to the Black Students' Association meeting. She looked at me funny, then started shaking her head like a baby who doesn't want what it sees on the spoon. "I'm not black," Joyce said. "I'm *multiracial*." Then she started telling me about her father, who *happened* to be Italian and was the sweetest man in the world; and her mother, who *happened* to be part African and part French and part Native American and part something else. "Why should I have to choose between them?" she asked me. Her voice cracked, and I thought she was going to cry. "It's not white people who are making me choose. Maybe it used to be that way, but now they're willing to treat me like a person. No – it's *black people* who always have to make everything racial. *They're* the ones making me choose. *They're* the ones who are telling me that I can't be who I am …"

They, they, they. That was the problem with people like Joyce. They talked about the richness of their multicultural heritage and it sounded real good, until you noticed that they avoided black people. It wasn't a matter of conscious choice, necessarily, just a matter of gravitational pull, the way integration always worked, a one-way street. The minority assimilated into the dominant culture, not the other way around. Only white culture could be neutral and objective. Only white culture could be nonracial, willing to adopt the occasional exotic into its ranks. Only white culture had individuals. And we, the half-breeds and the college-degreed, take a survey of the situation and think to ourselves, Why should we get lumped in with the losers if we don't have to? We become only so grateful to lose ourselves in the crowd, America's happy, faceless marketplace; and we're never so outraged as when a cabbie drives past us or the woman in the elevator clutches her purse, not so much because we're bothered by the fact that such indignities are what less fortunate coloreds have to put up with every single day of their lives – although that's what we tell ourselves – but because we're wearing a <u>Brooks Brothers</u> suit and speak impeccable English and yet have somehow been mistaken for an ordinary nigger. Don't you know who I am? I'm an *individual*! *(997 words)*

Barack Obama, Dreams from My Father, *New York: Broadway Books. 1995/2004, pp. 97–100*

Annotations
l. 22 *Oxy:* short for Occidental College: a private college in Los Angeles
l. 34 *Compton:* a suburb of Los Angeles notorious for gang violence and with a large, often poor black community
l. 37 *Watts:* a neighborhood in Southern Los Angeles, known for the 1965 Watts race riots and with a large, often poor black community
l. 69 *Brooks Brothers:* oldest men's clothier in the US, known for its high-end fashion

Lösungsvorschläge

1. *This task tests your text comprehension skills. You are supposed to describe Barack Obama's experiences at college, as he presents them in his autobiography. An assignment like this narrows down the text paragraphs relevant for your answer. You can start summarising the text from line 22 onwards. Frank's warnings that are depicted from line 1 to 21 are not part of this task because they do not refer to experiences at college.*
   You should mention the following points:
   - *quite a few Black students at college have their everyday worries and prefer to stay amongst themselves and not to be obsessed with race (cf. ll. 22–32)*
   - *difference between Black students from poorer communities and those insecure of their identity, such as Obama himself (cf. ll. 33–43)*
   - *example of Joyce: stress on multiracial instead of Black heritage, but avoidance of Black people; myth of non-racial White society (cf. ll. 44–71)*

The text is an excerpt from Barack Obama's memoirs *Dreams from My Father*, published in New York in 1995 and 2004. In the given passage, Obama remembers his experiences as a student at college in Los Angeles. — introduction

In general, he has the impression that in "monoracial" groups of only Black students, race is not an issue which is discussed much. Other everyday interests and worries, not unlike those of White students, occupy the young African Americans. — everyday worries among "monoracial" groups

Barack Obama himself, however, is more concerned with questions of race and identity. He attributes this to his status of being not from an all-Black, impoverished background. In other words, he has made it to the successful White-dominated society. At the same time this makes him lack a secure racial identity. — Obama's insecurity about racial identity

The example of his friend Joyce illustrates this conflict: When Barack asks her to accompany him to a meeting of the Black Students' Association, she bluntly refuses, protesting that she is not Black, but multiracial because of her ancestry of various ethnicities. She wants to be regarded as an individual and complains that Black people always make her choose and make everything racial, whereas White people accept her. In Barack's opinion, however, this integration is only superficial and ignores the fact that Black Americans are still confronted with prejudice and discrimination on a daily basis. Apparently, Joyce's feeling of being a part of the "White society" comes at the price of turning her back on her Black roots. *(245 words)* — Joyce's example: apparent integration at the price of denying one's roots

19

2. *For task 2, you need to find out which different attitudes to Black identity are described in the text and how they are expressed in terms of language. To solve the first part of the task, you can use your findings from task 1, where you have probably hinted at the different attitudes already. It makes for an especially elegant text when you manage to combine the description of the attitudes with the linguistic means used to illustrate them.*

You could mention the following aspects:

– *Frank's warnings as a kind of advance preparation for the difficulties to follow:*
  - *metaphors from world of education and finance ("advanced degree in compromise", l. 1; "real price of admission", ll. 8/9)*
  - *repetition ("Leaving your race at the door", "Leaving your people behind", l. 11)*
  - *examples of drastic language ("equal opportunity and the American way and all that shit", ll. 14/15; "they'll yank on your chain and let you know that you may be a well-trained, well-paid nigger, but you're a nigger just the same", ll. 17/18)*
– *attitude of Black people who stay in "monoracial" groups: ignorance of race:*
  - *metaphors to stress uniformity ("tribe", ll. 23/24; "traveling in packs", l. 25)*
  - *informal language for everyday experiences ("Surviving classes. Finding a well-paying gig after graduation. Trying to get laid.", l. 27)*
  - *anaphora to describe "one of the well-kept secrets about black people" ("that most of us weren't interested in revolt; that most of us were tired of thinking about race all the time; that if we preferred […]", ll. 28–32)*
– *race a bigger issue for "half-breeds" (l. 62), such as Obama himself:*
  - *rhetorical question ("So why couldn't I let it go?", l. 33)*
  - *seeming paradox of antithetical expressions ("luxury" of poverty, insecurity of having "nothing to escape from", cf. ll. 33–38)*
– *Joyce's way of denying her roots in order to belong:*
  - *comparison ("like a baby who doesn't want what it sees on the spoon", l. 46)*
  - *emphases in Joyce's hypocritical argumentation ("multiracial", l. 47; "happened to be", ll. 47/48; "black people"/"[t]hey"/"They, they, they.", ll. 53–55)*
  - *metaphors to underline dominance of White culture ("gravitational pull", l. 58; "one-way street", ll. 58/59)*
  - *sarcastic statements ("Only white culture could be neutral and objective. Only white culture could be nonracial […]. Only white culture had individuals.", ll. 60–62; "America's happy, faceless marketplace", ll. 64/65; "mistaken for an ordinary nigger", l. 70)*
  – *conclusion*

At the very beginning of the excerpt, Obama describes how his mentor Frank had warned him about the difficulties he as a Black student might encounter at college. That is why the whole section from line 1 to line 21 could be read as a kind of advance preparation for the issues to follow. By calling college "[a]n advanced degree in compromise" (l. 1) and talking of "[t]he real price of admission" (ll. 8/9), Frank uses imagery to make it clear that Black students' education is both challenging and costly for them, if not from a financial perspective, all the more so from a cultural one. What exactly it costs Black students is exemplified by the repetition of "[l]eaving your race at the door" and "[l]eaving your people behind" (l. 11). That Frank is not happy about the situation becomes clear in his partly drastic way of expressing his opinion. He doubts false promises of "equal opportunity" by calling "the American way" "all that shit" (ll. 14/15). Furthermore, his metaphor that Black college graduates, who aim for a leading role, are "yank[ed back] on [their] chain" (l. 17) as well as his repetition of the word "nigger" (l. 18) show that in Frank's eyes, all the talk about alleged racial justice is nothing but an illusion.

This sets the scene for the different attitudes Obama himself encountered at college. For him, there is a marked difference between Black students who stay in their closely-knit groups, their "tribe[s]" (ll. 23/24) and only "travel[…] in packs" (l. 25) and those who start to doubt their identity. By informally describing the problems and worries these "tribes" have as "[s]urviving classes", "[f]inding a well-paying gig after graduation" and "[t]rying to get laid" (l. 27) and by further stressing in an anaphora what he describes as "one of the well-kept secrets about black people", namely that they do not want to think and talk about race all the time (cf. ll. 28–32), Obama makes it clear that Black students' everyday life is not necessarily too different from that of their White peers.

All the more astounding for Obama is that he himself "couldn't […] let [the questions of racism] go" (l. 33). His attempt at explaining his obsession with race reveals a seeming paradox: Those who have the "luxury" (l. 33) of having grown up in areas marked by poverty and race conflicts are more secure about themselves than those like him who have "nothing to escape from" (l. 37). Their security lies in their firm rootedness in their identity while others, like Obama or other seemingly successful "half-breeds" (l. 62), can only "sputter" (l. 41) when asked about issues of race. On the surface, the successful Black Americans are part of an integrated society. Yet, Obama makes

Frank's warnings as advance preparation for difficulties to follow

ignorance of race in "monoracial" groups

race a bigger issue for multiracial people

21

it clear that his mentor Frank was right in pointing out that the alleged colour blindness is nothing but an illusion.

The example of his friend Joyce illustrates this. When Obama compares her initial reaction to his invitation to the Black Students' Association with "a baby who doesn't want what it sees on the spoon" (l. 46), she appears childish and naive in her refusal to seriously deal with her origins. The emphases used in her justification about why she does not want to go, namely that she is "multiracial" (l. 47) and that she does not want to choose one fixed racial identity, underline the hypocrisy of her argumentation. For instance, she stresses the coincidence of being born with a certain ethnic background by saying that her parents "happened to be" of certain origins (cf. ll. 47/48). Of course, this is true, yet her "[t]hey, they, they" (cf. ll. 53–55) attitude against Black people makes it obvious that she is not as neutral and open-minded as she presents herself to be. Instead, she has fallen victim to what Obama metaphorically describes as the "gravitational pull" (l. 58), the "one-way street" (ll. 58/59) of integration, which only seems to work when Black people deny both their origins and the structural racism in the USA in order to belong to "America's happy, faceless marketplace" (ll. 64/65).

Joyce's way of denying her roots

The text gets highly sarcastic when this attitude of Joyce and others who praise White culture in order to belong culminates in the statement that "Only white culture had individuals" (ll. 61/62). That it is exactly the general bias against people of colour that makes taxi drivers refuse to take on Black guests or that singles them out as the usual suspects of being criminals reveals the fallacy of this assumption. When even Black people themselves, who have made it, wonder how they can escape "get-[ting] lumped in with the losers" (l. 63) and "[being] mistaken for an ordinary nigger" (l. 70), the stigmatisation in people's heads seems shockingly effective.

sarcasm to criticise Joyce's attitude

All in all, Frank's initial warnings seem more than justified. When it comes to Black identity at college, ignoring race, either through informal segregation or through a pseudo-tolerant denial of its influence, seems to be the only feasible strategy.

conclusion

(845 words)

3.1 *Read the assignment carefully. The verb "discuss" means that you should present arguments both for the success of anti-racist movements and arguments that speak against ethnic minorities having equal rights in the US. There are many areas on which you could focus in order to examine racial equality or a lack thereof. Typical examples could be education, which is also the topic of the read-*

ing text, economic (in-)equality or politics, but of course, there are also other areas, such as the justice system, healthcare, etc., where there have been both steps forward and drawbacks. Also pay attention to the exact wording of the task: it asks you to consider different ways to overcome racism. So, make sure that you mention political and legislative changes, social justice groups, etc.
The sample solution includes the following points:
- *introduction: history of racism*
- *main part 1: progress in race relations:*
  - *education: Barack Obama as example of successful college graduate, desegregation (1954) and Little Rock Nine (1957), affirmative action programmes*
  - *work and employment: Equal Employment Opportunity Act*
  - *politics: Civil Rights Act, Voting Rights Act, examples of successful politicians (Barack Obama, Kamala Harris)*
- *transition to main part 2*
- *main part 2: still-existent disadvantages:*
  - *education: educational gap, ban of affirmative action in some states*
  - *economy: still-existent wealth gap, vicious circle of poverty and crime in problem districts*
  - *politics: renewed attempts at hindering Black people from voting (example: Georgia), Black Votes Matter*
- *conclusion: legal changes alone not sufficient, awareness-raising movements*

The USA has a long history of racism. Throughout the years, numerous steps have been taken to overcome it: From the abolition of slavery after the Civil War, over the Civil Rights Movement's achievements in the 1960s and up to Barack Obama's election as the country's first Black president, African Americans seem to have come a long way towards equality. Yet, the post-racial society that many expected to result from Obama's success is still a utopia in many respects. | introduction

Barack Obama himself seems to exemplify progress in several fields: In his memoir, he writes about his college education, which he takes more or less for granted while the generation of his elderly mentor Frank is still aware of a time when equal opportunities in education had to be fought for. | main part 1: progress in race relations: education

In 1954, the US Supreme Court finally ruled that schools be desegregated, and the system of bussing was introduced to improve ethnic diversity at America's schools. Despite these legal changes, the case of the Little Rock Nine, nine Black students who were hindered from entering a formerly White-only school by an angry mob in 1957, showed that racism in people's minds does not just stop because of a court ruling. Yet, it also proved the government's willingness to enforce the students' admission | desegregation of schools, Little Rock Nine against all opposition when even troops were sent to help the students enter the school.

In his memoir, Obama also mentions Black college friends from disadvantaged areas, such as Compton and Watts in Los Angeles. That they were able to enrol could be due to support initiatives or affirmative action programmes that definitely improved educational equality.

affirmative action

When it comes to work and employment, the system of affirmative action proved successful once more. Legislation, such as the Equal Employment Opportunity Act to protect Black people from discrimination in the labour market, helped countless African Americans to close the wealth gap between them and their White compatriots. In consequence, the number of well-to-do Black middle-class families rose. Obama himself comes from such a family, as he writes in his biography, and is again the perfect representative of equal opportunities.

work and employment

Similarly, in politics, Black Americans have come a long way since the days of the racially oppressive Jim Crow laws, when states with many Black inhabitants introduced a literacy test and a poll tax to suppress the Black vote. The Civil Rights Act and the Voting Rights Act of the 1960s abolished these racist practices and guaranteed Black people political participation. It was not only the number of Black voters, but also that of African Americans who actively take part in the running of the country that increased continually. Obama is again an outstanding example of a successful Black politician. So is Kamala Harris, the first Black, South Asian woman to become vice-president, among many others.

politics

However, although African Americans have made considerable progress so far, the American Dream of equality and acceptance for all, has not yet been fulfilled. Neither laws that mandate equal opportunities nor the singular success stories of people, such as Barack Obama, should make us blind to the fact that in general African Americans still face too many disadvantages.

transition to main part 2

In education, for example, Black Americans still lag behind White Americans, especially at the nation's prestigious universities and colleges. These institutions maintain that they are committed to diversity, but admissions of Black undergraduates continue to fall in many states, which might partly be due to the ban of affirmative action that is now in force in some of them.

main part 2: disadvantages: education

Despite the emergence of a fairly large Black middle class, many African American people continue to exist on the economic margins. America's ideal that anyone who works hard can achieve economic success is still beyond reach for many. On the whole, unemployment and poverty rates in the US are

economy

declining, but Black people are still poorer than Hispanic or White people. This becomes especially obvious in the still-existent problematic districts in some cities which are mainly populated by ethnic minorities and where a vicious circle of poverty and crime is often perpetuated from generation to generation.

In politics, several southern states have recently undertaken efforts to restrict voting of African Americans. Traditionally solid Republican states, such as Georgia, "flipped" Democratic in 2020, mainly because of Black voters who helped Joe Biden to win the state. Soon after, in 2021, the Georgian legislature renewed its attempts to disenfranchise Black voters by regulations and bans that particularly target that part of the population. Therefore, the Black Votes Matter movement, which was founded in Georgia to encourage African Americans to go to the polls and offers help with the voting procedure in order to increase the influence of Black communities, should not come as a surprise. `politics`

So, when even after monumental legal changes and the undeniable progress the Civil Rights Movement achieved, racism persists, the question of what more can be done is becoming increasingly desperate. The answer probably lies in asking and re-asking this question. Awareness is key and nothing seems as dangerous as tacitly accepting subtle racism as a given. That is what movements, like Black Votes Matter or Black Lives Matter, which mainly targets disproportionate police violence against Black Americans, attempt to achieve. *(865 words)* `conclusion: legal changes not sufficient, awareness-raising movements`

3.2 *This creative task requires you to take on the role of an exchange student at an American high school's debating society. So, be clear about that role in that you treat the USA as your host country not too unkindly in your speech. Of course, you may express criticism, but you should avoid sounding arrogant or condescending. Also bear in mind the type of text you need to write for this creative task. A speech should address your audience directly and include some linguistic devices, such as repetitions, anaphora, rhetorical questions, etc., which make it persuasive and easy to follow. When it comes to content, the assignment is quite open. So, you can address the topic of race relations from different angles. However, make sure to refer to the excerpt from Barack Obama's memoir as your starting point.*

The following points are discussed in the sample solution:
- *introduction: race relations in America as a challenging topic*
- *main part 1: race relations today:*
  - *improvements since the Civil Rights Movement (example: education)*
  - *"gravitational pull of white culture" as more subtle form of racism*

Hello everybody,

introduction

Phew, so we are to debate the current state of race relations in this country – what a tremendous challenge, as I would argue that the problem of racism is one of the most relevant, but also one of the most complex issues this nation, and with it the rest of the world, has to deal with. Yes, particularly for me as a foreign student, it might be difficult to really judge the situation. Nonetheless, the USA with its status of being a role model and trailblazer when it comes to values like liberty, justice and equality is so close to achieving real improvements and so far from them at the same time.

Let me start with the positive side: From a historical perspective, race relations have been improving considerably over the past decades. When we look at it from a legal point of view, the Civil Rights Movement has reached the tremendous goal of giving all Americans equality before the law, equal opportunities when it comes to education and employment as well as equal chances for political participation.

main part 1: race relations today: improvements (education)

And yet, I have got to know this country as more ambitious than that: it is not enough to have achieved something on paper, reality is what matters. And this is where countless challenges come to mind: just because African Americans can go to all colleges now does not mean that they can really live their racial identity proudly and openly. I recently read your former president Barack Obama's biography, in which he fittingly talked of the "gravitational pull of white culture" that he felt at college. What he meant was the only superficial acceptance of African Americans, who had to try so hard to belong that they often had to deny their real heritage and act as "White" as possible. Is that real equality or should we rather call it a more subtle form of racism?

more subtle forms of racism persist ("gravitational pull of white culture")

The same goes for the unconscious bias that Obama also talked about when he described "the woman in the elevator [who] clutches her purse" as soon as a Black person enters. Can we really talk of equal opportunities when your skin colour alone singles you out as a person to be afraid of, to be suspicious of, to be distrustful of? And while this might seem a rather harmless example, racial profiling and disproportionate police vio-

unconscious bias against Black people

26

lence are not. They really do threaten Black lives – and poison the atmosphere in this wonderful country.

So, when legally there should be nothing in the way of true equality, why is it so difficult to achieve peace and mutual understanding? Is the legacy of slavery still so strong? And if yes, what can be done to improve race relations? In my opinion, too many people favour the easy answer, so they ask for legal reforms and ultimately more laws to get inequalities under control. While I agree that reforms and many supportive measures are necessary to improve the lives in underprivileged communities, let me make one thing very clear: Laws will not bridge the racial divide. Laws will not heal wounds. Laws alone will not bring people together.

main part 2: appeal for change: laws alone are not the solution

Honesty and conversations will. Hard truths must be faced, the atrocities of the past and present must be dealt with and failures must be admitted. Only when the woman in the elevator does not subconsciously clutch her purse any longer will a true change have been achieved.

honest conversations necessary

Let me remind you again: what is so great about America and has brought the country so far is its wish to always improve and to never be content with a status quo that is only half good. So, yes, race relations have seen improvements, but let's tackle the rest of the prejudice, the rest of the injustice, the rest of what brings people apart. Then America will take another important step forward, as it did so often in its history.

conclusion

Thank you for your attention. *(654 words)*

Crime and Punishment in Literature and Film

Assignments

Comprehension

1. Outline the main events in Shujaa Graham's life.

Analysis

2.* Analyse the author's portrayal of Shujaa Graham.

> *Die Aufgabe 2 war in der ursprünglichen Prüfung in Aufgabe 2.1 und 2.2 unterteilt. Da für Ihre eigene Prüfung aber nur eine Aufgabe im* Analysis-*Teil vorgesehen ist, wurde 2.2 hier weggelassen.*

Comment / Creative Writing (Choose one.)

3.1 Discuss the pros and cons of capital punishment.
Refer both to the article and your coursework.

or

3.2 Imagine you are a German university student. At a party, you meet an exchange student from Texas named Ted Parker and start a discussion with him about capital punishment. Ted is a fervent supporter of capital punishment, but you disagree.
Write that discussion.

Capital Punishment Is Murder – Especially for the Wrongfully Accused
by Lindsay Bever

So far this year, 23 death row inmates have been executed in the US. One was killed by electrocution, the others by lethal injection. A 24th committed suicide. Among these prisoners, they served a total of 335 years as they were waiting to die. And there are 14 more Americans slated for execution by their government before the end 5 of the year.

We're told to believe they were guilty – of murder. What if they weren't? In fact, what if they were the victims – of prejudice, racism, corruption? In 1976, Shujaa Graham was one of them – wrongly sentenced to die and shipped to San Quentin prison in California. […]

10 It's chilling to think how many innocents may have lost their lives at the hands of the US criminal justice system since 1976 – when capital punishment was reinstated. Worse, according to the Death Penalty Information Center, there's no way to calculate how many were executed for crimes they didn't commit since courts typically won't consider claims of innocence when a defendant is dead. But with more than

28

15 250 exonerated by DNA testing – 17 of whom served time on death row – it's impossible to not think about the others who fell through the cracks – especially when looking at a man who almost did.

In many ways, Graham's life mirrors America's <u>Civil Rights Movement</u>. Graham grew up on a Southern plantation where his family worked as <u>sharecroppers</u>. In
20 1961, they moved to South Central Los Angeles to establish a better life and "that's where my trouble began", he said. As a teenager, Graham got caught up in gangs. He committed minor crimes. He spent much of his adolescence in <u>juvenile institutions</u>. And when he was 18, he went to Soledad Prison on a minor robbery charge.

Graham turned away from the gang life when he became influenced by the <u>Black</u>
25 <u>Panther Party</u> in prison and he took a leadership position in the black prison movement, working for prisoners' rights. Because of his leadership, he said, he was <u>framed</u> in the 1973 murder of a prison guard while serving out his sentence at the Deul Vocational Institute in Stockton, California. During Graham's second trial in 1976, he and his co-defendant, Eugene Allen, also an African American, were
30 charged with murder and sent to San Quentin's death house. It would take two more (all-white) trials and five more years before Graham would be freed, he said.

That was the story I expected to hear – one of a defunct criminal justice system, political corruption and racial bias. But ironically, Graham's story reveals his progressive attitudes against stereotypical 1970s America. Pacing back and forth in his
35 sunroom, he clutched a picture of those who worked on his defence committee around the time of his third trial in 1979. Among his supporters was 30-year-old Phyllis Prentice – who <u>stuck around</u>. Prentice, now 64, was a nurse in the county jail where Graham was being held while he awaited trial. "I thought she was a cop", he said, "because she was so nice to me – and white." But, on the heels of desegrega-
40 tion, Prentice, a political activist, and Graham, an African American political prisoner, became friends. She quit her job and joined his defence committee. And when Graham was finally exonerated and released in 1981, they started a life together.

Now, their home is filled with photographs of their three children and four grandchildren – perhaps another testament to Graham's willingness to break social
45 and political barriers. Prentice is still a nurse – a <u>palliative care nurse</u>. Graham has a landscaping business. But listening to their story, it's clear their passion still lies in the political work they started back in the 1970s. They are both on the board of Witness to Innocence, an organization dedicated to empowering exonerated death row survivors like Graham, who is vice chair. Graham still travels and speaks out against
50 issues of capital punishment, wrongful convictions and inhumane prison conditions, much like the ones he has lived through.

Graham's experience will forever be part of his history but, after I met him, I realized that his real story lies within the life he built because of – or maybe even in spite of – his past.
55 I sat in the sunroom staring at Graham through a camera lens. That's when he said something I'll never forget:

"I know why you're here. Perhaps if I'd never been on death row, you wouldn't be here today talking to me. That reminds me I should be looking at this as a great

thing – and it is – to get the chance to pass on my experience and hope that you'll
60 take it to another level. I promised the prisoners I would fight until the day I die."

(782 words)

Lindsay Bever, "Capital Punishment Is Murder – Especially for the Wrongfully Accused",
in: The Guardian, *27 August 2013, Copyright Guardian News & Media Ltd 2023*

Annotations

ll. 2/3	*[a]mong these prisoners:* here: all 24 prisoners together
l. 18	*Civil Rights Movement:* 1960s mass protest movement in the US, whose goal was to end racial segregation and discrimination against Black Americans
l. 19	*sharecroppers:* farmers who work on the fields of a landowner in return for a part of the harvest
l. 22	*juvenile institutions:* young criminals are detained here
ll. 24/25	*Black Panther Party:* a Black revolutionary socialist organization active in the United States from 1966 until 1982
l. 27	*(to) frame sb:* to pin the blame for a crime on an innocent person
l. 37	*(to) stick around:* here: to develop a close relationship with Graham
l. 45	*palliative care nurse:* nurse specialised in relieving pain

1. *For this task, you have to summarise the main events in Shujaa Graham's life. Focus on the essential points and write a coherent text using your own words and avoiding text quotations as far as possible. A summary should usually be written in the simple present. However, as you have to relate a number of events from Graham's past, you should also use past tense here. In your introduction, you should mention the basic facts about the text you have been given. You could mention the following aspects:*

   – *introduction*

   – *summary of main events in Shujaa Graham's life:*
     • *Graham's childhood on a plantation in the South (cf. ll. 18/19)*
     • *moves to Los Angeles, drawn into criminal circles, frequently spending time in juvenile institutions (cf. ll. 19–22)*
     • *first prison sentence at age 18: political activism for Black inmates' rights (cf. ll. 23–26)*
     • *1973: falsely accused of murdering a prison guard (cf. ll. 26–28)*
     • *1976: death sentence; sent to San Quentin prison (cf. ll. 7–9, 28–30)*
     • *1981: acquittal after several trials: fresh start with Phyllis Prentice, a White nurse supporting his activism (cf. ll. 30/31, 36–42)*
     • *happy family man, still active against the death penalty and the US justice system (cf. ll. 43/44, 46–51, 60)*

The article "Capital Punishment Is Murder – Especially for the Wrongfully Accused", written by Lindsay Bever and published in *The Guardian* on August 27, 2013, deals with the fact that innocent people might be on death row in the US. The author focuses on the example of Shujaa Graham, who was wrongfully sentenced to death, but was finally able to prove his innocence. introduction

Born into a family of sharecroppers, Graham lived on a plantation in the southern USA together with his family until 1961. In pursuit of a better life, the family eventually moved to South Central Los Angeles, where Graham got involved in gang life and started to commit several crimes. Subsequently he had to spend a lot of time in juvenile institutions. Aged 18, he was sent to Soledad Prison after being charged with robbery. There, Graham was influenced by the Black Panther Party and became leader of the Black prison movement. In 1973, one of the prison guards was murdered. Three years later, in 1976, Graham and another African American were charged with this murder, sentenced to death and sent to San Quentin to await their execution. Graham claims he was found guilty due to his leading role in the prison movement. After four trials, he finally managed to prove his innocence in 1981. summary of main events in Shujaa Graham's life

Today he is married to the White nurse Phyllis Prentice, whom he met in prison, and together they have a large family. Graham considers helping the wrongly convicted the task of his life and holds the position of vice chair on the board of Witness to Innocence. *(263 words)*

2. *This task deals with the way the author presents Shujaa Graham's case. You should keep in mind that a certain mode of presentation is usually chosen for a reason. So, also think about why Lindsay Bever has written her article. She seems to oppose the death penalty, which is what you should prove by quoting relevant parts of the article.*
   You could mention the following points:
   – *introduction: Lindsay Bever is against the death penalty*
   – *strong opposition to the death penalty and criticism of the US justice system:*
     • *headline*
     • *statistics, fact and figures: shocking numbers (cf. ll. 1–5)*
     • *questions that doubt the rightfulness of the decisions (cf. ll. 6/7)*
     • *system often not transparent (cf. ll. 12–14)*
     • *number of wrong judgements (cf. ll. 14–17)*
   – *personal example of Shujaa Graham to prove her point:*
     • *Shujaa Graham presented as a hero:*
       ◆ *allusion to "America's Civil Rights Movement" (l. 18)*
       ◆ *injustice and bias that led to his imprisonment: "he was framed" (ll. 26/27), "two more (all-white) trials" (ll. 30/31)*
     • *contrast between Graham's dark past and his happy present (cf. ll. 32–60):*
       ◆ *words that create a positive picture: "sunroom" (ll. 35, 55); "their home is filled with photographs of their three children and four grandchildren" (ll. 43/44)*
       ◆ *"passion" (l. 46) for political work*
       ◆ *memorable direct quote to finish the article (cf. ll. 57–60)*

In her article, Lindsay Bever clearly positions herself against capital punishment. Her main argument is based on the fact that such a sentence cannot be undone and that a lot of innocent people were executed in the past.

introduction

In the headline, Bever stresses her point by calling capital punishment "Murder", thus implying the state itself commits a crime by executing criminals. The afterthought "Especially for the Wrongfully Accused" refers to a serious problem as innocent people cannot be brought back to life once the death sentence has been enforced.

strong opposition to death penalty: headline

The author then cites statistics on the exertion of capital punishment in the year her article was published (cf. ll. 1–5). Not only do they help to underline the system's injustice already

statistics, facts and figures

32

hinted at in the headline, but by pointing out that the prisoners altogether "served a total of 335 years as they were waiting to die" (l. 3), Bever gives the impression that such punishment is inhumane and unreasonable.

Against the backdrop of these numbers Bever brings up her doubts concerning a possible bias and lack of competence as judges and juries should make sure that only people who have been found guilty beyond reasonable doubt are sentenced to death (cf. ll. 6/7). She also provides further statistics which state that 250 people have indeed been wrongfully accused of committing a capital crime (cf. ll. 14–17) since the death penalty was reintroduced in 1976. The fact that investigations into cases of already executed criminals are not granted on principle raises questions concerning the system's transparency in general (cf. ll. 12–14). criticism of the US justice system

Bever then introduces the case of Shujaa Graham to prove her point, but it is the way this story is presented that makes her line of argument really hit home. Before giving any further information on how Graham ended up on death row, Bever compares his life to the US Civil Rights Movement (cf. l. 18). As this movement was an important step towards racial equality and democracy, this conjures up a very positive image of Graham, who frequently had brushes with the law in his teenage years (cf. ll. 21–23). By pointing out that the African American "was framed" (ll. 26/27) because of his leading role in the Black prison movement, the author suggests that he is a victim of racism. Another hint is given by revealing that his trials were "all-white" (l. 31). personal example of Shujaa Graham

In the following paragraph, Graham is presented as a happy family man (cf. ll. 43/44), businessman (cf. ll. 45/46) and advocate for the rights of people who innocently ended up on death row (cf. ll. 46–51). Again, this depiction contrasts with his briefly mentioned criminal past and the murder of a prison guard he was accused of (cf. ll. 26–28). The interview takes place in Graham's "sunroom" (ll. 35, 55) that is "filled with photographs of […] children and […] grandchildren" (ll. 43/44). This description creates a favourable impression of Graham, whose heroic character is illustrated by the fact that he devoted his life to "empowering exonerated death row survivors" (ll. 48/49). At the end of the article, Graham's quote shows him to be neither unforgiving nor resentful: he instead points out the positive effects his experiences had on him, as he is now able to help and support other people in need (cf. ll. 57–60). It is strongly implied in those last paragraphs (cf. ll. 43–60) that capital punishment is obviously unjust as this contrast between Graham's dark past and his happy present charismatic and selfless person would have been wrongfully deprived of his life, had political activists not fought so hard for a reinvestigation of his case. *(610 words)*

3.1 *Collect arguments for and against the death penalty and structure them in a meaningful way. It makes sense to start with the arguments that speak against your own position and then oppose them with the (probably more convincing) counterarguments.*
Possible arguments for the death penalty could be:
– safety argument because there cannot be repeat offenses
– death penalty can serve as a deterrent
– the victims' families can feel vindicated
– death penalty might be cheaper than imprisonment for life
Possible arguments against the death penalty could be:
– killing another human being does not bring victims back to life
– miscarriages of justice can never be corrected
– death penalty is also expensive because of many re-trials, etc.
– right to life is a basic human right that should not be violated by the state

Lindsay Bever's article "Capital Punishment Is Murder – Especially for the Wrongfully Accused", published in *The Guardian* on August 27, 2013, rightly asks the question of whether the death penalty as a maximum sentence for a capital crime such as murder should be used in a modern democratic state. This crucial issue shall be dealt with as follows.

One of the main arguments for the death penalty surely is that it prevents society from further harm as executed murderers will never be able to commit any more crimes. Moreover, it is often claimed that the victims' families, who suffer from the loss of their loved one(s), might be able to make peace with the past and move on. As it is usually murderers who are sentenced to death in the Western world, the idea of the convict meeting the same fate as the victim appears to be just to the grieving relatives, as it follows the biblical rule of "an eye for an eye". In addition, it is widely believed that capital punishment might work as a deterrent. Knowing that certain crimes will result in the criminal's execution – provided he or she is caught and found guilty – might keep the perpetrator from following their initial plan. A further argument is the reduction of expenses. Convicts who are executed do not need to be provided for, contrary to inmates who serve their life sentence in prison and need medical attention, food, a fully-furnished cell and prison staff to look after them. In line with these arguments, many of the US federal states execute their convicts.

introduction

arguments for the death penalty

34

However, there are even stronger arguments against capital punishment. In connection with the death penalty people often talk about closure. But neither does the execution of the murderer end the suffering of those left behind nor can it bring the victim back to life. On the contrary, in the name of retaliation another murder is committed – this time by the state. Obviously, using the death penalty puts people in a godlike position, as they have to decide between life and death. In her article, Lindsay Bever shows the fallibility of such decisions and actions made by human beings: according to her research, 17 people on death row have been found not guilty (cf. ll. 14/ 15). Even if a person "only" served a long prison sentence and is cleared of all charges later, it is impossible to make up for what the convict was deprived of during all that time – no matter how much compensation is paid. If somebody is executed, by contrast, this person is gone forever. Furthermore, in some cases people have been waiting for their execution for several years. As verdicts can be revised and prisoners be reprieved by the US president or the governor of a federal state, it takes time until a person's execution is finally decided upon. This contradicts the idea that the death penalty is cheaper than having criminals sentenced to life imprisonment. As long as they are alive the taxpayer has to pay for their living costs. Thus, there is no advantage to serving a life sentence. Finally, in its Universal Declaration of Human Rights, the United Nations states the right to life for every human being. Taking somebody's life is thus wrong on principle – people as well as states, especially the ones that are considered democratic, should not violate this most basic human right. All in all, one can say that the disadvantages of the death penalty as a punishment for capital crime by far outweigh the advantages. *(591 words)*

arguments against the death penalty

3.2 *For this creative task, you should always keep in mind the fictional situation for which you are supposed to write your dialogue. You are to take the role of a German student meeting a Texan exchange student, Ted, at a party. It will probably not be easy to initiate a discussion about the death penalty in this atmosphere, but try to be creative and think about ways how to introduce the topic in a culturally appropriate manner. You can also use the article as a starting point although you do not have to refer to it. When it comes to language, you can use informal expressions as you are supposed to present a relaxed conversation between two young people at a party.*

When it comes to content, the same arguments as in task 3.1 could be applied here too. However, in this case, you should always directly juxtapose arguments

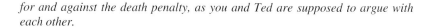

for and against the death penalty, as you and Ted are supposed to argue with each other.

Me: Hi, I'm Elias. I believe we've met before in Professor Lange's lecture. Aren't you one of the exchange students from America?

friendly small talk

Ted: Yeah, I'm Ted. I'm from Texas. I'm on an exchange year here in Hamburg. How are you?

Me: Fine, thanks. Texas must be a great place to live. I'd like to go there someday. Still, I'm a bit concerned about it as the people are said to be quite religious and crazy about guns. But …

introducing the topic of guns

Ted: Well, a lot of Americans are religious. I guess us being "crazy about guns" is a typically European perspective. Our constitution grants the right to carry guns to protect ourselves from dangerous situations.

Me: I'd be afraid that everybody I met on the street was probably carrying a gun with them. Do you not feel protected enough by the police and the law?

Ted: Well, the cops do a good job, basically. Of course, there are exceptions to the rules. And our justice system's ok, I guess – a bit slow perhaps. But with the death penalty we can at least get rid of the worst guys quite quickly …

transition to the topic of the death penalty

Me: Hearing you mention that, I read something in the paper the other day. Can I ask your opinion about it?

example from the article to express opposition

Ted: Yeah, sure!

Me: I came across the story of a man called Shujaa Graham. I don't know if you have heard of him … Anyway, as it turns out, he was wrongfully accused of murder and even put on death row although he was innocent. It took him a lot of effort and many years until he was finally found not guilty. That sounds awful to me. Just imagine if he had been executed!

Ted: I agree, it certainly is outrageous to put an innocent man on death row. But in most cases those murderers deserve to be executed. I mean, they have taken someone's life. You don't get sentenced to death for stealing a wallet. To boot, they acted against God's will. The bible says "an eye for an eye". It is only just to take a person's life if he or she has taken someone else's.

Ted's first argument for the death penalty: just retribution

Me: But "an eye for an eye" would mean that the victim should claim the perpetrator's life, which is impossible. If the state kills a murderer, this is retaliation at best and murder at worst. Because that is what happens, right? I've re-

first counterargument: another murder does not take back the first

36

cently seen a documentary on YouTube. They explained that the death certificate of the executed criminal states "murder" as cause of death. It's totally ironic and in some way it ridicules the idea of justice.

Ted: I guess it is murder. Can't deny that. But I can't see the point of paying for someone's life when he or she has committed a capital crime. Why should taxpayers have to give their money for someone who did harm to me or my fellow citizens? I mean, take a look at this guy Breivik from Norway. He killed about 80 innocent people. In America he'd have been sentenced to death without doubt. I can't imagine anyone would have been against it. Why should we pay for a person's well-being for the rest of their life when they've caused so much pain?

Ted's second argument: life imprisonment too expensive

Me: But killing him doesn't help the victims' families. It can't bring back their loved ones. You mentioned God's will, but in the ten commandments murder is forbidden. It's simply not in our hands to rule over other people's life and death. Just think about all those innocent people who died because some jury found them guilty. In some cases, all-White juries declared Black people guilty without any evidence at all. 250 people have been cleared of all charges after their cases were reinvestigated due to the latest methods of DNA testing. As long as the accused does not confess, we might never know whether they committed the crime or not. And even if they confess, those confessions might be forced or due to mental disturbance of the accused who just wants the trial to end. Executing somebody is a decision which can't be undone. There is no way back.

further counter-arguments: morally wrong to kill, particularly if people are wrongly accused

Ted: That's true. But either way you put it: I think the death penalty is an essential contribution to making the world a safer place. But let's not argue about basic opinions. We're at a party after all! Come on, let's have another one of those great German beers. *(724 words)*

conciliatory end of discussion

Crime and Punishment in Literature and Film

Assignments

Comprehension

1. Outline César's life and his criminal record up to this point.

Analysis

2. Analyse Zwilich's feelings towards César and how they are conveyed.

Comment / Creative Writing (Choose one.)

3.1 Discuss ways of dealing with juvenile delinquents like César. In your answer refer to both this excerpt and your coursework.

or

3.2 Soon after César's assault on Zwilich a status hearing is held – a discussion between a Family Court judge, the prosecution, Zwilich and the defendant, young César. Before the judge takes the final decision about what should happen to César, the prosecutor makes a statement in which he puts forward his views on the defendant, his criminal record and his possible reasons for committing crimes. He also gives a recommendation on how to deal with him in the future. Write the prosecutor's statement to the judge.

Tetanus

by Joyce Carol Oates

The following excerpt is taken from the short story "Tetanus" which is part of a collection of short stories by Joyce Carol Oates called Give Me Your Heart. *Here a social worker named Zwilich interviews an eleven-year-old boy called César about his latest crimes.*

1 "Well, César. So you've been busy."

Zwilich whistled through his teeth looking through the boy's file. He'd been taken into police custody five times, twice within the past three months. Vandalism, petty thefts, disturbances at home and at school, glue sniffing. A previous caseworker
5 had noted that one of the vandalism episodes included "desecration of a cemetery" and another the torture of a stray dog. It was noted that an older neighborhood boy had tied a rope around César's neck and had yanked him around, causing him to faint, when he'd been nine; another time César had fashioned a noose and stuck his own head into it; yet another time, more recently, he'd forced a noose over his six-
10 year-old brother's head. He'd been picked up with two older boys for stealing from a 7-*Eleven* store, and not long afterward he'd been arrested for vandalism in the rear lot

38

of the *7-Eleven* store. He'd been several times suspended from school. Following these incidents he'd been assessed by Family Services psychologists and counselors and given sentences of "supervised probation" with required therapy from Family Court judges who hadn't wanted to incarcerate so young a child. But Zwilich thought the next judge wasn't going to look kindly on all this.

The prosecutor for the case had told Zwilich that he intended to ask the judge to incarcerate the boy in a juvenile detention for thirty days minimum. César Diaz required psychiatric observation as well as treatment for the glue sniffing, and it was "high time" for the boy to learn that the law is serious. Sour, prim as a TV scold, Zwilich's colleague said, How are kids going to respect the law if there aren't consequences for their behavior?

Zwilich sneered: Who respects the law? Whose behavior has consequences? Politicians, mega-corporations?

He'd said, "Hell, this is a small child who's been arrested. Look at him, he's so small."

Now in the counseling room, Zwilich wasn't so sure. Fury quivered in César's tightly coiled little body; halfway you expected him to spring up at you, like a snake baring its fangs.

"… want to hurt your mother, César? Your little brother? You love them, don't you? Tell me."

"Didn't hurt nobody. Shit what Mama says."

"I think you love them. Sure you do. Why'd you want to scare them, César? Tell me."

César shrugged, sniggered. *You tell me.* […]

The boy was mimicking older boys he admired, neighborhood punks, dope dealers, the slatted rat-eyes, jeering laugh, junior macho swagger. In a boy so young the effect was as comical as a cartoon that, upon closer inspection, is pornographic.

Zwilich knew these kids. Some were "juvies", others were adolescents, "youths". Their souls' deepest utterances were rap lyrics.

He pitied them. He was sympathetic with them. He detested them. He feared them. He was grateful for them: they were his "work".

You would wish to think that César Diaz, so young, could be saved from them. Removed from the neighborhood, which was poisoning his soul, and placed – where? In a juvenile facility? But the youth facilities were overcrowded, understaffed. Zwilich admired some of the administrators of these facilities, for he knew of their idealism – their initial idealism, at least – but these places were in effect urban slum streets with walls around them. […] The boy's laughter was like a sharp shattering glass and getting on his nerves. If the boy was made to spend a single night in the juvenile facility, he'd be punished for that shriek of a laugh. He'd be punished for his runny nose, and for his smell, and for being a runt, a loser.

César was demanding to know where's Mama? was Mama here yet? and Zwilich said his Mama wasn't here, and César said, his voice rising, Where's Mama? I want Mama to take me home, and he wasn't laughing now, tears of indignation shone in his eyes, and Zwilich said, "César, your Mama told us to take you and keep you as long as we want to. Your mama said, 'I don't want César in the house anymore, I'm done with César, you keep him.'"

Zwilich was a perfect mimic of Mama's furious voice. Fixing his somber coun-
selor's eyes on César's face. [...] César stared at Zwilich now in stunned silence, his
60 mouth quivering. César couldn't be more respectful than if Zwilich had slapped him
on both cheeks, hard. You didn't tell an eleven-year-old that his mother didn't want
him, but the impulse had come to him, not for the first time in circumstances like
this, but for the first time with a child so young, an impulse as strong as sex, over-
powering, irresistible, a wish to create something – even misery, even self-disgust –
65 out of nothing.

[...] Zwilich relented. "César, hey." Stood and approached the stricken boy. César's eyes shone with tears, which gave him the look of a fierce little dog. When Zwilich touched him to comfort him, the boy cringed. "César, your mama didn't mean it.
She called us – a while ago and left a message for me. 'I love my –'"

70 So swiftly it happened then, Zwilich would live and relive the assault and never
quite comprehend how César grabbed his right hand and bit his forefinger before
Zwilich could shove him away.   *(874 words)*

Excerpt from GIVE ME YOUR HEART. TALES OF MYSTERY AND SUSPENSE *by Joyce Carol
Oates. Copyright © 2010 by The Ontario Review, Inc. Reprinted by permission of Houghton Mifflin
Harcourt Publishing company. All rights reserved.*

Annotations
l. 11   *7-Eleven:* convenience store, open 24 hours a day, seven days a week
l. 20   *TV scold:* someone who persistently voices criticism on TV
l. 39   *"juvies":* abbreviation for juvenile delinquents

40

Lösungsvorschläge

1. *Focus on eleven-year-old César Diaz's criminal record, but also summarise the*
   general information you get about his background.
   The following points should be mentioned in your solution:
   - *César's family background:*
     - *eleven years old (cf. introduction, l. 61)*
     - *rough neighbourhood (cf. ll. 6, 36/37, 44)*
     - *younger brother (cf. ll. 9/10, 30)*
     - *probably single mother who is overtaxed with César's education (cf. ll. 30,*
       52–57)
   - *César's criminal record:*
     - *vandalism (cf. ll. 3, 5, 11/12)*
     - *theft (from convenience store) (cf. ll. 3/4, 10/11)*
     - *anti-social behaviour at school and at home (cf. l. 4)*
     - *glue sniffing (cf. ll. 4, 19)*
     - *cruelty against dog (cf. l. 6)*
     - *violence against his younger brother (cf. ll. 9/10)*
   - *measures taken by the authorities:*
     - *in police custody several times (cf. ll. 2/3)*
     - *suspension from school (cf. l. 12)*
     - *assessment by Family Services psychologist and counselors (cf. l. 13)*
     - *"supervised probation" (Family Court judgement) (cf. ll. 14/15)*
     - *looming incarceration in juvenile detention facility (cf. l. 17/18, 45–51)*

César Diaz, whose life is described in the short story "Tetanus" by Joyce Carol Oates, is an 11-year-old boy who grew up in a rough neighbourhood. He probably comes from a broken family, as only his mother and a younger brother are mentioned. César's mother seems to have great difficulty in coping with her son's behaviour. Apparently, she has reached the end of her tether as she would consent to having her son taken care of by an institution. *[César's family background]*

Despite his young age, César Diaz has a remarkably long criminal record. The police file, which his social worker Zwilich reads, lists several occasions on which the boy has broken the law or shown anti-social behaviour. The more serious offences include theft from a convenience store and acts of vandalism. César has been in serious trouble at school several times, and this has led to his temporary suspension. He behaved violently towards his younger brother, nearly suffocating him, thus imitating mistreatment he himself had suffered at the hands of an older boy from his neighbourhood. César has also committed acts of cruelty against animals. In addition, he has been sniffing glue, which represents a health risk *[César's criminal record]*

41

for a child of his age and might be a first introduction to later drug use.

He has been detained in police custody five times and several efforts have been undertaken by the authorities, including Family Services and Family Court judges, to make him change his ways. Up to now this has been in vain.   *(250 words)*

measures taken by the authorities

2. *For this task, you should first of all come up with a general summary of social worker Zwilich's feelings towards César. After having established his ambivalent attitude towards the boy (cf. ll. 41/42) as a basis for your analysis, find further evidence in the text where this attitude is made apparent.*
    You could mention the following points:
    – *Zwilich feels sorry for César:*
      • *César was mistreated himself (cf. ll. 6–10)*
      • *bad role models (cf. ll. 10/11, 36–38)*
      • *bitter irony: "Who respects the law? Whose behavior has consequences? Politicians, mega-corporations?" (ll. 23/24)*
      • *repetition of "small" (ll. 25/26)*
      • *"the neighborhood, which was poisoning his soul" (l. 44)*
      • *examples of how César would suffer in a juvenile facility (cf. ll. 49–51)*
      • *the boy is hurt badly by his mother's rejection (cf. ll. 52–62)*
    – *Zwilich's anger at the boy:*
      • *comparison to aggressive animals (cf. ll. 28/29, 67)*
      • *figurative language: "In a boy so young the effect was as comical as a cartoon that, upon closer inspection, is pornographic." (ll. 37/38)*
      • *comparison: "The boy's laughter was like a sharp shattering glass and getting on his nerves." (ll. 48/49)*
      • *Zwilich's impulse to hurt César: "but the impulse had come to him, […], an impulse as strong as sex, overpowering, irresistible, a wish to create something – even misery, even self-disgust – out of nothing" (ll. 62–65)*
      • *César's assault seems to prove Zwilich right (cf. ll. 70–72)*
    – *narrative perspective: third-person personal (Zwilich's perspective)*

Zwilich, the social worker, has mixed feelings towards delinquents like César Diaz (cf. ll. 41/42). On the one hand, he feels sorry for him because he knows that growing up in a poor, rough neighbourhood like César's it is very hard to avoid getting into trouble (cf. ll. 43/44). Unable to understand the real nature and the consequences of the unlawful actions of drug dealers, thieves and robbers, young children tend to be impressed by older role models and will sooner or later try to follow their bad example. César's ill-fitting attempt to play it cool reminds Zwilich of older boys' behaviour – the social worker is even slightly amused by it (cf. ll. 36–38). In César's

Zwilich feeling sorry for César

case, the boy also seems to have learned that the stronger one is, the easier it is to dominate others, which is why he torments his younger brother just as he has been tormented by older boys (cf. ll. 6–10), and he seems to have learnt how to steal from older gang members (cf. ll. 10/11). From César's comments about his mother (cf. ll. 30–35) as well as from his criminal record (cf. ll. 2–15), Zwilich has to assume that there is nobody to give him proper guidance. His mother has obviously given up on César as she agreed for the authorities to take care of him (cf. ll. 55–57). Although the prosecutor in the current case wants César to spend at least thirty nights in a juvenile facility to teach him a lesson (cf. ll. 17–20), Zwilich feels that it would be unfair to punish the boy so severely when, at the same time, influential people and big companies get away with breaking the law (cf. ll. 23/24). Zwilich also points out that César is still very young (cf. ll. 25/26). He can see through César's insolent and aggressive behaviour during the interview and understands that this conduct is a kind of shield to help the boy pretend that he is strong and disinterested. Also, the social worker knows that César will be at the bottom of the pecking order in a juvenile facility (cf. ll. 49–51). Zwilich is aware that deep down the boy feels lost and abandoned and is longing for his mother. To a certain extent, César is a victim of circumstance, which is why the social worker pities him.

On the other hand, Zwilich is horrified and unnerved by César's disrespectful manners (cf. ll. 37/38, 48/49). Although he has been given yet another chance, the boy is not willing to cooperate (cf. l. 35). In addition, seen through the eyes of the social worker, the young offender resembles a small, but dangerous and aggressive animal whose reactions are hard to foresee, such as a snake (cf. ll. 28/29) or a dog (cf. l. 67). Both comparisons emphasise the potential danger of the wild and untamed nature of the boy. Zwilich feels helpless because he is running out of options to get the boy back on the right track. Out of frustration and as a last resort, he puts the child under pressure. Imitating the furious voice of his mother, he tells César that he is not wanted back home because his mother doesn't love him anymore (cf. ll. 55–58). Zwilich's realisation that in his job he is always dealing with hopeless cases like César Diaz makes him angry and increases the intense dislike for the child. At the same time, he is well aware that his impulsive behaviour is far from professional (cf. ll. 61–65), which he immediately regrets (cf. l. 66). When Zwilich touches the boy to make up for his unkind words, he is as-

Zwilich's anger at the boy

saulted, thus justifying his negative feelings towards César (cf. ll. 70–72).

Joyce Carol Oates uses the technique of third-person personal narration, which means she tells the story from Zwilich's per- narrative perspective
spective. This provides a deep insight into the social worker's feelings and thoughts. The reader can understand how Zwilich's frustration and anger develop. *(675 words)*

3.1 *You should think about ways of how to deal with young offenders like César Diaz. As the assignment says, you should take the excerpt as a basis. It already names two possible strategies: either stricter measures (as the prosecutor suggests) or a focus on an improved education and rehabilitation (as Zwilich suggests). Of course, you can also add your own ideas and background knowledge you have acquired in class.*

The sample solution mentions the following points:
- *introduction: reference to César Diaz's difficult case*
- *harsher punishments which could act as deterrents:*
  - *propagated by the prosecutor in the short story (cf. ll. 17–22)*
  - *former ways of punishing juvenile criminals (e. g. "borstals")*
  - *"three-strikes-law", "zero tolerance"*
- *focus on education and rehabilitation:*
  - *removal from a harmful environment (foster care)*
  - *educating young offenders and teaching them life skills*
  - *adventure-based therapy*
- *conclusion: society's responsibility towards young offenders*

A child who strays from the straight and narrow is a challenge for parents, educators, youth welfare services and juvenile law courts. César Diaz, the young boy who is interviewed in the short story "Tetanus" by Joyce Carol Oates, is a particularly difficult case. At just eleven years of age, César has an impressive criminal record: theft, assault, animal torture, problematic behaviour at home and at school as well as abuse of intoxicating substances (cf. ll. 2–12). After numerous failed attempts to bring the boy back on the right path again, the prosecutor and the social worker have different opinions about how to proceed. The fundamental question arises as to whether a stiffer penalty or a softer approach should be applied. introduction

The prosecutor's proposal "to incarcerate the boy in a juvenile detention for thirty days minimum" (ll. 17/18) reminds the reader of the harsh attitude towards juvenile delinquents in the past. The idea was to make them repent their wrongdoings and prevent them – and others – from breaking the law again. In Britain juvenile delinquents used to be sent to special de- harsher punishments

44

tention centres, so-called "borstals", which were supposed to offer them education and work but also teach them discipline and respect for authorities. The borstals were abolished in the 1980s. The more recent policies of "zero tolerance" and the "three-strikes-law" (= harsh punishment after the third offense has taken place) follow the same lines. They aim to demonstrate that offenses will be punished immediately. It is hoped that young offenders like César might straighten out when faced with the consequences of their deeds.

However, specialists concerned with juvenile crime put the stress on rehabilitation rather than punishment. They believe that crime and anti-social behaviour have social causes, such as poverty, poor housing, bad parenting and bad company. Therefore, dealing with a young offender like César requires a policy which will help him understand his failings, change his ways and thus integrate him into society again.

focus on educa-
tion and rehabili-
tation

Psychologists emphasise the importance of families in the shaping of a child's character and personality. Consequently, the next step in dealing with the young delinquent could be to remove him from his home and neighbourhood, a possibility Zwilich ponders (cf. l. 44). This might help to end César's involvement with older lawbreakers and reduce the risk that he will commit more serious crimes in the future. Hence, it is essential to find a foster family that will provide security and proper guidance.

removal from a
harmful environ-
ment

Another possibility, apart from foster care, is to make young delinquents take part in training courses to rebuild their personality. Under the supervision of psychologists and social workers, participants learn social skills such as self-control, respect and understanding for other people's feelings. Very often boys like César fail at school because of disruptive behaviour. They are often excluded from lessons and eventually drop out of school altogether. The young offenders are also taught how to work continuously towards a goal. In this way, it is hoped that they will eventually be able to pass examinations and thus improve their prospects for employment.

education and
teaching

A more recent method of dealing with young delinquents is what psychologists call "adventure-based therapy". In expeditions, teenagers are confronted with challenges, such as survival in an unfamiliar environment. The aim is to help them develop their personal skills and experience a feeling of independence and pride in their achievements.

adventure-based
therapy

All in all, there are several ways of dealing with juvenile offenders. Not all are successful, as Zwilich himself has experienced. The rate of re-offending is high. However, the deplor-

conclusion

able development of children like César is not exclusively their own fault – thus, society has to take responsibility for those teenagers who did not have a fair chance in life from the very beginning. *(622 words)*

3.2 *For this task, you should take the role of a prosecutor in César Diaz's case and write a recommendation statement on how to deal with the young criminal. Of course, there are different strategies you as the prosecutor could suggest. In the story, the prosecutor favours a stricter punishment of the young boy. However, you could also take his special circumstances and very young age into account and suggest educational measures, such as adventure-based therapy, instead of incarceration. Do not forget the formal elements typical of the required text form, such as an address as well as a final greeting of the court.*

The sample solution mentions the following points:
- *address*
- *introductory statement presenting César's case*
- *main part:*
  - *views on the defendant*
  - *criminal record*
  - *César's possible reasons for committing crimes*
  - *recommendation on how to deal with César in the future: rejection of initial idea of a harsh punishment in favour of re-education*
- *final greeting*

Judge Sullivan, Mr Zwilich, César,   address

Once again, we have come together for a status hearing concerning César Diaz. There is ample evidence that the boy is a real problem child. On many occasions Family Judges, counsellors and social workers have tried everything possible to make César understand that he is on the wrong path and must mend his ways. However, we all have to admit he has not changed his ways at all.   introductory statement

In the view of the prosecution, the defendant seems incorrigible. He is constantly getting deeper into trouble and has become more violent, aggressive and insolent since the authorities first had to deal with him. His teachers confirm that César is one of the worst and most unruly pupils in his class. He is lagging far behind in his command of the English language and his academic performance is way below average. Things cannot get much worse really, and if we do not take action now, it will soon be too late. César will be led astray by the criminal company he is currently keeping.   views on the defendant

The criminal record of the defendant lists numerous cases of assault against people as well as cruelty towards animals,   criminal record

46

property damage and offensive behaviour at home and at school. Recently, he has also committed serious offences such as stealing from a store. It has also been recorded that César has been sniffing glue. For an 11-year-old, this constitutes a serious health risk such as permanent damage to brain, liver and kidneys. César might also develop a chemical dependency and possibly be involved in drug trafficking.

So, what has gone wrong with César Diaz? How can we explain this intolerable behaviour? First of all, the boy has grown up in a deprived, crime-ridden neighbourhood. His mother finds it increasingly hard to control him. She has been in contact with Family Services more than once. Recently, she agreed to give César away. The environment he lives in and the company he keeps have a negative influence on him. There is evidence that he associates with criminals and police suspect that he has become a member of one of the gangs in the area. César's possible reasons for committing crimes

What can we do, how can we deal with the boy? César Diaz is a repeat offender who has been detained in police custody five times. Consequently, it is high time to make him feel the consequences of his unacceptable conduct and teach him that the law is to be taken seriously. As a first step, it is absolutely essential to remove the child from his environment, which has such a negative influence on him. This includes removing him from his home where he does not receive proper guidance. recommendation for future treatment of the boy

Initially, the prosecution had intended to have the boy incarcerated in a juvenile detention centre. However, after long discussions with Mr Zwilich, the social worker who has been dealing with the case of César Diaz for almost one year now, the prosecution agrees to give César one last chance to reform. In search of an alternative to imprisonment, Mr Zwilich has been trying for several weeks to find a foster family for the boy – so far in vain. Therefore, we recommend enlisting the defendant in an outdoor program for younger adolescents. Under the supervision of psychologists and counsellors he should learn to overcome difficult and challenging situations in a group of other young delinquents. Hopefully this new experience will help to rebuild his personality, increase his self-esteem and make him accept authority. I should make it quite clear, however, that this is the final opportunity for César's rehabilitation. It remains to be seen whether the measure will have any effect. Therefore I suggest another hearing once the program has finished. re-education in outdoor program instead of harsh punishment

Thank you.   *(619 words)*   final greeting

47

You will hear each recording **twice**. After each listening you will have time to complete your answers.

Task 1: Book Reviews   5 BE

You will hear five excerpts from radio reports in which the host reviews audiobooks. Match each book review (1 to 5) with one of the headings (A to G) by putting the corresponding letter into the correct box. For each book review there is only one answer which sums up the overall idea best. There are two more headings than you need. You have one minute to read the assignment.

Headings:

A Stealing to survive

B A cruel new parent

C Downfall of a nation

D Territorial expansion

E Frustration upon arrival

F History from a female perspective

G Hope in the face of financial difficulties

Book Review	1	2	3	4	5
Heading					

Task 2: Lunch   13 BE

You will hear a BBC report about how lunch breaks have changed.
While listening, fill in the missing information. You need not write complete sentences. Unless otherwise specified, name one aspect. You have one minute to read the assignment.

1. Role of lunch breaks in the past: *(Add two.)*	• enjoy food and drink • •
2. Reason for the return of lunch breaks in a Singapore institution:	

3. Purpose of lunch breaks in the banking district of London in the past:		
4. Changes in what is consumed: *(Name two.)*	• •	
5. Reason why business lunches have changed:		
6. Role of "Marks and Spencer":		
7. Reason why new kind of lunches are considered "democratic":		
8. Changes in the kind of food that can be purchased for lunch:		
9. Way the food is usually consumed:		
10. Result of an international study on the effect of extended lunches:		
11. Assessment of the current situation by the interviewee: *(Name one aspect.)*		

Task 3: A New Idea for Travelling   7 BE

You will hear an interview with the British adventurer Alastair Humphreys. While listening, tick (✓) the correct answer (a, b, c or d). There is only one correct answer. You have two minutes to read the assignment.

1. Having traveled the world, Alastair Humphreys turned to …
   a) ☐ package tours.
   b) ☐ survival training.
   c) ☐ nature preservation.
   d) ☐ unspectacular activities.

2. Humphreys says that the week's experience was …
   a) ☐ relaxing.
   b) ☐ manifold.
   c) ☐ dangerous.
   d) ☐ monotonous.

3. For Humphreys, the advantage of a microadventure is that it is …
   a) ☐ romantic.
   b) ☐ exclusive.
   c) ☐ inexpensive.
   d) ☐ uncomplicated.

4. His contribution to the microadventure concept is to have …
   a) ☐ popularized it.
   b) ☐ commercialized it.
   c) ☐ come up with the idea.
   d) ☐ placed more focus on sports activities.

5. Humphreys' concept motivates people to …
   a) ☐ live healthier lives.
   b) ☐ take random trails.
   c) ☐ cycle along motorways.
   d) ☐ explore the places around them.

6. For Humphreys, spending a night outside …
   a) ☐ unites the family.
   b) ☐ provides a new perspective.
   c) ☐ makes you feel insignificant.
   d) ☐ helps you understand the world.

7. Humphreys' main message is that you should …
   a) ☐ take more but shorter holidays.
   b) ☐ take a break from working too much.
   c) ☐ go on environmentally friendly holidays.
   d) ☐ enjoy ordinary things that fit in with your life.

Lösungsvorschläge

Text 1: Book reviews

1 **1** Today, I'd like to talk about a romantic historical fiction called *Ross Poldark*, written by Winston Graham and read by Oliver J. Hembrough. Captain Ross Poldark returns from America to his family home in Cornwall, where he finds much disappointment.

5 **2** Today, I'd like to talk about an intense debut children's book titled *One for the Murphys*, written by Lynda Mullaly Hunt and read by Nora Hunter. The last time 12-year-old Carley Connors cried was 384 days ago when her mother married an abusive stepfather.

3 Today, I'd like to talk about *The Book of Aron*, written by Jim Shepard and read by
10 Michael Goldstrom. This remarkable audio book is set in World War Two era Poland. The novel reveals the horrors of war through the eyes of the title character, Aron, and his band of child smugglers and petty thieves, who struggle to keep their families alive in the Warsaw ghettos.

4 Today, I'd like to talk about a thrilling narrative history book titled *Jacksonland*,
15 written and narrated by Steve Inskeep. This book is about the history of Andrew Jackson's land acquisition in what was the western United States, as well as Jackson's relationship with the Native American peoples who lived there.

5 Today, I'd like to tell you about the audio book titled *Capital Dames*, which is written and narrated by Cokie Roberts. This book focuses on Mary Todd Lincoln and
20 the other wives of significant leaders during and after the Civil War. Roberts's ability to weave information from letters, diaries and newspapers into a coherent and sometimes humorous whole is marvellous.

© *Audio File Magazine, https://audiofilemagazine.com/*

Book Review	1	2	3	4	5
Heading	E	B	A	D	F

Text 2: Lunch

1 **Julian Worricker,** *Host*: Whatever happened to the idea of the lunchbreak? Once upon a time, an hour or even two off work in the middle of the day to enjoy food and possibly drink was seen as a necessary means to recharge your batteries, socialise with colleagues, perhaps make some contacts. In some parts of the world, the
5 lunchbreak is, in fact, making a comeback. Earlier this month, for example, the Singapore Financial Exchange reintroduced lunch hours for its workers after scrapping them in 2013. The original aim was to boost the volume of business during the day, but too many traders complained of feeling overworked. Here, though, in the UK, the lunchbreak's decline seems to be continuing, as Elizabeth
10 Hodson now reports.

Elizabeth Hodson, *Byline*: Bankers and financiers in the city of London historically had business lunches to entertain clients and hopefully cement a lucrative contract or two. Not any longer, according to Justin Urquhart Stewart, a stalwart of the city for over four decades.

15 **Justin Urquhart Stewart:** What used to be a city lunch meant eating a lot, drinking probably too much, and of course, in those days, smoking a lot as well. Now, city lunches barely consist of anything at all. Various things have occurred. We don't have the whole attitude of drinking at lunchtime. That's gone. Smoking, that's gone … The other thing that has occurred is the regulators caught up with it. You
20 cannot just take someone out, "Let's go and have a decent lunch somewhere", because you have to declare it. And if I declare it as a reasonable sum of money, it could be seen as an incentive, something like a bribe. And therefore I'd be in breach of regulation, I could find myself, my business getting fined and I could actually lose my job. Here am I thoroughly enjoying my lime and soda.

25 **Hodson,** *Byline*: Convenience is now the buzz word when it comes to the midday meal. But buying a quick lunch on the go is a relatively new phenomenon, according to Polly Russell, a food historian and curator at the British Library.

Polly Russell: It's only in the last 35, 40 years that you can trace this buying what is a convenience meal at lunchtime in a prepack form in England. That was with the
30 launch of the prepack sandwich in the early 1980s by Marks and Spencer. This marks a moment where people are prepared to spend their money to save time, and it marks a real change in the relationship between leisure, money, work, labour. The sandwich is, in that sense, quite democratic that everybody, regardless of status or income, will probably at some point be buying a prepack sandwich.

35 **Hodson,** *Byline*: Whilst office workers once made do with an underwhelming sandwich, nowadays, more exotic and costly options are available. Outside a Thai café and takeaway, I asked workers in Central London how much they spent on lunches out.

Worker 1: About a fiver, I would say.
40 **Worker 2:** Maybe six quid.
Hodson, *Byline*: For lunch, how much would you spend?
Worker 3: At least six pounds.

Hodson, *Byline*: And how often do you eat out?

Worker 3: Every day. Thirty pounds a week. A hundred and twenty-eight pounds a
45   month and twelve hundred pounds a year, fifteen hundred dollars.

Hodson, *Byline*: A year?

Worker 3: Yeah.

Hodson, *Byline*: Although people seem happy to shell out for lunch, it's often still a
quick in-and-out-eat-at-the-desk type of experience. A long lunch might seem ra-
50   ther extravagant, but productivity statistics from the OECD reveal a rather interesting fact. Measured in US dollars per hour per worker, the French are 30 percent
more productive than their UK counterparts. Of course, there are lots of other factors at play, but it does beg an important question about the relationship between a
longer lunch and effectiveness at work. It was something I put to Justin Urquhart
55   Stewart, who we heard from earlier. Is it a good or a bad thing that lunch culture
has changed?

Urquhart Stewart: It's good that it has changed because frankly, what was there before
was unacceptable. It was lazy. It was actually taking advantage of the system.
Now, actually, I think sometimes it's gone too far the other way and you have to
60   be able to establish the rapport. It's not just about dealing with mathematics. The
city is still very dependent on actually the personal relationships and those relationships mean you have to sit down and talk to people and doing it over a meal is
the best way of doing it.

© *N. N. (25. 03. 2017) "Why Lunch is No Longer on a Worker's Menu"*. BBC News World Service,
www.bbc.co.uk/programmes/p04y01d3

1. Role of lunch breaks in the past:	*two of the following:* • recharge batteries • socialise with colleagues • make contacts
2. Reason for the return of lunch breaks in a Singapore institution:	people/traders (complained of) feeling overworked
3. Purpose of lunch breaks in the banking district of London in the past:	entertain clients/cement (lucrative) contracts
4. Changes in what is consumed:	*two of the following:* • no big lunches • lunches barely consist of anything at all • no drinking/no alcohol • no smoking
5. Reason why business lunches have changed:	business lunches can be seen as an incentive/a bribe/businesses can be fined/(business people) can lose (their) job

6. Role of "Marks and Spencer":	launched prepacked sandwiches (as a convenience meal to save time)
7. Reason why new kind of lunches are considered "democratic":	everybody (regardless of status or income) will buy it / consumed by all classes
8. Changes in the kind of food that can be purchased for lunch:	food more exotic / more costly / expensive / wider variety of food
9. Way the food is usually consumed:	quickly at the desk
10. Result of an international study on the effect of extended lunches:	French are more productive (than their UK counterparts) / long lunches increase effectiveness of work / productivity
11. Assessment of the current situation by the interviewee:	good that lunch culture has changed but changes have now sometimes gone too far / you have to be able to establish personal relationships / sit down and talk over a meal

Text 3: A New Idea for Travelling

1 **Alastair Humphreys:** I'd been doing big adventures for years, and I had this hunch that you didn't need to go to the ends of the world to have some sort of adventure. You didn't need to be in beautiful Patagonia to have this spirit of adventure. So, I decided to try and prove my theory by doing the most boring, ugly adventure I could
5 think of. And I came up with the idea of walking a lap of the M25 in the snow in January, which …

Winifred Robinson, *Reporter:* It's not legal!

Humphreys: Well, I was off the road.

Robinson, *Reporter:* OK.

10 **Humphreys:** I was in the fields and the villages and the footpaths and the towns alongside and it was quite an amusing and silly week, but it was very interesting because it felt like a genuine adventure. I was going places I'd never been. It was a physical challenge. I found pockets of wilderness. I met kind, interesting people just like you do when you're exploring the world. And time and again, as I walked
15 round the M25, I just kept thinking to myself, this experience is exactly the same as the four years I spent cycling around the world. Smaller, of course, a bit silly, but definitely felt like an adventure. And that's when I really started to come up with the idea of microadventures.

Robinson, *Reporter:* Travel companies say that microadventures are becoming part of
20 the mainstream holiday market and they talk about people travelling now, sometimes long distances to spend maybe ten days in the kind of place where they used

to spend three weeks, on safari maybe. Would you count that as a microadventure?

Humphreys: I personally wouldn't. I would say that's going on holiday, going on a
shorter holiday than you used to do. But who am I to complain if people are getting out and exploring the world? That's great. To my mind, the benefit of a microadventure is that it's local and it's simple and it fits in around your normal life.

Robinson, *Reporter:* Microadventures aren't a brand new concept. You started writing about them quite a few years ago now. Do you think they are now, though, just really taking off? And if they are, why now?

Humphreys: Well, I haven't invented anything. All I've been trying to do is say to people, "Hey, go camping, go ride your bike, go swim in a river!". Stuff that people have been doing for a long, long time. I think the only thing I've done was give it a, perhaps a clever name and harness social media and the power of hashtags to try and grow a community of people. I don't know why now, from my point of view, it's just growing from when I originally started it.

Robinson, *Reporter:* You've really got to choose your own adventure, though, haven't you? You've got to let your children choose their own adventures because there's nothing worse than somebody else's idea of a fabulous experience being foisted on you, is there?

Humphreys: Well, that could be miserable if ..., potentially. But also, I think one of the joys of microadventures is the planning, having the idea, getting out a map or looking out of your train window on the commute home and seeing a little woodland and being curious and then going to investigate it on your bike or even foot at the weekend. And certainly, I think it's a great thing to try and encourage children to do.

Robinson, *Reporter:* Okay, Alastair. Take me there then, into the woods at night. Tell me how that experience is transformed by the moonlight.

Humphreys: That's a good question. You must be good at this because I think there's a significant difference between going for, say, a day hike or a day bike ride, which I'm sure many people are familiar with, to then spending the night out in the place and returning the next day. That, in my mind, turns it into an adventure. And your natural caveman instinct says, "Oh, this is the time to be home in my bed." That's when it starts to feel like an adventure. The calm, the peace, the stillness, if you're by yourself. If you're with other people, it's often the time of great and interesting conversations. And the night is beautiful. We are, we humans are so boring these days. We so rarely spend time out in the darkness to see the stars and to see how the world feels different by night.

© *"Why Microadventures Are the Way to Holiday".* BBC Radio 4 You and Yours, *31 January 2018,*
http://www.bbc.co.uk/programmes/p05wpv38

1. Having traveled the world, Alastair Humphreys turned to …

   d) ✓ unspectacular activities.

2. Humphreys says that the week's experience was …

   b) ✓ manifold.

3. For Humphreys, the advantage of a microadventure is that it is …

   d) ✓ uncomplicated.

4. His contribution to the microadventure concept is to have …

   a) ✓ popularized it.

5. Humphreys' concept motivates people to …

   d) ✓ explore the places around them.

6. For Humphreys, spending a night outside …

   b) ✓ provides a new perspective.

7. Humphreys' main message is that you should …

   d) ✓ enjoy ordinary things that fit in with your life.

You will hear each recording **twice**. After each listening you will have time to complete your answers.

Task 1: Street Trees   7 BE

You will hear a podcast on trees in Detroit. While listening, answer the questions. You need not write complete sentences.

1. What are the advantages of street trees according to the presenter?
   (Name two.)
   - _____
   - _____
   - make streets look nicer

2. What did a study say about the effect of planting eleven more trees per block?
   _____

3. What was the paradoxical situation in Detroit between 2011 and 2014?
   _____

4. What was the aim of Christine Carmichael's campaign?
   _____

5. According to Christine Carmichael, what were some people in disadvantaged neighborhoods worried about?
   _____

6. What would change these people's attitude towards street trees?
   _____

You will hear a radio report about life on the Mexican-American border with the cities of El Paso on the American side, and Juarez on the Mexican side.
While listening tick (✓) the correct answer (a, b, c or d). There is only one correct answer.

1. According to the female presenter, how do young locals see the border?
   a) ☐ as a sad reality
   b) ☐ as separating families
   c) ☐ as having little importance
   d) ☐ as separating different cultures

2. How does Antonio Villasenor-Baca perceive the border?
   a) ☐ as a protective measure
   b) ☐ as a necessary measure
   c) ☐ as an annoying measure
   d) ☐ as a threatening measure

3. Why are some children from Juarez able to attend an American school?
   a) ☐ The school is run privately.
   b) ☐ The American school is in Mexico.
   c) ☐ They take part in a special program.
   d) ☐ They have an American and a Mexican passport.

4. What is said about the connection of the two border cities?
   a) ☐ They are twin cities.
   b) ☐ They are interdependent.
   c) ☐ Their police forces cooperate closely.
   d) ☐ El Paso dominates Juarez financially.

5. Why can Kenia Guerrero cross the border faster?
   a) ☐ She holds a Green Card.
   b) ☐ She uses the commercial lane.
   c) ☐ She only has a small backpack.
   d) ☐ She has bought a special document.

6. What has made crossing the border more difficult for Kenia?
   a) ☐ a change in politics
   b) ☐ rising drug trafficking
   c) ☐ increased illegal migration
   d) ☐ the introduction of body scans

You will hear an interview with Sam King, one of the passengers of the Empire Windrush, a ship that took about 500 people from Jamaica to Great Britain in 1948. While listening, fill in the missing information. You need not write complete sentences.

1. Why the economic situation in Jamaica was so serious in 1948:	
2. What Sam King's father wanted his son to do:	
3. Why Sam King had spent time away from Jamaica:	
4. What Sam King realized when back in Jamaica:	
5. What Sam King says about the fare for the passage: *(Name one aspect.)*	
6. What the journey of the *Windrush* led to:	
7. Why some middle-aged passengers found it hard to leave Jamaica:	
8. What some travellers did when learning a woman was on board illegally:	
9. Why Sam considered the food on board bad: *(Name one reason.)*	

10. How people spent their time on board: *(Name two activities.)*	• •
11. What some younger passengers worried about:	

Lösungsvorschläge

Text 1: Street Trees

1 **Jason G. Goldman:** This is "Scientific American, Sixty Seconds Science". I am Jason Goldman. Trees in cities do measurable good for biodiversity and for human health. They scrub pollution from the air. They provide habitat for wildlife. They make streets look nicer. And they even reduce stress and have been linked to re-

5 ductions in crime.

Back in 2015 a group of Toronto-based researchers discovered that planting just eleven more trees per city block could reduce heart-related conditions by the same amount as if everybody living on that block became a year and a half younger.

But in Detroit between 2011 and 2014 a quarter of eligible homeowners turned

10 down an offer from a local nonprofit for free street trees. Ironic, considering Detroit's nickname was once the City of Trees.

Christine Carmichael: It was actually over 1,800 trees that were rejected out of an eligible 7,425. So it was a big enough issue at that point where it warranted further investigation.

15 **Jason G. Goldman:** Forestry researcher Christine Carmichael, who did the research at Michigan State and has since moved to the University of Vermont.

The nonprofit created an education campaign to get more residents to accept the free trees, the assumption being that, if people had all the facts, they'd be more likely to take the trees. But when Carmichael talked to residents, she found that

20 they understood the benefits of trees. Their unease was about trust.

Christine Carmichael: Basically what I found was that opposition in Detroit to tree planting among some of these residents resulted primarily from negative past experiences with street trees, particularly in low-income neighborhoods that were grappling with blight from vacant properties, which created an additional burden

25 of care for their neighborhood.

Jason G. Goldman: In the last half-century or so, more than half a million Detroit trees died from disease and neglect. It was primarily low-income African American communities who were forced to deal with the consequences and the hazards, like falling limbs, posed by dead trees.

30 In speaking with residents, Carmichael found that they would be more willing to accept free trees if they could be more involved in the decision-making process. Locals wanted input on tree size and whether they produced flowers. They also very reasonably wanted to avoid trees that could drop rotting fruits or sap on cars and sidewalks.

1. What are the advantages of street trees according to the presenter?
two of the following:
* **good for biodiversity**
* **good for human health**
* **scrub pollution from the air**
* **provide habitat for wildlife**
* **reduce stress**
* **allegedly reduce crime**

2. What did a study say about the effect of planting eleven more trees per block?
would reduce heart-related conditions (as if people became one and a half years younger)/would improve health

3. What was the paradoxical situation in Detroit between 2011 and 2014?
people didn't want trees although they were offered them for free/ Detroit was once the City of Trees

4. What was the aim of Christine Carmichael's campaign?
get more residents to accept free trees

5. According to Christine Carmichael, what were some people in disadvantaged neighborhoods worried about?
negative past experiences with street trees/additional burden of care/hazards connected with dead trees

6. What would change these people's attitude towards street trees?
involve them in the decision-making process/ avoid planting trees that could become dangerous

Text 2: Border

1 **Ailsa Chang,** *Host*: Youth Radio's team covering the border spoke with young people from El Paso, Texas, and Juarez, Mexico, who grew up never seeing the border as a dividing line. Billy Cruz reports.

Billy Cruz, *Byline*: Along the dry, rocky desert of El Paso, past all the food chains and
5 shopping malls, a brown fence stretches for miles. Antonio Villasenor-Baca is 22. He was born here in El Paso, a huge borderplex that spans the Rio Grande River. But he has an uncle in Juarez. And growing up, Antonio's dad would take him back and forth a lot.

Villasenor-Baca: You know, like, you want to go out and party, you go to Juarez. You
10 have family in Juarez, but you live in El Paso, or vice versa. It really seems like just a huge hassle to, like, go through all of this stuff at the border.

Cruz: For young people like Antonio, life on the border isn't just about the momentous crossings we read about in the news. Commuting between two countries is a part of everyday life. There are even kids with dual citizenship who live in Juarez
15 with their parents and cross the border to go to school.

Villasenor-Baca: It's really weird because growing up as a kid, there's just other kids in your school. And it's not until you get older that you start seeing, well, it's the kids who speak Spanish who are the – doing the daily commute.

Cruz: Many people and goods flow between El Paso and Juarez every day. The cul-
20   ture and economies of both cities rely on each other. 23-year-old Kenia Guerrero is part of that flow. She grew up in Juarez but just finished college in El Paso. And she crosses the border every day to help out at her parents' cowboy boot shop.

Kenia Guerrero: Yeah, so we are at the Santa Fe Bridge. This is in the central part of El Paso. As you can see, like, cars are coming in from Juarez. It usually takes
25   about half an hour to three hours to cross to El Paso.

Cruz: To make her commute easier, Kenia got something called a SENTRI pass, which cuts down the time it takes to cross. Thousands of people in the El Paso-Juarez region pay the fees and go through the background checks to get one. Kenia says she feels equally at home in Juarez and here in El Paso.

30   **Guerrero:** It was pretty normal. And now it's not like that anymore because you're sometimes afraid.

Cruz: Now Kenia has to be extra careful whenever she crosses because she says agents have gotten stricter since President Trump took office. If she's caught with a prohibited item like even an apple she packed for lunch and forgot to throw
35   away, Kenia could lose her fastpass. Recently she had a close call.

Guerrero: Had a crushed candy in my cup holder. And the agent asked me, "Is that cocaine?". And I got nervous, not because it was cocaine but because it's just a question. Like, how can he think that I'm bringing cocaine?

© *Billy Cruz: "Young People Adapt to a Changing Life at the Texas-Mexico Border"*, NPR / Youth Radio, *20 July 2018, https://www.npr.org/2018/07/20/630076251/young-people-adapt-to-a-chang-ing-life-at-the-texas-mexico-border*

1. According to the female presenter, how do young locals see the border?

   c) ☑ as having little importance

2. How does Antonio Villasenor-Baca perceive the border?

   c) ☑ as an annoying measure

3. Why are some children from Juarez able to attend an American school?

   d) ☑ They have an American and a Mexican passport.

4. What is said about the connection of the two border cities?

   b) ☑ They are interdependent.

5. Why can Kenia Guerrero cross the border faster?

   d) ☑ She has bought a special document.

6. What has made crossing the border more difficult for Kenia?

   a) ☑ a change in politics

Text 3: Ship

1 **Alan Johnston, Host**: It is 1948 in Jamaica and the island is in bad shape. It's still re-
covering from a hurricane a few years earlier and Sam King remembers the
economy being in a desperate state.

Sam King: Things again were very bad because the coconuts were destroyed in '44. It
5 takes five to six years for the coconuts to rebuild. The whole structure of farming
was undermined. I didn't see any future. Of course, my father was very glad I was
there because I'm the eldest son and like him, eventually I would take over the
farm to pick pimento and to plant banana and all that and all that. But I had no intention of planting bananas.

10 **Alan Johnston**: Back then, Sam was just 22 years old, but he'd already seen the outside world. He'd volunteered during WWII and served in the Royal Air Force in
Britain. With the coming of peace, he'd returned to the hills of Eastern Jamaica.
But he knew he wouldn't stay. And within months, he spotted a chance to get
away.

15 **Sam King**: It was in the daily Jamaican newspaper that this troop ship would call to
Jamaica in about two weeks' time. And the passage was 28 pounds 10 shillings.
Let's get that straight: The average man didn't have 28 pounds 10 shillings. It was
equivalent to about three cows.

Alan Johnston: So you are sitting, reading the newspaper. And what goes through
20 your mind?

Sam King: I'm going back to England.

Alan Johnston: Eventually, nearly 500 passengers boarded the ship, bound for England and a new life. They would turn out to be pioneers. Their journey marked the
start of a new wave of migration. In the decade to come, a quarter of a million
25 West Indians would follow in the wake of the Windrush. Sam remembers the
mood that evening when she slips slowly out of Kingston harbour.

Sam King: People were waving, things were happening on the docks. Now for about
half of us, we had no intention of coming back to our colony. We were looking
forward, we were looking towards a new home. But there were some men in their
30 40s who had wife and children. They were looking back at the yard, they were
waving, they – but we, chiefly the young ones, we were not looking back, we
were looking forward.

Alan Johnston: Several stowaways had managed to smuggle themselves on board, one
was a woman and out of kindness, Sam and some of the other passengers clubbed
35 together and paid to buy her a ticket, enabling her to make the voyage legally. But
conditions on the troop ship in those first years after the war were far from luxuri-
ous.

Sam King: Sad to say, you have mashed potato in tins from New Zealand two years,
they put it on the table, mix it up with water. Now if you didn't eat it then, in the
40 evening they mix it with cabbage and if you didn't eat it then, in the morning they
fried it and called it bubble and squeak. I would eat it sometimes before, when I
was resident in Britain. Men were playing dominoes and things, but we had the

decks, were chiefly blankets and a few bunks. But the women were in cabins. So
we just mill around and in the evenings they have boxing competitions and things
like that and dance and all things. But the main thing is, it was to mentally get
yourself ready to land.

Alan Johnston: And the other young guys who, unlike you, hadn't seen Britain before,
were they asking lots of questions?

Sam King: Time and again they would come, "Sam, what, will I have a job?" They
were more concerned about jobs. I said, "Settle down." In the evening after supper
about 6.30, I would go on the lower deck to you know about ten of them I said,
"Look. Food is rationed in England, you can't grasp that, but work is all over the
place, so work is not the problem."

© *BBC World Service, 26 June 2011, Witness History, "The Voyage of the Empire Windrush",*
https://www.bbc.co.uk/programmes/p00h8xkq

1. Why the economic situation in Jamaica was so serious in 1948:	(recovering from) a (recent) hurricane (a few years earlier) / coconuts were destroyed (in 1944) / coconuts needed time to grow again / whole structure of farming was undermined
2. What Sam King's father wanted his son to do:	to take over the farm / to plant bananas / to pick pimento
3. Why Sam King had spent time away from Jamaica:	volunteered during WW II / served in Royal Air Force in Britain
4. What Sam King realized when back in Jamaica:	(he knew) he wouldn't stay
5. What Sam King says about the fare for the passage:	28 pounds, 10 shillings / the average man didn't have 28 pounds, 10 shillings / equivalent to about three cows / too expensive for average people
6. What the journey of the *Windrush* led to:	new wave of migration / a quarter of a million West Indians emigrated too
7. Why some middle-aged passengers found it hard to leave Jamaica:	had (to leave their) families / children and wives
8. What some travellers did when learning a woman was on board illegally:	clubbed together and paid to buy her a ticket / bought her a ticket
9. Why Sam considered the food on board bad:	old, tinned food / same food served over and over again

10. How people spent their time on board:	*two of the following:* • playing dominoes • milling around • boxing competitions • dances • mentally getting ready to land
11. What some younger passengers worried about:	finding a job (in England)

You will hear each recording **twice**. After each listening you will have time to complete your answers.

Task 1: Turning Pollution into Art   **9 BE**

Preparation time: 1:30 minutes

You will hear an interview with Angela Haseltine Pozzi, an artist living in Oregon. While listening, tick (✓) the correct answer (a, b or c). There is only one correct answer.

1. The Southern Oregon coast is known for its …
   a) ☐ flat islands.
   b) ☐ dramatic scenery.
   c) ☐ recreational value.

2. It is Angela's aim to …
   a) ☐ gather lots of plastic.
   b) ☐ make people collect plastic on shore.
   c) ☐ locate plastic items bitten into by animals.

3. Angela's pieces of art feature …
   a) ☐ extinct sea animals.
   b) ☐ fantasy sea animals.
   c) ☐ endangered sea animals.

4. Angela's intention of creating large sculptures is that …
   a) ☐ people notice them.
   b) ☐ stability can be ensured.
   c) ☐ a lot of waste is used up.

5. With her project, Angela hopes …
   a) ☐ to encourage other artists.
   b) ☐ to appeal to society as a whole.
   c) ☐ to cooperate with youth workers.

6. Angela's organisation Washed Ashore …
   a) ☐ gathers plastic waste from all over the US.
   b) ☐ puts together exhibitions throughout the nation.
   c) ☐ supports global campaigns for plastic-free oceans.

7. The Beijing Olympics is mentioned to show that ...
   a) ☐ plastic is a long-lasting problem.
   b) ☐ sports events create a lot of plastic trash.
   c) ☐ people find plastic products with logos attractive.

8. Angela is aware that plastic ...
   a) ☐ can be necessary.
   b) ☐ has to be replaced.
   c) ☐ should be disposed of properly.

9. When it comes to single-use plastic items, Angela suggests that ...
   a) ☐ they should be banned.
   b) ☐ engineers must solve the problem.
   c) ☐ the public is warned about the long-term effects.

Task 2: Sugar

5 BE

Preparation time: 30 seconds

You will hear five people talking about regulating sugar consumption.
Choose from the list (A–G) which heading best applies to which statement (1–5).
For each statement there is only one correct answer. There are two more headings
than you need.

Headings:

A Harming minors

B Business principles

C Prolonging life expectancy

D Attitude towards authorities

E Lowering the cost for health care

F Impact of prices on consumer groups

G Varied public health measures required

Statement	1	2	3	4	5
Heading					

Task 3: Modernising the Royal Family

Hinweis: Der Hörtext kann aus rechtlichen Gründen nicht abgedruckt werden und ist nicht in der MP3-Datei auf MySTARK enthalten. Eine ungekürzte Fassung des Beitrags ist bei der BBC unter folgendem Link abrufbar: https://www.bbc.co.uk/sounds/play/w3csywyp

Für die Bearbeitung von Task 3 sind die Minuten 00:10–03:24 und 03:45–04:07 relevant.

Preparation time: 1 minute

You will hear a radio programme on changes in the British Royal Family since 1992. Lucy Burns from the BBC speaks to Charles Anson, the former press secretary of the Royal Family.

While listening, answer the questions. You need not write complete sentences. Unless otherwise specified, name one aspect.

1. What did the Royal Family do in reaction to the situation in the early 1990s?	
2. How does the Queen remember 1992?	
3. What family matters affected the Royals in 1992? *(Name one.)*	
4. How did the media react to the royal events? *(Name two examples.)*	• •
5. What issue did the public raise?	
6. What happened in November 1992?	
7. What made Charles Anson's job more challenging at the time?	
8. How does Anson characterise the Queen during her long reign?	
9. Which change did Queen Elizabeth declare that affected the public directly?	

Lösungsvorschläge

Text 1: Turning Pollution into Art

1 **Rachel Martin,** *Host:* It is estimated that more than one million tons of plastic garbage contaminates the world's oceans every year. But one artist on the Oregon coast is making a small dent in that. NPR's Kirk Siegler has the story from the seaside village of Bandon in southern Oregon.

5 **Kirk Siegler,** *Byline:* Here at Coquille Point, the wind is tumultuous and the sea violent. Huge waves crash up against the giant moss-covered rocks perched off the beach. The rugged Oregon coast is famous for being pristine and wild, but train your eyes down a little closer to the beach and sand itself and even here you find bits of plastic.

10 **Angela Haseltine Pozzi:** Well, I think the most disturbing thing I find is detergent bottles and bleach bottles with giant bite marks out of them by fish.

Siegler: Artist and teacher Angela Haseltine Pozzi has made it her mission to collect as much of this shameful garbage as possible, washing ashore from Asia, Europe, California, right here in Oregon.

15 **Pozzi:** Right, hear this.

(Soundbite of Rummaging)

Siegler: In her gallery nearby, she takes these plastic bottle caps, cocktail toothpicks, shotgun shell casings, anything and turns them into jaw-dropping sculptures of the very marine life threatened by all this plastic.

20 **Pozzi:** This piece over here is a giant weedy seadragon, and it's 18 feet long and ten feet tall.

Siegler: Its neck made of suction cups from vacuum cleaners; its eye is a black water bottle cap.

Pozzi: And the idea is that you can't ignore something that's really big, and it grabs
25 your attention.

Siegler: Like the jellyfish sculpted from golf balls or the puffin bird whose feathers are made from fastened-together flip flops and plastic lighters and the life-sized replica of a juvenile humpback whale's rib cage made of – you guessed it – plastic household bleach bottles. You can walk under it and even bang on it like a drum.

30 *(Soundbite of Banging)*

Pozzi: My goal in creating this project is to reach the general public, not the art connoisseurs and the environmentalists. I want to reach everybody. I want to reach kids. I want to reach people who might throw something on the beach and not think about it. And I want to make them start to think about it.

35 **Siegler:** A few years ago, she founded a nonprofit called Washed Ashore. They've built 80 sculptures made out of 26 tons of garbage collected from the Oregon coast. They've been displayed across the country, from the zoo in Tacoma, Washington, to the Smithsonian in Washington, D.C. One of the most popular sculp-

tures, though, is right here in the gallery – a six-foot-wide sea star made from indi-
40 vidual-use plastic water bottles.

Pozzi: A lot of these right here are actually washed in from the 2008 Beijing Olympics that still wash up on our beaches. They have the insignia on them.

Siegler: 2008?

Pozzi: Yep, yep. And they're still coming in.

45 **Siegler:** And you can play this one like a drum, too. It's a hit with kids.

(Soundbite of Banging)

Pozzi: It's more sound than music *(laughter)*.

Siegler: Angela is not on a crusade to end all plastics. She knows we have to use them in our phones or medical equipment. But will these enormous plastic sculptures
50 make us rethink how much we use?

Pozzi: Single-use plastics are the most dangerous because you use it, and in five minutes, you're done with it. And then it lasts a thousand years. And we were never taught that. You know, if we were taught that, we'd think differently, I think. And that's part of the thing is education.

55 **Siegler:** Education, she says, can make a difference. And after all, we invented all these convenient plastics, so why can't we invent our way out of the crisis? Kirk Siegler, NPR News, Bandon, Oregon.

(Soundbite of Vurez's "Glorious Crystal Gleam [Mmx2 – Crystal Snail Stage]")

https://www.houstonpublicmedia.org/npr/2019/12/04/784416386/on-the-oregon-coast-turning-pollution-into-art-with-a-purpose/

Task one is a multiple choice task that asks you to listen for detail. First, read the beginnings of the sentences 1 to 9 as well as the possible sentence endings carefully and underline key words. While listening, pay attention to precisely these key words (or synonyms/paraphrases/expressions from the same word family), as they might give you a hint at the correct solution. Be aware that the wording in the answers may not be the same as in the text.

These text passages will help you find the correct answer:

1 *"the wind is tumultuous and the sea violent. Huge waves crash up against the giant moss-covered rocks [...]. The rugged Oregon coast is famous for being pristine and wild" (ll. 5–7)*

2 *"Angela Haseltine Pozzi has made it her mission to collect as much of this shameful garbage as possible" (ll. 12/13)*

3 *"In her gallery nearby, she takes these plastic bottle caps [...] and turns them into jaw-dropping sculptures of the very marine life threatened by all this plastic." (ll. 17–19)*

4 *"And the idea is that you can't ignore something that's really big, and it grabs your attention." (ll. 24/25)*

5 *"My goal in creating this project is to reach the general public [...]. I want to reach everybody. I want to reach kids. I want to reach people who might throw something on the beach and not think about it." (ll. 31–34)*

1. The Southern Oregon coast is known for its ...

   b) ☑ dramatic scenery.

2. It is Angela's aim to ...

   a) ☑ gather lots of plastic.

3. Angela's pieces of art feature ...

   c) ☑ endangered sea animals.

4. Angela's intention of creating large sculptures is that ...

   a) ☑ people notice them.

5. With her project, Angela hopes ...

   b) ☑ to appeal to society as a whole.

6. Angela's organisation Washed Ashore ...

   b) ☑ puts together exhibitions throughout the nation.

7. The Beijing Olympics is mentioned to show that ...

   a) ☑ plastic is a long-lasting problem.

8. Angela is aware that plastic ...

   a) ☑ can be necessary.

9. When it comes to single-use plastic items, Angela suggests that ...

   c) ☑ the public is warned about the long-term effects.

Text 2: Sugar

1 **Speaker 1:** Well, I mean, it's interesting when you look at any forms of suggested
regulation, any government approaches to this, there's fundamentally a view that
says government does not have a role in what we eat or drink, regulation is a bad
thing of any form. And what we've found over the last 40 years is that the en-
5 emies of regulation have become the enemies of science.

Speaker 2: Well, I think the issue is that the industry are driving demand and consumption and it's in their interest to do that. Highly processed foods, many of
which are high in sugar, are very cheap to produce. There's a very high profit
margin. You try and find an apple in a car-parking station or an airport. It's much
10 easier to find a packet of chips and a soft drink. And we have, we are surrounded
by advertising, marketing, promotion of these foods.

Speaker 3: So there definitely has been a change in purchasing habits. And there was
a study published in 2015 in the BMG that looked at 50,000 Mexican families and
what happened next. And what they found was that purchases of sugared drinks
15 decreased and purchases of untaxed bottled water increased. And this was an effect that was seen across all parts of the socio-economic grouping scale, particularly in poorer families. So that change seemed to be most marked in people that
had less money to start off with.

Speaker 4: Well, certainly the Council of Presidents of Medical Colleges had a sum-
20 mit about obesity. And one of the issues that was clearly flagged was the need for
financial incentives to create an effective strategy and to start really early and with
the whole family. And that means prevention, really almost pre-conception. And,
you know, well, there's not a lot of evidence that education alone does a lot in this
space.

25 **Speaker 5:** We know that these products are very heavily, high-sugar products are
heavily marketed to young people, and they develop their tastes when they're
young, particularly for sweetness. And we know that adolescents, in particular, are
very high consumers of sugary drinks, particularly boys, and are way exceeding
the World Health Organization guidelines. But also very young children are start-
30 ing to drink these drinks very, very early. And that's something that we haven't
seen before either. So it's a huge source of added sugar in the diet.

eigene Zusammenstellung nach https://www.bbc.co.uk/programmes/b07414dg,
https://www.abc.net.au/radionational/programs/healthreport/is-it-time-for-a-sugar-tax/9224258

Here you have to match each statement (1–5) with one of the headings (A–G) by putting the corresponding letter into the correct box. Note that two more headings than you need are given. Use the preparation time to underline key words in the headings. Try to think of synonyms or expressions from the same word family or word field that might be mentioned in the recording and listen out for these signals. These text passages will help you find the correct answer:

1 *"there's fundamentally a view that says government does not have a role in what we eat or drink, regulation is a bad thing of any form." (ll. 2–4)*

2 *"the industry are driving demand and consumption and it's in their interest to do that. Highly processed foods, many of which are high in sugar, are very cheap to produce. There's a very high profit margin." (ll. 6–9); "we are surrounded by advertising, marketing, promotion of these foods." (ll. 10/11)*

3 *"purchases of sugared drinks decreased and purchases of untaxed bottled water increased. And this was an effect that was seen across all parts of the socio-economic grouping scale, particularly in poorer families. So that change seemed to be most marked in people that had less money to start off with." (ll. 14–18)*

4 *"And one of the issues that was clearly flagged was the need for financial incentives to create an effective strategy" (ll. 20/21), "there's not a lot of evidence that education alone does a lot in this space." (ll. 23/24)*

5 *"high-sugar products are heavily marketed to young people" (ll. 25/26); "And we know that adolescents, in particular, are very high consumers of sugary drinks, particularly boys, and are way exceeding the World Health Organization guidelines." (ll. 27–29); "also very young children are starting to drink these drinks very, very early. [...] So it's a huge source of added sugar in the diet." (ll. 29–31)*

Statement	1	2	3	4	5
Heading	D	B	F	G	A

Text 3: Modernising the Royal Family

Hinweis: Der Hörtext kann aus rechtlichen Gründen nicht abgedruckt werden und ist nicht in der MP3-Datei auf MySTARK enthalten. Eine ungekürzte Fassung des Beitrags ist bei der BBC unter folgendem Link abrufbar: https://www.bbc.co.uk/sounds/play/w3csywyp

Für die Bearbeitung von Task 3 sind die Minuten 00:10–03:24 und 03:45–04:07 relevant.

Task three is a note-taking task. Before you start, it can be useful to highlight the key words in the task. It may also help you to pay attention to which speaker is most likely to give certain information. Note that the questions in the task are in chronological order. This gives you a rough idea as to when the information will be mentioned in the text. During the first listening you can note down which answers are likely to be correct. In the second listening, you can then confirm these answers. You are allowed to use bullet points and don't have to write full sentences. Be brief and precise in your answers. More than one option may be correct for each question but you are not supposed to give more than one item per question except for item 4.

These text passages will help you find the correct answer:

1 *Listen carefully to the presenter Lucy Burns at the beginning of the recording, when she refers to the 1990s.*

2 *Here you need to listen carefully to the Queen and look out for the key word "1992" from the task. Queen Elizabeth II refers to that year as an "annus horribilis". Lucy Burns also explains the English meaning of this Latin word ("horrible year") – you can use that in your answer too.*

3 *The key word from the task is "family matters". So pay attention when the words "family", "Royal Family" or the names of different family members are mentioned in the recording. The speaker of the media report lists more family matters than you need to complete this task. You just have to write down one of them. Relevant expressions and passages mentioned in the recording are, for example, "Duke and Duchess of York separated", "Princess Anne ended 18 years of marriage" and "divorce" as well as "a torrent of stories about the state of [the Prince and Princess of Wales's] marriage".*

4 *The key word "media" from question 4 is referred to as "press" in the recording. The speaker lists several reactions of the media, but you just have to name two. The relevant phrases are "Press interest in the Royal Family was relentless", "Scandals were splashed", "Tapes were leaked" and "There were even premium rate phone lines that members of the public could call to listen to the recordings themselves".*

5 *The expression "issue [...] raise[d]" in question 5 is taken up in the phrase "Questions were [...] being asked" in the recording. The information you need is mentioned right after that.*

6 *The key words from the task are "November 1992", which are also mentioned in the text. The right answer is given in the following media report.*

7 *To answer the question, listen carefully when Charles Anson starts to speak. The relevant passage is introduced with the words "it made the job [...] a little more difficult".*

8 *Here you have to listen carefully to Charles Anson again when he starts his sentence with: "But what made the job completely doable". Note that you do not have to write down everything he says about the Queen. One adjective or noun is enough.*

9 *Note that Lucy Burns names two changes that the Queen declared but you have to just name one of them. Only the changes that affected the public directly are correct. The setting up of the Way Ahead group, for instance, would therefore be an incorrect answer. The relevant passage starts with the words "the Queen announced".*

1.	What did the Royal Family do in reaction to the situation in the early 1990s?	set up the Way Ahead Group / plan reforms / plan for the future
2.	How does the Queen remember 1992?	as a terrible / horrible year / with sadness
3.	What family matters affected the Royals in 1992?	breakup / separation / divorce / marriage troubles
4.	How did the media react to the royal events?	*two of the following:* • showed relentless interest • splashed scandals (across front pages) • leaked tapes (of intimate phone calls) • phone lines people could call (to listen to recordings of intimate phone calls)
5.	What issue did the public raise?	how much the Royal Family cost (the taxpayer)
6.	What happened in November 1992?	Windsor Castle fire / castle was consumed by fire
7.	What made Charles Anson's job more challenging at the time?	(to talk about the public duties when) people asked about the private lives (of the Royal Family)
8.	How does Anson characterise the Queen during her long reign?	did her job with steadiness / steady / calm (in difficult times)
9.	Which change did Queen Elizabeth declare that affected the public directly?	she would start paying income tax / tax payer would not pay for junior members of the Royal Family

You will hear each recording **twice**. After each listening you will have time to complete your answers.

Task 1: Book Reviews   **5 BE**

Preparation time: 40 seconds

You will hear the beginnings of five book reviews.
Choose from the list (A–G) which description best applies to which book review (1–5). For each book review there is only one correct answer. There are two more descriptions than you need.

Descriptions:

A Dealing with characters' secrets

B Describing a character's dreams

C Tracing a character's self-exploration

D Inspired by very different historical events

E Presenting the lives of prominent individuals

F Telling the story of formerly overlooked people

G Based on historical events and connected to current issues

Book Review	1	2	3	4	5
Description					

Task 2: Baroness Trumpington   **14 BE**

Preparation time: 1:30 minutes

You will hear a radio report about Lady Jean Trumpington (born Jean Campbell-Harris, 1922–2018, a British politician).
While listening, fill in the missing information. You need not write complete sentences. Unless otherwise specified, name one aspect.

1. Why did Lady Trumpington's departure from politics attract so much attention?	

77

2. Why does the host of a TV show mention the invention of television?	
3. Which incident made Lady Trumpington widely known?	
4. What is said about her education?	
5. In which two different fields of work was she active during World War II?	• •
6. Why did she return to Great Britain?	
7. What did she change in her life during her time in Cambridge?	
8. Why did she choose the title "Baroness Trumpington"?	
9. What was special about her holding her governmental position at the end of the 1980s?	
10. What did she do in Downing Street that helped her keep her position?	
11. What was her duty as Baroness in Waiting?	

12. Which interest will she continue to pursue after retiring?	

Now think of the text as a whole. Tick (✓) the correct answer (a, b or c). There is only one correct answer.

13. In the radio report, Lady Trumpington's personality is presented as being ...

a) ☐ charitable and caring.

b) ☐ cautious and level-headed.

c) ☐ self-confident and unconventional.

Task 3: Sea Otters   6 BE

Preparation time: 1:30 minutes

You will hear a radio report about research on sea otters in Canada.
While listening, tick (✓) the correct answer (a, b or c). There is only one correct answer.

1. The research focusses on the ...

a) ☐ effects of sea otter populations on the local economy.

b) ☐ behavioural patterns of sea otters living close to humans.

c) ☐ consequences of climate change for sea otter populations.

2. There was more seafood in the area after the Europeans had arrived because ...

a) ☐ sea otters were exterminated.

b) ☐ Europeans relied mainly on farming.

c) ☐ the native population was moved inland.

3. The scientists have chosen Vancouver Island for their research project because ...

a) ☐ university facilities are readily available.

b) ☐ a particular species of sea otters lives there.

c) ☐ the place is suitable for comparative field studies.

4. The sea otters affect the ecosystem because ...

a) ☐ they tend to destroy habitats of other species.

b) ☐ their feeding behaviour enables the growth of fish.

c) ☐ they help to reduce the impact of invasive species.

5. Ecologist Edward Gregr addresses the issue that …
   a) ☐ visits to the area need to be regulated.
   b) ☐ not everyone in the area profits in the same way.
   c) ☐ too many sea otters threaten the fragile ecosystem.

6. Native Canadians living in isolated communities perceive the growing population of sea otters as …
   a) ☐ a potential threat.
   b) ☐ a minor nuisance.
   c) ☐ a welcome source of income.

Lösungsvorschläge

Text 1: Book Reviews

1 **1** Welcome to Book Club and a novel that's set in the aftermath of the First World War but crackles with contemporary relevance. James Meek's novel *The People's Act of Love* is set in the wastes of Siberia in 1919. And in a way, it is a Russian novel, because its action springs from the turmoil of that country in its dark history.

5 **2** Hello and welcome to Book Club from Swansea. Sheers's book is a psychological thriller that mixes suspense – Michael, the central character, tries to conceal an awful event out of fear – with a story of the relationship between two men who both have something to hide.

3 Hello. If you look at *The New York Times* for October 4th, 1951, you will see two
10 headlines jostling together on the front page, one reporting that "Giants win over the Brooklyn Dodgers in a famous baseball game", the other saying, "Soviets explode atomic bomb". Well, when Don DeLillo looked at those headlines in the early nineties, 40 years on, the prickle of excitement started him on a journey of the imagination that led to *Underworld*.

15 **4** Hello and welcome to Book Club and a biographical feast. We're talking this month about the story of two interlocked families, and at the head of them, the two most glamorous figures of the late Victorian stage, Sir Henry Irving and Ellen Terry. They're the joint subjects of one of our most admired literary biographers, Michael Holroyd, now in his eighties, who's our guest today.

20 **5** Hello and welcome to Book Club. This month's book is funny and breezy, but don't be misled by that. *Rachel's Holiday* is also a journey into darkness with Rachel discovering the depths of her drug addiction and its threat to her whole life. Her holiday is, in fact, a trip into rehab, away from the high life she's been enjoying in New York to a clinic in Dublin, the Cloisters, where she imagines that she'll get away
25 from it all, but instead discovers more about herself than she expected.

based on: bbc.co.uk/sounds/play/m000dxtp; bbc.co.uk/sounds/play/m0007b4t; bbc.co.uk/sounds/play/b07sxttn; bbc.co.uk/sounds/play/b072htqw; bbc.co.uk/sounds/play/m000fw1j

You do not have a lot of time to read through the task, so concentrate on highlighting the key words which sum up the main idea of each description. Also mark words you think are essential for comprehension. You will have a very short break before and in between sets to look them up, but do not overestimate the time frame. The listening comprehension in your exam takes its complexity not only from the level of sophistication of the audio files, but also from the speed with which you have to solve the tasks.

– 1 – G: The key phrases in the description are "historical events" as well as "connected to current issues" (= "contemporary relevance", l. 2), which is the main difference when compared to description D, which only speaks of "historical events". It also differs from D in that it does not deal with "very different histori-

81

cal events" but rather focuses on a specific historical period of a specific country.
- **2 – A:** *The key word here is "secret", which is indirectly mentioned several times: The review talks about the protagonist "tr[ying] to conceal" (l. 6) something and about two men "hav[ing] something to hide" (ll. 7/8).*
- **3 – D:** *The fact that the review talks about "headlines jostling" (l. 10) points towards "very different historical events", as mentioned in **D**. If you don't know the word "jostling", the headlines give you an even stronger clue: One is about a baseball game (cf. ll. 10/11), the other about the explosion of an atomic bomb (cf. ll. 11/12), which do not have anything in common.*
- **4 – E:** *Finding the correct solution can be tricky here, because you might mistake the word "interlocked" (l. 16) for "overlooked". In this case, you might be tempted to choose **F** ("story of [...] overlooked people") as an answer. It is, however, stated that the book deals with "the two most glamorous figures of the late Victorian stage" (ll. 16/17), which then leaves **E** ("prominent individuals") as the correct solution.*
- **5 – C:** *This review hints at the correct description quite often. It is about "self-exploration", which is expressed in phrases like "journey into darkness" (l. 21), with the protagonist "discovering the depths of her drug addiction" (l. 22) and "discover[ing] more about herself than she expected" (l. 25).*

Book Review	1	2	3	4	5
Description	G	A	D	E	C

Text 2: Baroness Trumpington

1 **Edward Stourton:** It should surely not come as a shock when a nonagenarian decides to retire. But Lady Trumpington's decision to leave the House of Lords when she reaches 95 this month made a splash. Perhaps that's because she's been part of the place for so long no one can quite imagine the scene without her.

5 **TV host:** It would be ungallant of me to tell you Her Ladyship's age. So let's just say she was born before this programme started. And before BBC One started. And before television started. Please welcome Baroness Trumpington.

Stourton: She began among pearls and ermine, and she's ending her long career in similar territory. On the way, she's lived our history and known most of the peo-
10 ple who made it. But she only really became famous in her late eighties when she was caught by the cameras making a V-sign at one of her fellow peers, as the comedian Jack Whitehall reminded her on "Have I Got News for You?".

Jack Whitehall: Did you regret swearing at him or …?

Baroness Trumpington: No, because I regretted what he said, which was that people of
15 my age were starting to look very, very, very old. Well, wouldn't you do that if you …?

Jack Whitehall: Yeah, I can see …

Stourton: Jean Campbell-Harris was born in 1922. Her father was a former major in the Bengal Lancers with the right connections. Her mother was the heir to a Chicago paint fortune. Her formal education was limited, as was often the way for women then. And she says she's never taken an exam. But finishing school in Paris gave her good French and German. The war began when she was 16.

Old news report: Down on the farm, the land girls are doing their bit and a bit more.

Stourton: Like thousands of other young women, Jean Campbell-Harris was sent to work as a land girl, filling the gap left when the countryside's young men went to fight. In 1940, she took her language skills to the secret codebreaking centre of Bletchley Park. She was a cipher clerk. Jean worked on Madison Avenue in the post-war Mad Men days, and it was in the United States that she met her very English husband, Alan Barker, a historian, then working at the Ivy League University, Yale. His career brought him back to a teaching post at Eton and then to the headmaster's job at the Leys, a private school in Cambridge. *[excerpt from song]* And it was during her years as a headmaster's wife that Jean Barker, as she then was, really turned her attention to politics.

Georgina Morley: She became a councillor in Cambridge and then ultimately mayor of Cambridge, and I think she rather loved being mayor.

Stourton: Cambridge local politics was a long way from life in Mayfair and Manhattan, and her early political career was hard graft. She tried and failed to become an MP. The political scene was dominated by another powerful woman, Margaret Thatcher. In 1980, Jean Barker was given a peerage by the new Tory government. She already had contacts in the House of Lords, including the Tory peer, Viscount Astor, whose mother had been Jean's friend and fellow clerk at Bletchley.

Viscount Astor: Jean took to the House of Lords like a duck to water, as it were, because she could actually kind of deflate someone who was being pompous, for example.

Stourton: There remained the little matter of deciding on a title. Her reputation for a robust speaking style was already established, so she rejected Baroness Barker. She explained her final decision to the prominent eighties Tory John Gummer, now Lord Deben.

Lord Deben: So, she said, "I had to choose the village nearest to me". And there were two possibilities. One was Trumpington and the other was Six Mile Bottom. She thought that was not a good idea. So, Trumpington it was.

Stourton: Lady Trumpington's husband Alan died after a stroke in 1988, leaving her a widow in her mid-sixties. She was serving as a minister at Agriculture at the time, the first ever woman minister there, and threw herself into her work. She survived at the ministry when John Major succeeded Margaret Thatcher until …

Georgina Morley: At one point she was called into Downing Street. And John Major, it turned out, had decided that the time had come for her to retire from the front bench, and she was not expecting this. And she told me afterwards, shamelessly, that she cried. Whereupon the Prime Minister patted her on the shoulder and said,

83

60 "There, there, all right then, well, never mind, we'll leave you as you are." So, she stayed on.

Stourton: By 1992, she was the oldest ever serving woman minister, and during John Major's second term, she became a Baroness in Waiting, representing the Queen on formal occasions until the Tories lost power in 1997. Lady Trumpington isn't

65 giving up all her passions. Her enthusiasm for horse racing, for example, is as fierce as ever. But her son, Adam, says that by giving up the Lords, she's giving up more than a job.

Adam Barker: The Lords became her family.

based on: bbc.co.uk/sounds/play/b098bqr1

This task requires an in-depth knowledge of vocabulary, the ability to distinguish be-tween several native speakers talking, and the skill to understand various accents of British English. You also have to cope with inferior sound quality in bits of historic audio documents. However, do not worry too much, as you can rely on the order of the questions following the chronology of the recording and you mostly need to note down only one aspect out of several mentioned.

1 *There are several reasons why "Lady Trumpington's decision to leave the House of Lords" (l. 2), or in other words "politics", attracted attention or "made a splash" (l. 3): "she's been part of the place for so long" (ll. 3/4), "no one can quite imagine the scene without her" (l. 4), and also "she reaches 95 this month" (ll. 2/3).*

2 *By mentioning the invention of television the host reveals Lady Trumpington's age in an indirect and humorous way ("It would be ungallant of me to tell you Her Ladyship's age.", l. 5): "So let's just say she was born before this programme started. And before BBC One started. And before television started." (ll. 5–7)*

3 *You do not need to know that the "V-sign" is a rude gesture (when the palm is facing towards the person making the sign) – it is enough to recognise the host mentioning that "she only really became famous in her late eighties when she was caught by the cameras making a V-sign at one of her fellow peers" (ll. 10/11). In the next sentence it becomes clear that she was swearing at him (cf. l. 13).*

4 *The show continues with milestones in Baroness Trumpington's life. Be careful, however, because this task only asks for Trumpington's education. You only need to note down one aspect from lines 20 to 22: "formal education was limited […] she's never taken an exam […] finishing school in Paris […] good French and German."*

5 *Listen closely here: The short clipping from a wartime news report serves as a distractor and the term "land girl(s)" (ll. 23, 25) is mentioned quite fast, meaning that she worked on a farm during the war. Her second job as a "cipher clerk" (l. 27) is not only hard to understand, but also no longer common and you need to know "clerk" as another word for "secretary" or "office worker". Bletchley Park was a facility of the British Intelligence Service to decode secret German mes-sages in World War II. If you know that, you can also give "intelligence work" or "code breaking" as an answer.*

6 *Here, you need to deduct the answer from what is said about Trumpington's hus-*

84

band, whom she met in the United States (cf. ll. 28/29) and who was "a historian, then working at [...] Yale. His career brought him back to [...] Eton and then to [...] a private school in Cambridge" (ll. 29–31), so Jean Barker, as she was now called, became "a headmaster's wife" (l. 32) in England.

7   In order to answer this question correctly, you must not lose track of the audio. It ends with the story of Trumpington's husband who got a job in Cambridge. And here, the Baroness "turned her attention to politics" (l. 33) by becoming councillor and mayor (cf. l. 34) there.

8   Listen particularly closely after the key word "title" (l. 45). As Trumpington "rejected [the title of] Baroness Barker" (l. 46), she then "had to choose the village nearest to [her]" (l. 49) and as she refused to be called "Six Mile Bottom", she chose the other village called "Trumpington" (cf. ll. 50/51).

9   Pay attention when the year 1988 is mentioned (cf. l. 52), which points towards the question of "her governmental position at the end of the 1980s". The audio says that "[s]he was serving as a minister at Agriculture at the time, the first ever woman minister there" (ll. 53/54) and that she still was "at the ministry when John Major succeeded Margaret Thatcher" (l. 55).

10 Here, "Downing Street" is the key word. Pay attention to what Lady Trumpington did when she was asked to resign by John Major, then Prime Minister: "she cried" (l. 59), which led to "the Prime Minister patt[ing] her on the shoulder" and leaving her in office (cf. ll. 59–61).

11 The moment the audio mentions "Baroness in Waiting" (l. 63), it is explained that she was "representing the Queen on formal occasions" (ll. 63/64).

12 This information is also given very fast and rather at the end of the audio when your concentration might be decreasing. It is stated that the Baroness has a passion for horse racing (cf. l. 65), so you can deduce that this is what she will continue to follow after retiring.

13 Here you need to understand the general character of Baroness Trumpington. By having a look at your answers in tasks 1 to 12, there is nothing that hints towards "charitable and caring" (**a**). If that were the case, the audio would have given some examples. The same goes for "cautious and level-headed" (**b**). A person who became a politician without formal education (cf. ll. 20–22, 32–35), went to the United States on her own (cf. ll. 27/28), gave inappropriate hand signs towards a colleague (cf. ll. 10–16), and was still active in her 90s (cf. ll. 1–4) can be nothing more than "self-confident and unconventional" (**c**).

1. Why did Lady Trumpington's departure from politics attract so much attention?	she had been there for so long / she retired at the age of 95 / hard to imagine House of Lords without her
2. Why does the host of a TV show mention the invention of television?	to show/allude to Lady Trumpington's (advanced) age / because Lady Trumpington had been born before TV was invented / to introduce a guest in a humorous way

3.	Which incident made Lady Trumpington widely known?	making V-sign / swearing (at a fellow peer) / making a rude gesture
4.	What is said about her education?	limited formal education / has never taken an exam / (went to) finishing school (in Paris) / (fairly) typical of women's education at the time / good command of German and French
5.	In which two different fields of work was she active during World War II?	• farming / agriculture / (work as) land girl • code breaking / intelligence / office work / (work as) cipher clerk
6.	Why did she return to Great Britain?	followed her (English) husband / because of her husband's job
7.	What did she change in her life during her time in Cambridge?	started her political career / became councillor/mayor
8.	Why did she choose the title "Baroness Trumpington"?	(name of / refers to) nearest village / did not like other options (Barker/Six Mile Bottom)
9.	What was special about her holding her governmental position at the end of the 1980s?	first (ever) female Minister at Agriculture / first (ever) woman holding that position / stayed in office when the Prime Minister changed
10.	What did she do in Downing Street that helped her keep her position?	she cried / she made the Prime Minister feel sorry for her
11.	What was her duty as Baroness in Waiting?	representing the Queen on formal occasions
12.	Which interest will she continue to pursue after retiring?	horse racing

13. In the radio report, Lady Trumpington's personality is presented as being …

    c) ☑ self-confident and unconventional.

Text 3: Sea Otters

1 **Ari Shapiro**, *host*: Let's talk about sea otters. They float on the water, cuddle their little babies. Same time, they're voracious eaters that gobble up shellfish. And that has brought them into conflict with people who rely on shellfish for their livelihoods. NPR's Nell Greenfieldboyce reports that scientists have now assessed the eco-

5 nomic impact of restoring sea otters to their historic homes.

    Nell Greenfieldboyce, *byline*: Sea otters are pretty big. They can weigh 60 pounds or more. To survive in the cold waters of the Northern Pacific, they need to eat a lot.

    Jane Watson: And so a sea otter is going to eat about a quarter of its body mass, its body weight, in food each day.

10 **Greenfieldboyce:** Jane Watson is a researcher with Vancouver Island University in Canada. She says historically sea otters coexisted with Indigenous people. But when the Europeans arrived, hunters with the fur trade wiped the otters out.

    Watson: All of a sudden, all of the prey that otters eat no longer had their principal predator eating them anymore.

15 **Greenfieldboyce:** Clams, crabs, sea urchins – their populations took off, and people got used to the abundance. Well, a few decades ago, sea otters were reintroduced to the west coast of Vancouver Island. Edward Gregr is an ecologist at the University of British Columbia. He says further down the coast from where the otters now live, there's another spot where the otters haven't yet moved in.

20 **Edward Gregr:** And so we thought, this is, you know, this is a perfect natural experiment to compare what the ecosystem looks like with and without sea otters.

    Greenfieldboyce: In the journal *Science*, they say otters do eat up clams and crabs worth millions of dollars. They also devour sea urchins, and that allows kelp to flourish. The kelp supports fish species that are worth a lot of money. What's

25 more, tourists will pay to watch the otters frolic. Gregr says, all in all, the financial benefits of otters are more than seven times greater than the losses. But, he says...

    Gregr: We want to make sure we don't lose sight of the caveats around that, mainly the fact that, you know, these costs and benefits are not going to be distributed equally across fisheries or communities.

30 **Greenfieldboyce:** Tourism, for example, isn't necessarily a realistic or attractive option for people who live in remote areas where access to food is a real issue. Barbara Wilson is a member of the Haida Nation who's studied Indigenous people's feelings about the sea otters.

    Barbara Wilson: The impact for us is fairly critical.

₃₅ **Greenfieldboyce:** She says Canadian law currently protects the otters. The otters have a right to eat, but so do people. Nell Greenfieldboyce, NPR News.

This task can be difficult insofar as the vocabulary is rather sophisticated or technical and the correct answer is often hidden behind complex expressions. Take your time before the first listening round to look up key words to which you should pay attention while listening to the text.

1 *The scientists are doing research on the impact sea otters have on the local economy (cf. **a**): in lines 2 and 3 the host mentions "gobbl[ing] up shellfish […] brought [the otters] into conflict with people who rely on shellfish for their livelihoods" and in lines 4 and 5 he says that "scientists have now assessed the economic impact of restoring sea otters to their historic homes".*

2 *The audio mentions that otters were "wiped out" (another word for being "exterminated", cf. **a**) by the Europeans (cf. l. 12). Next, the podcast explains that "all of the prey that otters eat no longer had their principal predator eating them anymore" (ll. 13/14), which eventually led to an "abundance" (l. 16) of seafood in the area.*

3 *A scientist explains why Vancouver Island is the perfect place for a "natural experiment to compare what the ecosystem looks like with and without sea otters" (ll. 20/21). A key word which helps you find the correct answer is "comparative" (cf. **c**), which is the adjective of the verb "compare" that is mentioned in the audio.*

4 *Here you need to find out that in places where there are sea otters the fish population increases. The following sentence explains why: "[The otters] also devour sea urchins, and that allows kelp to flourish. The kelp supports fish species that are worth a lot of money" (ll. 23/24), which means that "their feeding behaviour enables the growth of fish" (**b**). The other options ("destroy habitats", **a**, and "help to reduce the impact of invasive species", **c**) are not mentioned in the text.*

5 *The solution can be found in lines 28 and 29: "these costs and benefits are not going to be distributed equally across fisheries or communities." A potential threat to the ecosystem (cf. **c**) is not mentioned in the audio and although one might be tempted to tick **a** because of tourists visiting the area (cf. l. 25), this is not called an issue at all.*

6 *The correct solution lies in the quote by Barbara Wilson, who is a representative of the Haida and expresses "Indigenous people's feelings about the sea otters" (ll. 32/33). She explicitly states that "The impact [of the growing population of sea otters] for us is fairly critical" (l. 34). This is too severe a way of talking about that issue to call it "a minor nuisance" (**b**), while "a welcome source of income" (**c**) is not mentioned at all.*

1. The research focusses on the …

   a) ☑ effects of sea otter populations on the local economy.

2. There was more seafood in the area after the Europeans had arrived because …

   a) ☑ sea otters were exterminated.

3. The scientists have chosen Vancouver Island for their research project because …

   c) ☑ the place is suitable for comparative field studies.

4. The sea otters affect the ecosystem because …

   b) ☑ their feeding behaviour enables the growth of fish.

5. Ecologist Edward Gregr addresses the issue that …

   b) ☑ not everyone in the area profits in the same way.

6. Native Canadians living in isolated communities perceive the growing population of sea otters as …

   a) ☑ a potential threat.

You will hear each recording **twice**. After each listening you will have time to complete your answers.

Task 1: Book Reviews   **5 BE**

Preparation time: 45 seconds

You will hear five excerpts from a panel discussion about novels. Choose from the list (A–G) which description best applies to which book review (1–5). For each book review, there is only one correct answer. There are two more descriptions than you need.

Descriptions:

A Various reactions to a kidnapping

B Expecting a meeting after a long time

C A familiar approach to scientific progress

D Clearing up a crime in a dystopian setting

E Looking for information on different issues

F Presenting a field of expertise in its complexity

G An adolescent in challenging social circumstances

Book review	1	2	3	4	5
Description					

Task 2: A Migration Story   **9 BE**

Preparation time: 1:30 minutes

You will hear an excerpt from the recording of an event where people tell their migration stories on stage. The speaker's name is Banke. While listening, tick (✓) the correct answer (a, b or c). There is only one correct answer.

1. When in the Netherlands, Banke's ...
   a) ☐ father had a temporary job there.
   b) ☐ family intended to stay permanently.
   c) ☐ parents worried about being sent home.

2. When she later moved to America, Banke …
   a) ☐ took language classes.
   b) ☐ adopted a different way of speaking.
   c) ☐ regretted they did not move to Britain.

3. According to Banke, people in England seem to think that …
   a) ☐ your pronunciation stays the same.
   b) ☐ language is important for a legal career.
   c) ☐ immigrants should adopt standard English.

4. In England, Banke used her language skills to …
   a) ☐ get into a good university.
   b) ☐ pretend to be from the US.
   c) ☐ show others how educated she is.

5. Banke had come to England with the aim of …
   a) ☐ applying for citizenship.
   b) ☐ developing professionally.
   c) ☐ reconnecting with other Nigerians.

6. In London, she has …
   a) ☐ joined a political party.
   b) ☐ met with good and bad.
   c) ☐ had financial difficulties.

7. In London, Banke feels she belongs because many people …
   a) ☐ are like her.
   b) ☐ ignore their origins.
   c) ☐ live life to the fullest.

8. After Brexit, Banke became aware of how …
   a) ☐ London lost its fascination for her.
   b) ☐ Londoners treated her as a foreigner.
   c) ☐ London differs from the rest of England.

9. Due to Brexit, Banke decided to …
   a) ☐ leave the UK.
   b) ☐ participate in local politics.
   c) ☐ keep up her language strategy.

Preparation time: 1 minute

You will hear a BBC report about the UK scientist Kevin Warwick.
While listening, fill in the missing information. You need not write complete sentences. Unless otherwise specified, name one aspect.

1. What Kevin Warwick is remembered for:	
2. Former purpose of technology used by Warwick:	
3. Infrastructure available to Warwick:	
4. Reasons why Warwick decided to be the test subject himself: *(Name two.)*	• •
5. Basic operational principle:	
6. Examples of practical use of the device: *(Name two.)*	• •
7. How the research group felt about the experiment:	
8. Reaction from a Californian writer:	

9. The title which best fits the overall message of the report is:

  a) ☐ Entering new scientific territory

  b) ☐ Carrying out an immoral experiment

  c) ☐ Finding inspiration for science fiction

Lösungsvorschläge

Text 1: Book Reviews

1 A cruel landscape, volcano-studded. There are hardly any roads in and out. And in that sort of bleak place, in the first chapter, two little girls, sisters, go missing. They're lured into a shiny black car by a stranger. But what comes after that isn't a thriller. What you get, chapter by chapter, each chapter moves the novel forward a month and it's told by a different woman in the community ... And as the shock waves of the girls' abduction is *[sic]* rippling throughout, everybody's affected in a different way.

2 It is a coming-of-age novel about a high-school debate star and his psychiatrist parents in Topeka, Kansas, in the 1990s. And the central conflicts are the mother's growing fame as a feminist author and the strains that that puts on the family. And then also the ambiguously bullying relationship between the protagonist, the debate star, and an alienated, marginalized learning-disabled boy that they're kind of bringing into their circle.

3 Ted Chiang is a really interesting writer. He is, by day, a technology manual writer. If that makes this book sound boring or dry, trust me, this must be, like, his version of, like, rap singing, you know, or rapping or, like, dancing in the middle of the night because it's very engaging and it certainly is about technology, but it's so much deeper than that. It is about really the ways in which technologies inherently involves *[sic]* humans and what technologies, both existing and potential future technologies, mean for humanity.

4 A family on a road trip. A husband. A wife. The kids are in the back seat. The couple's marriage is in crisis, but they're on a road trip anyway to the southern border. They share an interest in immigration. The husband is trying to document historic migration patterns involving Native Americans, and she is trying to locate the children of a woman who immigrated to the United States from Mexico, and her children followed her and disappeared, presumably into US custody. So, these themes are embedded in the sort of story of the road trip.

5 It concerns two guys named Charlie and Maurice, two Irish drug smugglers in their 50s. They find themselves, sort of overnight, at a port town in northern Spain at a ferry terminal, waiting for Maurice's estranged 23-year-old daughter to hopefully show up. He hasn't seen her in two or three years. She's in her early 20s and she's fallen in with a sort of group of New-Age-type characters who, you know, float around the world. And so they're hoping that she'll arrive either coming or going from Tangier. They've gotten a tip that that's where she'll be.

"Talking About the 10 Best Books of 2019." The New York Times Book Review Podcast. Zugriff am 22. 11. 2020 von https://www.nytimes.com/2019/11/26/books/review/podcast-10-best-books-2019.html

These text passages will help you find the correct answer:

1 Description 1 is about a "kidnapping" (**A**): "two little girls, sisters, go missing. They're lured into a shiny black car by a stranger." (ll. 2/3) It is also about "[v]arious reactions" to the crime, or as the text puts it, "everybody's affected in a different way" (l. 6).

2 In being "a coming-of-age novel" (l. 7), the book reviewed in description 2 is about an "adolescent" (**G**). That this teenager is living "in challenging social circumstances" can be concluded from words like "the central conflicts" (l. 8) or "strains" (l. 9).

3 "Ted Chiang is [...] a technology manual writer." (l. 13) So, technology is his "field of expertise" (**F**). He presents it "in its complexity" because his book "certainly is about technology, but it's so much deeper than that" (ll. 16/17).

4 Description 4 is probably the most difficult to identify. However, it can help to cross out all the descriptions you have already allocated. Then you might be able to gauge that both husband and wife in description 4 are looking for something, "migration patterns" and "the children of a woman who immigrated to the United States from Mexico" respectively (cf. ll. 22–24). So, "Looking for information on different issues" (**E**) is correct here.

5 The two men mentioned in description 5 are "waiting for Maurice's estranged 23-year-old daughter to hopefully show up" (l. 29). As "[h]e hasn't seen her in two or three years" (l. 30), this novel is about "a meeting after a long time" (**B**).

Book review	1	2	3	4	5
Description	A	G	F	E	B

Text 2: A Migration Story

1 When I was four years old, my family moved from Nigeria to the Netherlands and to us, we weren't migrants at all. My dad was moving there for four years for work. That was the only reason we were there. And in four years we were going to move back. A few years later, when I was 16, I moved to the United States and went to college,

5 worked for a few years and went to law school. So when I moved to Holland, my sisters and I couldn't even speak English and we learned English very quickly at a British school and had some kind of weird expat British accent, moved to America and tried to integrate as quickly as possible with an American accent. The thing I learned in England, for most of my life, an accent was an aspirational thing. It was something that you

10 chose to do and you went forward and you learned it and you spoke in whatever accent you wanted. Since moving to England, apparently an accent is something that you're born with and you have to stick with for the rest of your life. And so I, when I moved to England, I went to college, law school, and then I moved to London to be a lawyer. And as soon as I moved here, I discovered that the categories of immigrants or mi-

15 grants had nothing to do with the colour of your skin, but it was more about what ac-

94

cent you had. And because I'm a very smart woman, I decided that I was going to be
American. And British people tend to treat Americans with a great deal of respect and
curiosity. So that worked out very well for me. The funny thing about it is I've now
been in England for six years and I have a British passport now, but it wasn't some-
20 thing I ever intended to do. I've never moved anywhere with the intention of staying
there forever. So even moving here was because I wanted to move back to Nigeria
eventually, but I wanted to work somewhere where I could get international work experience that I could take back with me. And even though I've stayed here longer, in
the city of London, longer than I've ever stayed in any city of my life, it hasn't been
25 easy. Like London is the first place in my entire life that I've heard myself referred to
as the N-word twice. The funny thing about London is London is probably the place
that I've paid the most taxes and been the most active in terms of citizenry. But I've
also just had some of the most amazing experiences here. And I've decided that my
favourite kind of people are the people, when you ask them, "Where are you from?",
30 and they pause, and they don't know how to explain where they're from. And that's
definitely me. Because when you hear, when someone asked me, "Where are you
from?", especially after we've already been in conversation, I want to know why. I'm
like, "Are you asking me because of my name or are you asking me because of my
accent, or are you asking me where my passport is from?" Because it's all very dif-
35 ferent stories. And for the most part, I felt that London was home because it had the
greatest collection of people who were from everywhere. And you can go out every
night in London and meet someone from a different country. But I think in recent
times, with Brexit, it's the first time in my life where I felt like London is part of a
bigger country that may not be as welcoming as London itself is. And perhaps Lon-
40 don is only welcoming because it does have the biggest collection of people from
everywhere, or people who don't even have, like, a very direct story about where it is
that they're from. I think when I got my British passport, I decided I was going to go
back to my Nigerian accent and just not talk in an American accent anymore. But
after Brexit, I thought, maybe I'll hold on to it for a little bit longer.

Special: "Migration – Daniel & Banke". Spark – True Stories Live. Zugriff am 22. 11. 2020 von
https://podtail.com/en/podcast/spark-true-stories-live/special-migration-daniel-banke/

These text passages will help you find the correct answer:
1 *"My dad was moving there for four years for work. That was the only reason we*
  were there. And in four years we were going to move back." (ll. 2/3)
2 *"we […] had some kind of weird expat British accent, moved to America and tried*
  to integrate as quickly as possible with an American accent." (ll. 6–8)
3 *"Since moving to England, apparently an accent is something that you're born*
  with and you have to stick with for the rest of your life." (ll. 11/12)
4 *"And because I'm a very smart woman, I decided that I was going to be Ameri-*
  can. And British people tend to treat Americans with a great deal of respect and
  curiosity. So that worked out very well for me." (ll. 16–18)
5 *"I have a British passport now, but it wasn't something I ever intended to do. I've*
  never moved anywhere with the intention of staying there forever. So even moving
  here was because I wanted to move back to Nigeria eventually, but I wanted to

work somewhere where I could get international work experience that I could take
back with me." (ll. 19–23)

6 *"it hasn't been easy. Like London is the first place in my entire life that I've heard*
myself referred to as the N-word twice. [...] But I've also just had some of the
most amazing experiences here." (ll. 24–28)

7 *Banke "felt that London was home because it had the greatest collection of people*
who were from everywhere" (ll. 35/36) and in that "they don't know how to ex-
plain where they're from" (l. 30), they are very much like her (cf. ll. 30/31).

8 *"But I think in recent times, with Brexit, it's the first time in my life where I felt*
like London is part of a bigger country that may not be as welcoming as London
itself is." (ll. 37–39)

9 *"I think when I got my British passport, I decided I was going to go back to my*
Nigerian accent and just not talk in an American accent anymore. But after Brexit, I
thought, maybe I'll hold on to it for a little bit longer." (ll. 42–44)

1. When in the Netherlands, Banke's …
   a) ☑ father had a temporary job there.

2. When she later moved to America, Banke …
   b) ☑ adopted a different way of speaking.

3. According to Banke, people in England seem to think that …
   a) ☑ your pronunciation stays the same.

4. In England, Banke used her language skills to …
   b) ☑ pretend to be from the US.

5. Banke had come to England with the aim of …
   b) ☑ developing professionally.

6. In London, she has …
   b) ☑ met with good and bad.

7. In London, Banke feels she belongs because many people …
   a) ☑ are like her.

8. After Brexit, Banke became aware of how …
   c) ☑ London differs from the rest of England.

9. Due to Brexit, Banke decided to …
   c) ☑ keep up her language strategy.

Text 3: Science

1 **Farhana Haider:** Hello, this is the "Witness History" podcast with me, Farhana Haider. And today I'm taking you back to August 1998, when a British scientist became the first known person to have a silicon chip surgically implanted into his body. He was Professor Kevin Warwick of Reading University. The chip could commu-
5 nicate with a computer at his university campus, which meant that Professor War-wick became a more enhanced version of himself, and as a result, the world's first cyborg, a man-machine hybrid. Kevin was a professor of cybernetics at the University of Reading in England when the idea of implanting the chip occurred to him and his team of researchers. The technology itself was not new. Silicon chips
10 were already used in many countries to identify pets. However, this implant was able to interact with computers.

Warwick: We actually had the technology we could use, and we had the building which was wired up as an intelligent building so that, well, let's put the two to-gether. Maybe the technology wouldn't work. We didn't, you know, we weren't
15 sure until we actually tried it.

Haider: Having decided to try it, next came the question of who would actually have the implant because there were risks involved.

Warwick: We thought about one of the researchers having it, but there were dangers. It could have gone wrong. It wasn't designed realistically as an implant. So, be-
20 cause of the dangers, it's me that wants to do it, so I should face the dangers. And also I wanted to feel what it actually was like to experience things myself.

Haider: So having decided that he was the one that would go through the experience, on the morning of 24 August 1998, the silicon chip transponder was implanted into Kevin's upper left arm. Kevin emerged a more enhanced version of himself.
25 The implant, a radio frequency identification device, identified him to the comput-er in the intelligent building at his university campus, which was equipped with sensors. As he strolled through the building, the implant emitted signals that let him interact with his surroundings.

Warwick: When I went down the corridor of my building, the computer knew it was
30 me and the lights came on in the building because of me, in fact because of the implant. When I walked towards my laboratory, the door opened automatically for me. When I came through the front door, it said, "Hello, Professor Warwick."

Haider: The implant only worked in the intelligent building at the university. So in the evenings when he went home, he could have some downtime. The team were very
35 excited by how well the implant and the computers were communicating.

Warwick: There was an awful lot of publicity from all around the world …

Haider: …as well as the media interest. The experiment also led to some interesting mail.

Warwick: I got a message from some guy in California about two days after I'd gone
40 ahead with the experiment and he said, "Well, look, I was just writing about this as a science-fiction story, and you've gone and done it." So he was quite annoyed

with me for ruining his story. What was being written as futuristic would actually happen, so he had to change his storyline quite a bit.

Haider, F. (2019, 19. August). "Witness History: The First Human Cyborg". BBC World Service. Zugriff am 22. 11. 2020 von https://www.bbc.co.uk/sounds/play/w3csywxs

These text passages will help you find the correct answer:

1 *"a British scientist became the first known person to have a silicon chip surgically implanted into his body. He was Professor Kevin Warwick of Reading University. [...] Professor Warwick became a more enhanced version of himself, and as a result, the world's first cyborg, a man-machine hybrid." (ll. 2–7)*

2 *"The technology itself was not new. Silicon chips were already used in many countries to identify pets." (ll. 9/10)*

3 *"we had the building which was wired up as an intelligent building" (ll. 12/13)*

4 *"So, because of the dangers, it's me that wants to do it, so I should face the dangers. And also I wanted to feel what it actually was like to experience things myself." (ll. 19–21)*

5 *"the silicon chip transponder was implanted into Kevin's upper left arm. [...] The implant, a radio frequency identification device, identified him to the computer in the intelligent building at his university campus, which was equipped with sensors. As he strolled through the building, the implant emitted signals that let him interact with his surroundings." (ll. 23–28)*

6 *"When I went down the corridor of my building, the computer knew it was me and the lights came on in the building because of me, in fact because of the implant. When I walked towards my laboratory, the door opened automatically for me. When I came through the front door, it said, 'Hello, Professor Warwick.'" (ll. 29–32)*

7 *"The team were very excited by how well the implant and the computers were communicating." (ll. 34/35)*

8 *"I got a message from some guy in California [...] and he said, 'Well, look, I was just writing about this as a science-fiction story, and you've gone and done it.' So he was quite annoyed with me for ruining his story. What was being written as futuristic would actually happen, so he had to change his storyline quite a bit." (ll. 39–43)*

9 *The team around Kevin Warwick were "[e]ntering new scientific territory" (**a**), which is indicated by expressions such as "[he] became the first known person to have a silicon chip surgically implanted into his body" (ll. 2/3) or "the world's first cyborg" (ll. 6/7). The uncertainties around the project ("Maybe the technology wouldn't work. [...] we weren't sure until we actually tried it.", ll. 14/15; "It could have gone wrong. It wasn't designed realistically as an implant.", l. 19) also show that what Professor Warwick and his team did had not been done before. Consequently, the experiment was somehow risky, yet there is no moral judgement throughout the article (cf. **b**). Warwick's last statement (cf. ll. 39–43) connects his experiment with the area of science fiction, however not in the way implied by answer **c**. It is rather the opposite which is true: Because of Warwick's experiment, an idea formerly regarded as futuristic was no longer unrealistic.*

1.	What Kevin Warwick is remembered for:	became the first human to be implanted a silicon chip / first human cyborg / first man-machine hybrid
2.	Former purpose of technology used by Warwick:	identifying pets
3.	Infrastructure available to Warwick:	"intelligent" building
4.	Reasons why Warwick decided to be the test subject himself:	• did not want others to face dangers for him • wanted to experience things himself
5.	Basic operational principle:	the silicon chip implanted into Warwick's skin could be identified by a computer / emitted signals that could be recognised by the "intelligent" building
6.	Examples of practical use of the device:	*two of the following:* • the lights came on when he entered the building • the door of his laboratory opened when he approached • he was personally greeted by the front door of his building
7.	How the research group felt about the experiment:	they were excited
8.	Reaction from a Californian writer:	he was angry because the experiment had ruined his science-fiction story / because he had to change his story

9. The title which best fits the overall message of the report is:

a) ☑ Entering new scientific territory

You will hear each recording **twice**. After each listening you will have time to complete your answers.

Task 1: Focus on Africa   6 BE

Preparation time: 45 seconds

You will hear six statements about the BBC radio programme "Focus on Africa". Choose from the list (A–G) which heading best applies to which statement (1–6). For each statement there is only one correct answer. There is one more heading than you need.

Headings:

A Internal debates

B Greater reliability

C Ordinary opinions

D Historical situation

E Under investigation

F Despite resentment

G Recent advancements

Statement	1	2	3	4	5	6
Heading						

Task 2: The Founding of Google   11 BE

Preparation time: 2 minutes

You will hear an interview with computer scientist Tamara Munzner, who attended Stanford University with the two founders of Google, Larry Page and Sergey Brin. While listening, tick (✓) the correct answer (a, b or c). There is only one correct answer.

1. In the mid-1990s, the atmosphere in Silicon Valley was …

   a) ☐ relaxed.

   b) ☐ euphoric.

   c) ☐ competitive.

2. Employment opportunities often opened up …
   a) ☐ in informal settings.
   b) ☐ on the basis of sympathy.
   c) ☐ based on scholarly excellence.

3. New business enterprises were often …
   a) ☐ extremely profitable.
   b) ☐ financed from abroad.
   c) ☐ initiated by rich investors.

4. Tamara Munzner portrays young Larry Page and Sergey Brin as …
   a) ☐ being well-liked.
   b) ☐ willing to take risks.
   c) ☐ enjoying heated conversations.

5. For Page and Brin, a good search engine would have to …
   a) ☐ be thorough and reliable.
   b) ☐ take preferences into account.
   c) ☐ undergo constant re-evaluation.

6. BackRub was a tool that was …
   a) ☐ intensively used.
   b) ☐ faulty in some areas.
   c) ☐ restricted to college students.

7. Page and Brin gave their search engine its name Google …
   a) ☐ after taking a survey.
   b) ☐ against Munzner's explicit advice.
   c) ☐ following a creative exchange of ideas.

8. The first *Google Doodle* was …
   a) ☐ a way of advertising a cultural event.
   b) ☐ the equivalent of an out of office sign.
   c) ☐ part of the Google marketing strategy.

9. After starting Google, Page and Brin …
   a) ☐ struggled to find qualified staff.
   b) ☐ received job offers from several colleges.
   c) ☐ had reason to be confident about the future.

10. Munzner did not join Google because she was …
   a) ☐ bypassed by Page and Brin.
   b) ☐ eager to run her own company.
   c) ☐ determined to complete her doctorate.

Now think of the text as a whole:

11. Munzner talks about her experiences in 1990s California in a …
   a) ☐ casual tone.
   b) ☐ sentimental tone.
   c) ☐ self-righteous tone.

Task 3: American Sign Language   8 BE

Preparation time: 1:30 minutes

You will listen to an NPR radio program from 2020.
While listening, answer the questions. You need not write complete sentences. Unless otherwise specified, name one aspect.

1. What is special about the shorthand name signs used for widely-known people?

_____

2. How is Donald Trump's name expressed in American Sign Language?

_____

3. Why was a sign that alluded to Joe Biden's aviator glasses ruled out? *(two aspects)*
   • _____
   • _____

4. According to Felicia Williams, what role does the internet play in the sign-finding process?

_____

5. Why is a plant considered for Kamala Harris's sign?

_____

6. What is Williams's suggestion about the sign-finding process?

_____

Now think of the text as a whole: Tick (✓) the correct answer (a, b or c). There is only one correct answer.

7. The tone of the report is …
   a) ☐ critical.
   b) ☐ concerned.
   c) ☐ conversational.

Lösungsvorschläge

Text 1: Focus on Africa

1 **1** "Focus on Africa" was born in the year of Africa, 1960. As people in 17 countries celebrated independence, they could now hear their stories on the BBC's first ever news programme broadcast to the whole of Africa.

2 With now so many platforms for news and information, now it's not about where
5 you can get the news, but it's where you can get the correct news, you know? So I think you look at different platforms or listen to different platforms for different things, and I think particularly BBC "Focus on Africa", we know on this platform we'll get this kind of information.

3 What "Focus" really, really does is that it allows you to see momentous events,
10 you know, big world events as well, not just African events, through the eyes of actual people. So, we don't just talk to leaders and, you know, doers and shakers and all of that. We actually talk to the people that are affected by these things.

4 It's not just the content, it's also the platforms. We have embraced new technology. "Focus on Africa" can be listened to not just on the radio, but also on all digital plat-
15 forms, via mobile phones, via our website. We can be listened to live and on demand.

5 We often find that we have to push back against attitudes that people might hold in the wider BBC about how certain African stories are covered or, you know, or a take on a story. So we often find ourselves in heated conversation sometimes about what a particular perspective is on a story or why we object to the way a certain story is be-
20 ing presented or being approached.

6 Our network of local correspondents are there on the ground. We also bring contacts. We bring names that would normally not agree to be interviewed by the BBC, the wider BBC, that they see, still see to a certain extent, as a sort of imperialist organisation.

based on: https://www.bbc.co.uk/programmes/p08n6jxr;
https://www.bbc.co.uk/sounds/play/p08nngd7 (u. a.)

/ *You do not have a lot of time to read through the task. However, highlight a buzz-*
/ *word for each description given. While listening, note down words that might fit one*
/ *of the descriptions. This listening comprehension takes its complexity not only from*
/ *the level of sophistication of the audio files, but also from the speed in which you*
/ *have to solve the tasks.*
/ *– 1 – D: The year 1960 is given (cf. l. 1), when several African countries gained in-*
/ *dependence (cf. l. 2). It is also mentioned that people in the whole of Africa were*
/ *now able to hear "their stories" on the BBC (cf. ll. 2/3).*
/ *– 2 – B: The buzzword here is "reliability" which hints to l. 5: "you can get the cor-*
/ *rect news".*
/ *– 3 – C: Here, it is not about the opinions of stars or politicians, but about what nor-*

mal, ordinary people think: "through the eyes of actual people [...] the people that are affected by these things." (ll. 10–12)
- **4 – G:** "Recent advancements" can be equated with "We have embraced new technology" (l. 13), such as "digital platforms, [...] mobile phones, [...] website [...] live and on demand" (ll. 14/15).
- **5 – A:** The buzzword "debates" hints towards a synonym mentioned by speaker 5, which is "heated conversation" (l. 18).
- **6 – F:** Speaker 6 mentions people who "would normally not agree to be interviewed by the BBC" (l. 22) because they see this broadcaster as an "imperialist organisation" (ll. 23/24). They resent being interviewed by the BBC but not by "local correspondents" (l. 21).

Statement	1	2	3	4	5	6
Heading	D	B	C	G	A	F

Text 2: The Founding of Google

1 **Farhana Haider:** Larry Page was from Michigan, Sergey Brin was born in Russia. Both had academics as parents, and both came to Stanford to do computer science PhDs. When they met in 1995, California's Silicon Valley was a place of possibilities.

Tamara Munzner: Everything was sort of bubbling and in ferment and everything was
5 possible. And the amazing thing about the mid-90s was every single time you'd go to a party, you would get like multiple really amazing, cool-sounding job offers. So I had to re-decide not to drop out of grad school every week. The start-up explosion was very pervasive. Something like a quarter of all grad students at the time were doing start-ups. All the faculty had start-ups as well. So, most of the Stanford
10 professors at the time were already multi-millionaires from previous start-ups. As a computer scientist, it was an amazing place to be.

(excerpt from song "California Dreamin'")

Farhana Haider: At Stanford, Tamara shared an office with Larry Page and three others.

Tamara Munzner: If you meet Larry, you meet Sergey because they always hung out
15 together. Even then, they were already very much this sort of dynamic duo.

Farhana Haider: I mean, they have famously said that they found each other obnoxious when they first met. But what was your first impression of Sergey Brin and Larry Page?

Tamara Munzner: I'm not sure if obnoxious is exactly the first word I would use, but
20 let's just say they were really, really good at getting you sucked into arguments. I mean, I do know that I learned how to program with headphones exactly so that I would not get sucked into every single argument that happened in the office. Otherwise I never would have gotten anything done.

Farhana Haider: Page and Brin realised that when you're looking for a webpage, you want it to be not only relevant but seen as valuable by previous users. So if, say, you're searching for advice on how to bake a chocolate cake, you don't just want lots of mentions of the word "chocolate cake". You want the page which other people rate as the best chocolate cake page. This breakthrough idea, called page ranking, was inspired by the process of peer reviewing academic articles, which Page and Brin were familiar with from their parents. It needed a complex bit of mathematics called an algorithm to work. The algorithm was in a search engine called BackRub, which Page and Brin launched in 1996. BackRub was so popular that it regularly crashed the Stanford Internet connection, but the founders thought it needed a new name. And during a brainstorming session that has become the stuff of tech folklore, they came up with Google and wrote it on their Stanford white-board. The word may or may not have been an intentional misspelling of a math-ematical term.

Tamara Munzner: It was yet another one of these long, freewheeling discussions. It was, you know, like, "Hey, what should our new name be?". I do know that I came in the next day and I'm like, "Oh my God, you guys, you spelled it wrong. What the hell?" Because we're talking about G-O-O-G-O-L, googol, the mathematical thing, you know, of the ten to the a hundred. Not G-O-O-G-L-E. Turns out Google had legs.

Farhana Haider: On September 15, 1997, the Google.com domain was registered. Not long after, the first *Google Doodle*, the changes that are made to the Google logo to mark important occasions or celebrate important figures, appeared. It was a Burning Man figure that was intended to let everyone know that both Page and Brin were at the festival in Nevada.

Tamara Munzner: Google did a lot of things that didn't feel corporate, like this whole thing about the *Google Doodles*, you know how there's these little pictures at the top. It really did start out where it was like, "Oh, we're going to be at Burning Man, and we want people to know that, like, if the thing crashes, we aren't gonna be here to fix it for a while." So, they made this little doodle of, you know, this lit-tle sketch of the Burning Man thing for the Google logo to sort of visually signify, "Hey, we're gonna be gone."

Farhana Haider: The next year Page and Brin moved out of the campus at Stanford University and famously launched their company from a friend's garage after rais-ing $1 million from family, friends and other investors. The search engine was easy to use. All you had to do was type a word or two into its simple interface. The com-pany started to expand rapidly. Tamara is now a professor at the University of British Columbia. But does she now kick herself for not joining Google at the be-ginning and possibly becoming a tech billionaire?

Tamara Munzner: I was tempted to the point where I seriously thought about it. I sort of seriously thought, you know, "Should I be employee three or employee 30 or employee 3,000?" I think if I tried to be like a single-digit employee, I would have killed them, and they would have killed me. That was just clearly not gonna work. It's, like, our styles are sufficiently different that it was like, "No, no, no, no, no.

105

We'll drive each other crazy." Also, I wanted to finish my PhD and do visualisation and so, clearly that wouldn't happen if I'd gone off and done that start-up.

based on: bbc.co.uk/sounds/play/w3cszms7

The order of the questions follows the order in the audio file, and you need to tick one aspect out of three. However, the vocabulary is rather sophisticated and technical, and the correct answer is often hidden behind complex expressions. Moreover, the audio recording contains a lot of information in a rather short amount of time, so there is hardly any time to think about a certain aspect in too much detail. Therefore, also try to get the global message of the podcast. Take the two minutes before the first listening and look up unknown words in the task.

1 *Several words and phrases hint towards the correct answer: "a place of possibilities" (l. 3), "[e]verything was sort of bubbling and in ferment" (l. 4), "everything was possible" (ll. 4/5).*

2 *"Employment opportunities often opened up in informal settings" (**a**): "every single time you'd go to a party, you would get like multiple really amazing, cool-sounding job offers." (ll. 5/6)*

3 *Munzner speaks about "start-ups" (ll. 7–10), which refers to "[n]ew business enterprises". She then explains that people "at the time were already multi-millionaires from previous start-ups" (l. 10), which means that these new businesses must have been "extremely profitable" (**a**).*

4 *Page and Brin "were really, really good at getting you sucked into arguments" (l. 20), which means they "enjoy[ed] heated conversations" (**c**).*

5 *Haider explains the idea of "page ranking", which takes into account what others have already preferred (cf. ll. 27–29).*

6 *The information that BackRub was a tool that was intensively used is mentioned rather fast by Haider, who tells the story of it "crash[ing] the Stanford Internet connection" on a regular basis because it "was so popular" (ll. 32/33).*

7 *There are two expressions that lead towards the correct answer. Haider mentions "a brainstorming session" (l. 34) and Munzner speaks about "long, free-wheeling discussions" (l. 38). Next, she explains the actual process of Google getting its name (cf. ll. 38/39), which is the "creative exchange of ideas" (**c**) mentioned in the task.*

8 *Here, you need to understand that Page and Brin wanted to go to the Burning Man festival and used the first* Google Doodle *to let people know (cf. ll. 45–48). The connection between the burning man sketch and an "out of office sign" (**b**) is explained in detail from line 50 onwards: they wanted to "visually signify, 'Hey, we're gonna be gone.'" (ll. 54/55)*

9 *"After starting Google, Page and Brin had reason to be confident about the future" (**c**), as "[t]he company started to expand rapidly." (ll. 59/60)*

10 *At the very end of the audio recording, Munzner mentions briefly that she "wanted to finish [her] PhD" (l. 68).*

11 *Munzner talks in a "casual tone" (**a**) (in the sense of German „beiläufig", „lässig", „salopp"). For instance, she uses exaggerations, such as "I would have*

106

*killed them, and they would have killed me" (ll. 65/66). Although she remembers the past fondly (cf. ll. 4–11), her tone is not "sentimental" (**b**), i. e. overly emotional. Neither is she "self-righteous" (**c**): she talks about Page and Brin with respect and describes her decision not to join Google in a rather neutral and friendly manner (cf. ll. 63–69).*

1. In the mid-1990s, the atmosphere in Silicon Valley was …
   b) ☑ euphoric.

2. Employment opportunities often opened up …
   a) ☑ in informal settings.

3. New business enterprises were often …
   a) ☑ extremely profitable.

4. Tamara Munzner portrays young Larry Page and Sergey Brin as …
   c) ☑ enjoying heated conversations.

5. For Page and Brin, a good search engine would have to …
   b) ☑ take preferences into account.

6. BackRub was a tool that was …
   a) ☑ intensively used.

7. Page and Brin gave their search engine its name Google …
   c) ☑ following a creative exchange of ideas.

8. The first *Google Doodle* was …
   b) ☑ the equivalent of an out of office sign.

9. After starting Google, Page and Brin …
   c) ☑ had reason to be confident about the future.

10. Munzner did not join Google because she was …
    c) ☑ determined to complete her doctorate.

11. Munzner talks about her experiences in 1990s California in a …
    a) ☑ casual tone.

Text 3: American Sign Language

1 **Ari Shapiro**, *host*: What do you call President elect Joe Biden? Well, Joe Biden in spoken English. But that question is a source of ongoing debate in the deaf community.

Marie Louise Kelly, *host*: Yeah. Right now, American Sign Language users spell it out B-I-D-E-N. But public figures, like the president, usually get shorthand name signs
5 based on a recognizable trait.

Shapiro: One of President Trump's, for example, is a fluttering hand above the head, resembling his hair in the wind. But for the president elect …

Julie Hochgesang, *through interpreter*: What is an iconic sign or iconic about Joe Biden?

Shapiro: Julie Hochgesang is an associate professor of linguistics at Gallaudet Uni-
10 versity. She is deaf and spoke with us through an interpreter.

Hochgesang, *through interpreter*: Some people are saying his hair. Some people are saying his glasses. Some are saying his smile.

Kelly: Biden's aviator glasses were a front-runner, signed by making the letter C near the eyes. Then it was pointed out that C is also the symbol for the street gang *The*
15 *Crips*, which could endanger some people who use the sign.

Felicia Williams, *through interpreter*: You know, some people don't have experience with that, but other people who do don't want to use that. So, we're opening up the conversation and becoming more sensitive. We don't want to create something that is going to really be negatively or pejoratively associated with the president elect.

20 **Shapiro**: Felicia Williams is also on faculty at Gallaudet. She is deaf and African American. And she told us through an interpreter that a lively debate is now playing out online.

Williams, *through interpreter*: Technology has really allowed us to exchange information and allowed us to have an open dialogue through social media. Without that, I
25 don't know how we would become more definitive.

Kelly: Social media has also allowed people who are deaf, African Americans, South Asians to weigh in on a possible sign for Vice President elect Kamala Harris. A sign based on the lotus flower is one idea, a reference to her first name's meaning in Sanskrit.

30 **Shapiro**: There is no official authority to make a final call. The community will eventually coalesce around something. And Williams stressed that there is no rush to decide.

Williams, *through interpreter*: I think that we need to just slow down and back up and have White deaf people respect the space and have the process be organic. Don't
35 force it.

Kelly: Until then, Williams said, B-I-D-E-N – that'll work just fine.

Again, the order of the questions follows the order in the audio file, and you mostly need to give only one aspect out of several. Often you can just write down what the speaker says. However, an in-depth knowledge of vocabulary and the ability to distinguish between several native speakers talking are required. Additionally, each speaker speaks rather fast and to the point, without elaborating very much.

1 *"But public figures, like the president, usually get shorthand name signs based on a recognizable trait." (ll. 4/5)*

2 *"One of President Trump's, for example, is a fluttering hand above the head, resembling his hair in the wind." (ll. 6/7)*

3 *You need only give two aspects: "Then it was pointed out that C is also the symbol for the street gang* The Crips, *which could endanger some people who use the sign." (ll. 14/15); "You know, some people don't have experience with that, but other people who do don't want to use that. [...] We don't want to create something that is going to really be negatively or pejoratively associated with the president elect." (ll. 16–19)*

4 *Here it is enough to mention one of two things: "Technology has really allowed us to exchange information and allowed us to have an open dialogue through social media." (ll. 23/24)*

5 *"A sign based on the lotus flower is one idea, a reference to her first name's meaning in Sanskrit." (ll. 27–29)*

6 *There are some suggestions given, but only one needs to be mentioned: "And Williams stressed that there is no rush to decide." (ll. 31/32), "I think that we need to just slow down and back up and have White deaf people respect the space and have the process be organic. Don't force it." (ll. 33–35)*

7 *The way the topic is talked about can be best described as "conversational" (**c**). Williams's last remarks (cf. ll. 33–35), for example, show that the general approach to the topic is rather relaxed.*

1. What is special about the shorthand name signs used for widely-known people?
based on recognisable trait / iconic about person

2. How is Donald Trump's name expressed in American Sign Language?
fluttering hand above head

3. Why was a sign that alluded to Joe Biden's aviator glasses ruled out?
- **could be confused with symbol (used) for (street) gang *(The Crips)***
- **(could be a) danger for users**
- **some people don't want to use it**
- **(could) be negatively/pejoratively associated with President elect/Joe Biden**

4. According to Felicia Williams, what role does the internet play in the sign-finding process?
(allows) to exchange information / to have an open dialogue

5. Why is a plant considered for Kamala Harris's sign?
(lotus flower =) her first name's meaning (in Sanskrit)

6. What is Williams's suggestion about the sign-finding process?
   no rush to decide/White deaf people should respect the space/let the process be organic/slow down and do not force it

7. The tone of the report is …
   c) ☑ conversational.

Assignment

Your Irish friend is considering a gap year and wants to know what Germans think about this issue.
Based on the article, write him/her an email, outlining the expectations and reservations involved.

Mut zur Lücke!

Von Deike Uhtenwoldt

Ferne Länder sehen, bedrohte Tiere retten, Sprachen lernen: Ein Gap Year zwischen Abitur und Studium ist beliebt und oft nützlich für den weiteren Lebensweg. Manche Angebote allerdings sind völlig überteuert oder wenig sinnvoll für die Karriere.

1 Die Lücke zwischen Abi und Studium, in der Familie Brößling ist sie Pflichtprogramm. „Die Kinder kommen durch das G8-Abi sehr jung aus der Schule und haben angesichts des steigenden Rentenalters noch genug Zeit, etwas anderes zu machen, als gleich zum Studium zu rennen", erklärt Mutter Katja Brößling, warum ihre Kin-
5 der nach der Schule einen Freiwilligendienst antreten sollen. Die Betriebswirtin zeigt sich offen für die Zukunftspläne der Kinder, ob Ausbildung oder Studium. Was genau es werden soll, dürfen sie selbst bestimmen – solange sie vorher ein Jahr lang bewiesen haben, dass sie auf eigenen Beinen stehen können. „Ich finde dieses Jahr unglaublich praktisch für die jungen Leute", sagt sie. „Sie können sich ausprobieren.
10 Ohne den Druck, gleich wieder im ersten Semester eine Leistung abliefern zu müssen."

Brößlings Sohn ist gerade 18 geworden und wird ab September einen Bundesfreiwilligendienst in der Seehundauffangstation in Norden-Norddeich absolvieren. Die Tochter hat noch ein Jahr bis zum Abi, sie will sich politisch engagieren, am
15 liebsten in Frankreich, und fragt gerade bei Parteiorganisationen im Nachbarland an. Zwischendurch hatte die 16-Jährige auch mal mit einer Auszeit in Neuseeland geliebäugelt, aber ihre Eltern hatten ziemlich schnell deutlich gemacht, dass das Jahr selbst finanziert werden muss – und möglichst gesellschaftlich sinnvoll sein soll […].

Seehunde retten, abgeschieden mit anderen Freiwilligen zusammenwohnen oder
20 möglichst viel von der Welt entdecken und sie hier und da ein wenig besser machen – für die unterschiedlichen Zielvorstellungen junger Schulabgänger gibt es inzwischen einen Begriff: das „Gap Year", ein Lückenjahr also. Aber mit Pause und Nichtstun hat es wenig zu tun: „Es geht um die Phase zwischen zwei Lebensabschnitten, die eine neue Erfahrung mit sich bringt, über eine längere Zeit andauert und häu-
25 fig mit einem Auslandsaufenthalt junger Menschen in Verbindung gebracht wird", sagt die Geographin Manuela Bauer. Die Wissenschaftlerin schließt gerade ihre Promotion über „Gap-Year-Reisen" ab und hat typische „Gappers" befragt, wie sie sagt.

111

Auszubildende nach der Lehre, Studierende zwischen Bachelor- und Masterab-
schluss, Abiturienten.

30 „Die Schulabgänger sind die zahlenmäßig größte Gruppe", sagt Bauer. Schon
die Altersverteilung ihrer Erhebung macht es deutlich: 18,9 Jahre alt waren die Pro-
banden im Schnitt, als sie ihre Reise antraten. Um diese jungen Erwachsenen ohne
Berufserfahrung oder Studienabschluss für sich zu gewinnen, sie mit Papieren wie
Arbeitsvisum und Krankenversicherung zu versorgen oder sie vor Ort zu betreuen,

35 sei ein „Gap-Year-Markt" entstanden, der regelrecht mit der Auszeit nach dem Schul-
abschluss wirbt, so Bauer. […]

Aber gerade die Volunteer Tourismus-Angebote sind umstritten: „Es ist überhaupt nicht hilfreich, wenn junge Menschen für drei Wochen nach Nepal gehen, um
dort mal eben ein wenig Entwicklungshilfe zu leisten", sagt die Berufsberaterin Birte

40 Biebuyck. Das gelte finanziell – von 1 000 Euro, die ein Freiwilliger für seinen Aus-
landseinsatz zahlt, kämen gerade mal 17 vor Ort an –, aber auch menschlich: „Kin-
derprojekte sind beliebt, aber ständig wechselnde Bezugspersonen und zu wenig vor-
bereitete Freiwillige schaden", so die studierte Theologin.   *(499 Wörter)*

Lösungsvorschläge

For this mediation task, you are supposed to write an email based on a German newspaper article, to an Irish friend. In this email, expectations and reservations connected with gap years are to be explained. That you are writing to an Irish friend should be obvious from the style of language you use, but also from your choice of appropriate content. Think twice about including information such as the "G8-con-cept" in German schools, for example, which a foreign reader might not immediately grasp. Rather write something like, "school leavers getting younger and working longer years". Also pay attention to using email conventions, such as the way you address your friend, a personal introduction and a greeting to end your email. When it comes to structure, you can use the one suggested in the task and describe advantages of gap years before focussing on potential disadvantages.

You should include the following points:
- *expectations/advantages of gap years:*
  - *not going to university or starting to work straight after school, avoiding the same stress (cf. ll. 2–4, 9–11)*
  - *gaining independence (also financial independence), contributing to society (cf. ll. 7/8, 16–18)*
  - *testing oneself and one's abilities and talents (cf. l. 9)*
  - *working abroad, gaining new experiences (cf. ll. 23–25)*
- *reservations/disadvantages of gap years:*
  - *commercial interests of "gap year market" (cf. ll. 32–36)*
  - *developing countries do not profit financially or economically (cf. ll. 37–41)*
  - *some work can even be damaging (work with children) (cf. ll. 41–43)*

Dear Bridget,

> address and personal introduction

I think it's a brilliant idea to consider a gap year. Perhaps it might be an option for me too once I've finished school. As to your question about what Germans think about this issue, here is what I found in an article in a German newspaper.

Those who support a gap year believe it's a good idea for school leavers not to go to university or start working straight after school. Instead, as they get ever younger and will probably have to work longer until retirement, people should take the opportunity to do something new without the immediate pressure to be successful. That way they can test themselves and find out what they are good at. Working abroad in particular expands young people's horizons tremendously. When they also earn their own money and apply for work in a meaningful project, they learn a lot about taking responsibility and becoming more mature.

> expectations/advantages

While all this sounds really good, there are also downsides, especially for the developing countries, which should be profiting from gappers' work there. Instead, it is often commercial organisations and not the countries themselves that profit financially or econom-

> reservations/disadvantages

113

ically. In addition, helping in a children's project, which is very popular, can even be bad for the kids, when gap year helpers come and go all the time and are not properly trained to work with children.

So, all in all, there are ups and downs, and it also depends on what you decide to do. I, for my part, would enjoy a gap year and can't wait to hear what you will do.

personal greeting

Take care,
Florian

(270 words)

Assignment

Your US exchange partner has to give a presentation in class about a German tradition and decides to talk about travelling journeymen, as he/she saw one in your hometown last summer. He/She asks you for some help.
Using the information in the text, write an email in which you present the tradition of travelling journeymen and the situation now.

Mit Stock und Hut auf Wanderschaft gehen
Von Andrea Döring

1 Hut, Stock und ein Bündel – der freundliche junge Mann mit den langen Rasta-Locken ist unschwer als Wandergeselle zu erkennen. An einer Raststätte an der
5 A61 in Rheinland-Pfalz fragt er nach einer Mitfahrgelegenheit.

Bis Worms passen die Pläne zusammen, und das kleine Bündel, auch Charlottenburger genannt, hat locker
10 Platz im Kofferraum. Konstantin Schäfer stammt aus Saarlouis und ist Zimmermann. Gerade kommt der 24-Jährige von einer Feier in der Eifel. Jetzt ist er auf dem Weg zu seinem bislang letzten Arbeitgeber im südhessischen Heppenheim. Der soll ihm in seinem Wanderbuch noch ein Zeugnis ausstellen.

15 Das Wanderbuch, der knotige Stock, auch Stenz genannt, und das Bündel gehören zur Grundausstattung jedes Wandergesellen dazu. Stolz trägt Schäfer den traditionellen schwarzen Hut, einen Ohrring, ein weißes Hemd, darüber eine Weste mit acht Perlmuttknöpfen, ein Jackett und weite Schlaghosen. Seine Kluft ist schwarz. Das weist ihn als Zimmermann aus, denn jedes Gewerk hat seine ei-
20 gene Farbe.

Wer Meister werden wollte, musste vom Spätmittelalter bis zur beginnenden Industrialisierung auf Wanderschaft gehen. Arbeits- und Lebenserfahrung sollten die jungen Männer sammeln. In ungefähr 35 Handwerken ist das bis heute möglich: Bäcker, Betonbauer, Bootsbauer, Goldschmiede, Köche, Landwirte, Maurer
25 und Schneider gehören etwa dazu.

„Es ist wunderbar, wenn junge Menschen Erfahrungen sammeln. In der Bäckerei habe ich Wandersleute allerdings noch nie gesehen", erzählt Peter Görtz, Inhaber einer großen Bäckerei-Kette in Ludwigshafen und Umgebung. „Ich würde sofort 20 nehmen."

30 Maternus Burauen von der IG Bau und erster Sekretär der Conföderation Europäischer Gesellenzünfte (CCEG) schätzt, dass derzeit etwa 450 bis 550 Gesellen auf der <u>Walz</u> sind. Eine offizielle Statistik gibt es nicht. Aktuell seien schätzungsweise zehn bis zwanzig Prozent der Wandersleute Frauen. [...]

Seit 2014 gehört die Walz in Deutschland zum immateriellen Kulturerbe der 35 UNESCO. Wer sich auf sie begeben will, muss einige Regeln beachten: Er muss in einem Handwerk einen Gesellenbrief erlangt haben, unverheiratet sowie schuldenfrei sein. Die Wanderschaft dauert zwei oder drei Jahre – und einen Tag. In dieser Zeit darf man sich seinem Heimatort bis auf 50 Kilometer nicht nähern. Ursprünglich war dies als Marktkontrolle für die Meister gedacht – ihre Gesellen 40 sollten woanders ihr Glück finden und ihnen keine Konkurrenz machen.

„Ich hatte Fernweh", sagt Schäfer. Seit fast zwei Jahren ist er schon unterwegs. Durch Holland, Belgien, Frankreich, Österreich, die Schweiz und Israel führte ihn bereits sein Weg. „Viele unterschiedliche Arbeitstechniken habe ich kennengelernt, aber wichtiger als die handwerkliche ist die Erfahrung mit Men- 45 schen und die Selbsterkenntnis", sagt er.

„Beim Österreichischen Hospiz in Jerusalem habe ich am Eingangsportal Schusslöcher zugespachtelt", berichtet er. Welche Arbeitgeber Schäfer nach seinem Besuch in Heppenheim findet, ist offen. Der Geselle will nach Norwegen. „Die zahlen gut", hofft er. Der Lohn richtet sich nach den ortsüblichen Tarifen. 50 Üblich ist oft auch Kost und Logis.

In Worms am Dom ist die gemeinsame Fahrt zu Ende, es bleibt noch der Weg bis Heppenheim. Dort hat sich Schäfers zwischenzeitlicher Arbeitgeber und früherer Altgeselle Jerome Schmitt bereits mit 25 Jahren selbstständig gemacht. „Ich habe ihn unter meine Fittiche genommen, habe ihm beigebracht, wie das Le- 55 ben auf der Landstraße funktioniert, wie man Arbeit findet, als ich vor zwei Jahren selber noch unterwegs war", berichtet Schmitt. „Wer auf Wanderschaft geht, hat schon ein gewisses handwerkliches Know-how. Man lernt mehr im Bereich des Menschlichen", erzählt er. „Wichtig ist das vor allem bei problematischen Kunden. Man ist pragmatisch und zielorientiert, wirft nicht so schnell die Flinte 60 ins Korn", sagt er zum Wert der alten Traditionen. „Man gibt sein Wort, man lässt sich festnageln."·

Festnageln ist dabei im buchstäblichen Sinne gemeint. „Man wird auch heute noch mit dem Ohrläppchen an einen Balken genagelt. Dann bekommt man Ringe an die Ohren. Ursprünglich waren die dazu da, die Beerdigung zu bezahlen, 65 wenn man unterwegs stirbt", sagt Schmitt. Im Zeitalter von Piercings und Tattoos wirkt das aber gar nicht mehr so archaisch. Und ganz modern erscheint auch die Idee der Walz, an verschiedenen Orten zu leben und zu arbeiten. *(639 Wörter)*

Andrea Döring: „Mit Stock und Hut auf Wanderschaft gehen" in: Frankfurter Rundschau, *29. Mai 2018, © dpa Deutsche Presse-Agentur GmbH;*
Bild: © picture alliance / Andrea Döring / dpa | Andrea Döring

Anmerkungen
Z. 19 Gewerk: Handwerk
Z. 32 Walz: Wanderschaft eines Handwerksgesellen

Lösungsvorschläge

Before you start writing, pay close attention to the assignment. It tells you for whom you have to summarise the information (an American exchange partner) and in what form (a personal email). This will determine the style you should use: write in correct, formal language because your friend needs the information for a presentation at school. However, do not forget to use a more colloquial style when you address your friend and his/her situation. When it comes to content, you should only sum up the pieces of information that are relevant for your friend's presentation: so leave out the concrete personal examples mentioned in the article. Instead, focus on what makes the tradition of travelling journeymen special, where it comes from and why and how it is still practised today.

You should include the following aspects:
- *appearance of travelling journeymen:*
  - *equipment: bindle, hiking pole, logbook (cf. ll. 15/16)*
  - *traditional clothing: hat, waistcoat, jacket, flared trousers, shirt (cf. ll. 16–18)*
  - *colour of clothes different depending on craft (cf. ll. 18–20)*
  - *earring (traditional and current custom of being "nailed down"; original use: payment for funeral costs) (cf. ll. 62–65)*
- *rules for travelling journeymen:*
  - *completed apprenticeship, unmarried, no debts, travel for two or three years and one day (cf. ll. 35–37)*
  - *staying away at least 50 km from hometown (cf. ll. 37–40)*
- *history of the tradition:*
  - *dates back to Middle Ages (cf. l. 21)*
  - *obligatory to become masters until the beginnings of industrialisation (cf. ll. 21/22)*
- *present situation:*
  - *450–550 journeying craftspeople, ten to 20 per cent women (cf. ll. 31–33)*
  - *custom recognised by UNESCO since 2014 (cf. ll. 34/35)*
  - *many also work abroad (cf. ll. 42/43, 66/67)*
  - *normal pay, often free board and lodging (cf. ll. 49/50)*
- *reasons for travelling:*
  - *improve skills and learn new techniques (cf. ll. 22/23, 43/44)*
  - *gain new experiences, learn about the world and oneself (cf. ll. 22/23, 44/45, 57–60)*

Hello Cheryl, greeting

Thanks for your email. That's an interesting subject for your presentation. I'd be glad to help you with some information I found in a German newspaper. introduction

As you might remember from last summer, travelling journeymen can easily be recognised by their traditional clothing, consisting of a hat, a waistcoat, a jacket, flared trousers and a shirt. The colour of these depends on the journeymen's craft. They carry a bindle, a appearance of travelling journeymen

117

pole and a logbook to record their journey. Another interesting feature is the earring they all wear. Originally, the rings were meant to pay for their funeral in case they died on the trip. They are also reminders of the tradition of nailing the journeymen's earlobes to a post. This custom is still being practised as a symbol of the craftsmen's reliability.

There are more strict rules to observe: the journeymen must have finished their apprenticeship and must be unmarried, free of debt and prepared to travel for two to three years and one day. They must also keep a distance of at least 50 km from their hometown to avoid competing with their masters.

rules for travelling journeymen

The tradition of travelling began in the late Middle Ages. Until the beginning of the Industrial Age, travelling in this way was obligatory for anyone who wanted to become a master of their craft.

history of the tradition

Currently, there are about 450 to 550 journeying craftspeople, ten to 20 per cent of whom are women. They are paid at the standard rate for their trade, with board and lodging often being free. In 2014, the UNESCO recognised the custom's cultural value by giving it world heritage status.

present situation

There are several reasons for its ongoing popularity: the journeymen, who often travel abroad these days, can improve their learned trade by acquiring new techniques. Moreover, they meet many people, gain experiences and learn skills, such as perseverance and pragmatism. All of this can prove helpful when dealing with customers, especially with difficult ones.

reasons for travelling

I hope you'll find this information useful. Please tell me how your presentation went.

ending (fitting to text form)

Love,
Lily   *(341 words)*

Assignment

In your social studies class, you and students at your American partner school are working on the joint e-learning project "Changing Lifestyles".
Write an article for the project website, outlining why people have lived in shared accommodation in the past and present.

„Fast niemand zieht mehr aus Überzeugung in eine WG"
Von David Gutensohn

1 **ZEIT Campus ONLINE: Immer mehr Menschen leben in Wohngemeinschaften. Seit wann liegt die WG im Trend?**

<u>Clemens Albrecht</u>: Menschen, die nicht miteinander verwandt sind, aber einen Haushalt teilen, gab es schon im Römischen Reich. Das ganze europäische Mittelalter war
5 geprägt von Lebensformen, in denen Familien, ihr Dienstpersonal und andere Personen sich ein Haus teilten. Eigentlich ist die Wohngemeinschaft die normale Lebensform.

Seit wann leben Familien nicht mehr in Wohngemeinschaften?

Zumindest bis in die Mitte des 19. Jahrhunderts war das die Regel. Danach lebte die
10 Kernfamilie verstärkt im eigenen Heim, allerdings in der Oberschicht immer noch mit Personal. Als die Dienstboten dann in den 1950er- und 1960er-Jahren durch Maschinen ersetzt wurden, wurde die Kernfamilie mit eigenem Haushalt zum Standard. Die Männer gingen arbeiten, die Frauen blieben zu Hause und kümmerten sich um die Kinder.

15 **Wie hat das Modell der Wohngemeinschaft trotzdem überlebt?**

Wie so viele gesellschaftliche Strukturen wurde auch diese von der <u>68er-Bewegung</u> aufgebrochen. Ihre Wohngemeinschaftsprojekte läuteten das Comeback der alten Wohnform ein. Das damals Neue an der Wohngemeinschaft war, dass sie egalitär organisiert wurde. Es gab keine patriarchalen Strukturen innerhalb von Wohngemein-
20 schaften. Das ist bis heute so geblieben, wenn man mal davon absieht, dass es Haupt- und Untermieter gibt. Die Wohngemeinschaft der 68er war immer ein gesellschaftsreformerisches Projekt. Doch die Hoffnung, dass irgendwann alle Menschen frei und gleich zusammenleben würden, erwies sich als große Illusion.

Wieso ist die Idee gescheitert?

25 Heute entscheiden sich Studierende pragmatisch statt politisch für eine Wohngemeinschaft. Ist das Studium beendet und die Familie gegründet, verlässt man die WG und zieht ins Reihenhaus. Einige Jahre später wird der Nachwuchs denselben Kreislauf

durchlaufen. Die WG ist zu einer Lebensform auf Zeit geworden – vor allem für gut gebildete 20- bis 30-Jährige. Fast niemand zieht mehr aus Überzeugung in eine Wohn-
30 gemeinschaft.

Warum sonst? Eine Studie vom Centrum für Hochschulentwicklung (CHE) zeigt, dass die WG-Quote kontinuierlich steigt und mittlerweile jeder und jede dritte Studierende in einer Wohngemeinschaft lebt. Für sie ist die WG zur beliebtesten Wohnform geworden.

35 Rein pragmatisch ist die WG für viele Studierende einfach die beste Lösung. Sie haben oft zu wenig Einkommen, um sich eine eigene Wohnung leisten zu können. Vor allem in angesagten Städten sind Ein- oder Zweizimmerwohnungen besonders teuer. Dort sind nicht nur Studierende auf Wohngemeinschaften angewiesen. Auch Erwachsene, die im Berufsleben stehen, bleiben oder ziehen heute in Wohngemein-
40 schaften. Oft nur, weil das finanzierbar ist und sie ohnehin mobiler und flexibler arbeiten und leben als früher.

Entscheiden sich Menschen heute nur noch aus finanziellen Gründen für eine WG?

Zum Teil. Es ist aber auch ein anderer Trend zu beobachten: Einige Menschen leben
45 explizit asketisch und minimalistisch. Es gibt eine ganze Bewegung von Menschen, die bewusst Verzicht üben und möglichst wenig besitzen möchten. Da kann man sich mit keiner Wohnform besser identifizieren als mit der Wohngemeinschaft. Die WG kann also auch Teil eines Lebensstils sein und Identifikation schaffen. Einige machen damit aus der Not eine Tugend: Sie bloggen über ihren Lebensstil und integrieren das
50 kleine WG-Zimmer in ihr positives Selbstbild.

Andere wiederum wünschen sich nur, dass abends jemand zu Hause ist, oder?

Wohngemeinschaften können auch eine Art Familienersatz sein. Wir Soziologen unterscheiden zwischen Gemeinschaft und Gesellschaft. Gemeinschaft, das sind Freunde und Familie, unsere engsten Beziehungen, die immer mit sozialer Kontrolle ver-
55 bunden sind. Daraus möchten viele fliehen, ohne in die völlige Anonymität der großen Städte zu geraten. Ihnen kann die WG wiederum Gemeinschaft bieten, ohne so eng wie Familie zu sein: Menschen, die da sind und sich um einen kümmern, vor denen man sich aber nicht für den alltäglichen Lebenswandel verantworten muss.

(579 Wörter)

Gutensohn, David (2019, 19. April). „Fast niemand zieht mehr aus Überzeugung in eine WG". Zeit Campus Online vom 13. 01. 2020, https://www.zeit.de/campus/2019-04/wohngemeinschaften-studierende-bezahlbarer-wohnraum-clemens-albrecht

Anmerkungen
Z. 3   Clemens Albrecht: Professor für Kultursoziologie, Universität Bonn
Z. 16 68er-Bewegung: (hier) die westdeutsche Studentenprotestbewegung der späten 1960er-Jahre

Lösungsvorschläge

In this task you are required to write an article for the project website of a joint e-learning project called "Changing lifestyles" which your school and your American partner school are working on. In your article you are supposed to outline why people have lived in shared accommodation. Include an appropriate headline*, a brief introduction to the topic, clear paragraphs as well as a brief conclusion. Note that these do not have to be as long as in the following example, which is slightly longer than it would be required for this task. You are supposed to focus on reasons for sharing a home in the past and in the present, that is, your main part should be divided into two parts. Avoid including your own opinion on the topic or unnecessary details from the material. As the article is part of a school project you should avoid slang or colloquial expressions and aim for a rather neutral tone.*

The following information should be included in your text:

- *reasons for living in shared homes in the past:*
  - *common way of life → people from different families used to share accommodation (cf. ll. 3–7)*
  - *servants usually lived in the master's household until the mid-20th century (cf. ll. 9–12)*
  - *new political ideas in the 1960s: disapproval of patriarchal structures, egalitarian ideal of people living together freely and equally → more people living together again and sharing homes (cf. ll. 16–22)*
- *reasons for living in shared homes in the present:*
  - *students and young professionals share homes temporarily and for pragmatic reasons:*
    - *rents in cities are too high and cannot be afforded by these groups (cf. ll. 35–40)*
    - *high degree of flexibility and mobility in their professional and private lives (cf. ll. 40/41)*
  - *for some, sharing accommodation is an alternative lifestyle they prefer:*
    - *free decision against gathering possessions, leading a minimalist lifestyle → give up on unnecessary things, comforts and enjoyment (cf. ll. 44–48)*
    - *escape from constraints and social control in their parents' homes without living a life in anonymity → flatmates as family substitutes who offer company and support (cf. ll. 52–58)*

Shared home, sweet home? – Why sharing accommodation is a growing trend   headline

Having a roof over your head is a basic human need just like having access to food and drink. Both in the past and still today, people shared accommodation. Interestingly, the number of people from different families living together in a shared flat or house is increasing. However, the reasons for this trend are different today than they were some decades ago.   introduction

121

For centuries, sharing a household was pretty normal. Masters and their servants usually lived in the same household up until the mid-20th century. This changed once upper-class families did not have servants any longer due to the increasing use of machines. From then on, living together with only one's core family became the social norm.

reasons for sharing homes in the past: masters and servants living together

When new political ideas came up in the late 1960s, more and more people again started living together in shared homes. They often disapproved of the patriarchal structures they were faced with in their family homes and thought to enjoy more freedom and equality when living together with peers.

1960s: ideal of freedom and equality

Today, young people in particular still share accommodation, but their reasons are different than in the past. They rather share homes temporarily and for pragmatic reasons. They usually cannot afford to pay high prices for flats in cities plus they show a high degree of flexibility and mobility in their professional and private lives. Thus, sharing a flat is the obvious choice for them.

reasons for sharing homes today: pragmatic reasons

For others, sharing accommodation is an alternative lifestyle they prefer. They regard it as a deliberate decision against accumulating possessions. Choosing a minimalist lifestyle by having one room for themselves and sharing others like the kitchen means abstaining from unnecessary material comforts and pleasures. They also often want to escape from pressure and constraints in their parents' homes. However, they require company and support from peers as a family substitute. Thus, they prefer sharing a home and not living by themselves.

alternative lifestyle

Sharing accommodation is a growing trend all over Germany as more and more people are sharing a home. What has changed, though, are the motives for living this way. Today, people share flats out of necessity and lifestyle rather than out of political conviction.

conclusion

(355 words)

122

Assignment

You are taking part in a German-American youth project in which the participants share information about changing traditions. You have decided to focus on the role of porcelain in Germany. Based on the interview below, write an article for the project website in which you describe the current situation of manufacturing and using porcelain in Germany and the developments responsible for it.

Zurück zur Tischkultur
Interview von Sophie Hilgenstock

1 **Herr Holler, ist das nur so ein Gefühl, oder erlebt Porzellan tatsächlich gerade eine Renaissance?**

Nein, anhand der Zahlen können wir leider nicht erkennen, dass es eine Renaissance gibt. In diesem Jahr hatten die deutschen Porzellanhersteller im Vergleich zum Vor-
5 jahr einen Umsatzrückgang von 5,1 Prozent. Ähnlich sah es im letzten Jahr aus. Daher ist es schwierig zu behaupten, Porzellan erlebe eine Renaissance. Lediglich im Projektgeschäft, also im professionellen Bereich, ist die Nachfrage zuletzt gestiegen. In Gaststätten, Seniorenwohnanlagen und Krankenhäusern wird neuerdings wieder mehr Wert auf gutes Geschirr gelegt, dort konnten die deutschen Porzellanhersteller
10 in den vergangenen Jahren große Erfolge feiern.

Wie sieht es in Privathaushalten aus? Spätestens zu Weihnachten ist gutes Geschirr doch der Renner.

Das ist richtig. Je näher Weihnachten rückt, umso besser läuft das Geschäft. Viele Kunden haben es dabei vor allem auf die Weihnachtskollektionen abgesehen, die viele
15 Hersteller im Angebot haben. Gemeint ist Porzellan mit Weihnachtsdekor, also mit Tannenbäumen, Glocken und Nikoläusen. Diese Porzellanlinien funktionieren gut, speziell bei Familien mit Kindern.

Woran liegt es, dass Porzellan ansonsten aus der Mode ist?

Das hat mehrere Gründe. Der wohl wichtigste Faktor ist, dass jüngere Generationen
20 weniger Wert auf hochwertiges Porzellan und Essen am gedeckten Tisch legen. Die sonntägliche Kaffeetafel, Familienfeiern zu Hause, Gäste zum Abendessen – die Anlässe, das gute Geschirr aus dem Schrank zu holen, sind aus der Mode gekommen. Wer greift heute noch zur Kaffeekanne aus Porzellan? Man stellt seinen Becher direkt unter den Kaffeeautomaten oder läuft mit Thermobecher aus dem Haus. Das ist
25 ein Kulturwandel, den man nur in Teilen auffangen kann – etwa, indem die Geschirrhersteller Coffee-to-go-Becher aus Porzellan herstellen, die man immer wieder verwenden kann. Aber den Trend halten wir nicht auf.

Einst war die Porzellanmarke identitätsstiftend. Gilt Porzellan heute noch als Statussymbol?

30 Nicht mehr so wie früher. Es ist nicht mehr die Regel, dass jede Familie ein gutes Geschirr besitzt oder auf eine bestimmte Marke schwört. Porzellan gehört auch nicht mehr typischerweise zur <u>Aussteuer</u>. Es gibt zwar noch Hochzeitspaare, die zur Trauung ein bestimmtes Service bekommen, aber die sind aus unserer Sicht viel zu selten geworden – die meisten wünschen sich Geld für die Hochzeitsreise. Schaut man sich 35 an, wofür junge Menschen heute Geld ausgeben, liegen die Prioritäten ganz klar woanders: Es ist kein Problem, sich für 800 Euro ein Handy zu kaufen, bei hochwertigem Porzellan sieht es oft anders aus.

Wie wollen Sie das ändern?

Mit modernem Design, guter Qualität und pfiffigen Ideen. Das Ziel muss es sein, 40 sich von den Billigimporten aus Asien abzuheben. Außerdem müssen wir Online als Vertriebsweg ausbauen. Uns sterben zunehmend die Fachhändler weg – gab es früher in jeder Kleinstadt ein klassisches Haushaltswarengeschäft, machen heute etwa 40 Fachgeschäfte pro Jahr in den Innenstädten dicht. Aber Porzellan will man anfassen, bevor man es kauft. Der Onlinehandel ist damit eine Herausforderung.

45 **Deutschland war einmal Porzellanland. Was ist schiefgelaufen?**

Deutschland ist in Europa weiterhin der größte Standort der Porzellanherstellung, und ich bin sicher, das wird auch so bleiben. Die Herausforderungen allerdings werden nicht kleiner. Der Endverbraucher greift oft lieber zur Dumpingware aus China – also zu Porzellan, das weit unter Herstellungskosten auf den Markt geschwemmt 50 wird. Inzwischen gibt es deshalb auf chinesische Importware Strafzölle. Aber damit sind die Probleme nicht vom Tisch: Die politischen Rahmenbedingungen für die deutschen Porzellanhersteller sind schwierig. Sie haben europaweit die höchsten Energiekosten und die höchste Abgabenlast. […]

Wie schaffen es altehrwürdige Häuser wie Meissen, <u>KPM</u> oder Fürstenberg,
55 **sich am Markt zu halten?**

In den letzten Jahren sind mit Russland oder dem Vorderen Orient wichtige Exportmärkte weggebrochen. Je mehr Krisen und Kriege die Welt erschüttern, umso schwieriger wird es auch für die Produzenten von kunsthandwerklich hergestelltem Porzellan. Nichtsdestoweniger gibt es weiterhin ein großes Interesse an individuellen, 60 hochwertigen Produkten – von Porzellanfiguren über handbemalte Vasen bis hin zu aufwendig gestalteten Tellern. Wer heute noch am Markt ist, hat bewiesen, dass er sich trotz schwierigster Rahmenbedingungen mit seinen Produkten durchsetzen kann – von daher sehe ich nicht schwarz. *(642 Wörter)*

Hilgenstock, S. (2018, 10. Dezember). „Zurück zur Tischkultur: Ein Besuch in der Manufaktur Fürstenberg“. Leipziger Volkszeitung. https://www.lvz.de/Nachrichten/Panorama/Zurueck-zur-Tischkultur-Ein-Besuch-in-der-Porzellanmanufaktur-Fuerstenberg [Zugriff am 22. September 2020]

Anmerkungen

Z. 1 Christoph René Holler: Hauptgeschäftsführer des Bundesverbands Keramische Industrie

Z. 21 Kaffeetafel: ein festlich gedeckter Tisch für Kaffee und Kuchen am Nachmittag

Z. 32 Aussteuer: Ausstattung für den künftigen Haushalt, die eine Braut traditionell von ihrer Familie zur Hochzeit geschenkt bekam

Z. 54 KPM: Königliche Porzellan-Manufaktur Berlin

Lösungsvorschläge

Before you start writing, pay close attention to the assignment. It tells you for what aim you have to summarise the information (a German-American youth project) and in what form (an article for the project website). This will determine the style you should use: generally write in correct, formal language, but as your addressees are the participants of a youth project, some more colloquial expressions are also allowed. Do not forget the formal elements an article requires, such as a headline, a clear structure into paragraphs, etc. When it comes to content, focus on the current situation of the German porcelain industry on the one hand and on developments responsible for this situation on the other.
You should include the following aspects:
- *headline (fitting to text form)*
- *introductory paragraph: summary of the current situation of the German porcelain industry:*
  - *difficult situation, decline in sales in recent years (cf. ll. 3–5)*
  - *however, Germany is still Europe's biggest manufacturer (cf. l. 46)*
- *reasons for difficulties:*
  - *changing eating traditions ("to-go" culture instead of fixed family dinners) (cf. ll. 19–24)*
  - *porcelain no longer a status symbol or a typical wedding present (cf. ll. 28–34)*
  - *young people often have other spending priorities (holidays, smartphones, etc.) (cf. ll. 34–37)*
  - *competition from cheap products from Asia (cf. ll. 40, 48–50)*
  - *many shop closures of homeware stores, online trade is not really taking off (cf. ll. 41–44)*
  - *German manufacturers have to pay high energy costs and other expenses (cf. ll. 51–53)*
  - *difficult political circumstances: crises challenging for luxury goods, such as porcelain, markets in some countries lost for political reasons (cf. ll. 56–59)*
- *still, partly hopeful outlook on the future:*
  - *professional branches (restaurants, hospitals, retirement homes) still have a demand for high-quality products (cf. ll. 6–10)*
  - *Christmas collections are also sought after (cf. ll. 13–17)*
  - *strategy for the future: focus on quality (cf. ll. 39/40, 59–61) and adapting to new modern ways (cf. ll. 25–27, 40/41)*

The times are a-changing: Is German porcelain on the way out?   headline

Germany has a history of high-quality porcelain production and the country still is the biggest manufacturer in Europe. Yet in recent years, there has been a steady decline in sales.   introduction

The reasons for this are manifold: Due to changing eating habits, such as takeaway meals often replacing fixed family dinners, using high-quality cups and plates is no longer as important as it used to be. Consequently, porcelain has lost its attractiveness as a status   reasons for difficulties: changing traditions

126

symbol or a typical wedding present. Generally, young people nowadays often have other spending priorities.

Another challenge lies in the sale venues: Quite a significant number of homeware shops have closed all over Germany and online selling has not really taken off yet. When it comes to the porcelain market, customers usually want to lay their hands on a product before they buy it.

shop closures and difficulties of online trade

Moreover, manufacturers have to compete with cheap products from China. This is especially difficult because of the high costs that make production in Germany expensive.

competition from China

Furthermore, in times of crises, people tend to buy fewer "unnecessary" luxury items. Another consequence of recent political developments is that some of the main German export markets in Russia and the Middle East have become more difficult to access.

difficult political circumstances

Still, the future of German porcelain production does not look entirely grim: Restaurants, hospitals and retirement homes are showing an increasing demand for high-quality crockery. Christmas collections are also exceptionally sought after. So, by keeping their standards high and at the same time adapting to some of the challenges of modern times, the German porcelain industry could well prove that change can be an opportunity rather than a threat.

hopeful outlook on the future

(272 words)

Assignment

As an intern at an American newspaper, you have been asked for information on diversity initiatives in Germany.
Write an email to the editor in which you present the "Neue deutsche Medienmacher*innen" (NdM) and their campaign #WeatherCorrection.

Wetter migrantisch: Tief Ahmet, Hoch Dragica
Von Andrea Dernbach

1 Ahmet hatte schon seinen Einsatz. Demnächst dürften Bartosz und Cemal, Bozena und Chana über Deutschland kommen. Sturm und gutes Wetter tragen ab sofort und vorerst keine traditionsdeutschen Namen mehr: Auch der Wetterbericht bekommt Migrationshintergrund. Die ersten Tief- und Hochdruckgebiete erhalten 2021 türki-
5 sche, rumänische, polnische oder arabische Namen, also die der am stärksten vertretenen Herkunftskulturen. Dem Turnus folgend gibt es zwölf Monate lang Männernamen für die Tiefs, Frauennamen für die Hochs.

   Der Grund für den migrantisch-meteorologischen Jahresbeginn: Die Neuen deutschen Medienmacher*innen haben die Patenschaften für die ersten Wetterlagen im
10 neuen Jahr übernommen, das deutsche Wetter „gekapert", wie es auf ihrer Website heißt. Die NdM sind ein Zusammenschluss von Journalistinnen und Journalisten aus Familien mit und ohne Einwanderungsgeschichte, die sich für mehr Vielfalt im Journalismus einsetzen.

   „Wir leben in einem Einwanderungsland. Trotzdem tragen die Wetterhochs und
15 -tiefs fast immer nur Namen wie Gisela und Helmut. Zeit, dass sich das ändert." Deutsche hießen „schließlich auch Ahmet, Chana, Khuê und Romani". Und bis das endlich bei allen angekommen sei, werde man „nicht aufhören, Wirbel zu machen".

   Es ist nicht die erste <u>Spaßguerilla-Aktion</u> der NdM vor dem durchaus ernsten Hintergrund eines erheblichen Diversitätsproblems im deutschen Journalismus: Wäh-
20 rend inzwischen ein gutes Viertel der deutschen Bevölkerung Migrationshintergrund hat (26 Prozent), gilt das lediglich für fünf bis zehn Prozent der Belegschaften in den Redaktionen. Tendenz nur langsam steigend. Weil das aus NdM-Sicht auch auf den Journalismus durchschlägt, der so entsteht, haben sie etwa für die „unterirdischste" Berichterstattung eines Jahres den Anti-Preis „Goldene Kartoffel" ausgelobt – und
25 dies nicht nur mit deren Wachstum unter der Erde begründet: Die Kartoffel sei auch das deutscheste Gemüse überhaupt, habe aber gleichzeitig eine lupenreine südamerikanische Migrationsgeschichte. [...]

   Nun also die Aktion #wetterberichtigung, mit der die NdM symbolisch auf die reale Vielfalt in den drei deutschsprachigen Ländern aufmerksam machen wollen.
30 Mit dabei sind die Schwesterorganisation „Neue Schweizer Medienmacher*innen"

und österreichische Initiativen – auch Idee und Umsetzung kamen aus Wien, von den Kreativen Goran Golik und M. Alexander Trybus. Das Geld für die Aktion – auch Wetterpatenschaften kosten – kam durch Sponsoring zusammen.

Die Wettertaufen sind übrigens eine sehr berlinische Angelegenheit: 1954 mach-
35 te sich am Institut für Meteorologie der Freien Universität die damalige Studentin und spätere ZDF-Meteorologin Karla Wege dafür stark, das US-Modell zu überneh-men. Dort hatten seit dem Zweiten Weltkrieg die pazifischen Taifune Namen. Gab es mehrere zugleich, ließ sich so besser der Überblick behalten.

Erst nach der Einheit nahm auch der Rest Deutschlands Orkane namens Wiebke
40 und Vivian wahr. Berlin vergibt die Namen seither für alle weiter; der Deutsche Wet-terdienst war einverstanden. Seit einer kleinen Debatte Ende der 1990er Jahre dar-über, ob nicht Frauen diskriminiert werden, heißen jährlich wechselnd mal die Tiefs und mal die Hochs nach Männern, dann wieder nach Frauen.

Ausgerechnet in geschlechterpolitischer Hinsicht sahen sich nun die diversitäts-
45 bewegten NdM zu einem Rückschritt gezwungen: Sie sind Patinnen für etliche Män-ner, aber nur für drei Frauen: „Wir wollten den gesamten Januar übernehmen", erläu-tert die Vorsitzende Ferda Ataman. „Aber im Januar gibt es nun mal nicht so viele Hochs."

Deshalb dürfen vorerst nur die Hochs Bozena, Dragica – Erinnerung an die jugo-
50 slawischen „Gast"arbeiterinnen und -arbeiter – und Chana ran. Danach übernimmt wieder eine Elke. Tiefdruckmann Kasper hat seinen Einsatz erst nach zehn Migran-ten – von Ahmet und Bartosz bis Jussuf und Irek.   *(531 Wörter)*

Dernbach, Andrea. „Tief Ahmet, Hoch Dragica". Der Tagesspiegel. 5. Jan. 2021.
Zugriff am 28. Jan. 2021 von https://www.tagesspiegel.de/politik/wetter-migrantisch-tief-ahmet-hoch-dragica/26771256.html

Anmerkung
Z. 18 Spaßguerilla-Aktion: provokative Aktion, um auf politische Anliegen aufmerksam zu machen

Lösungsvorschläge

Your task here is to "present" the information given in the German text. This means that you are not supposed to include your own opinion. Just summarise what it says in the text about the project. You should present the information in the form of an email. As you are an intern who is writing to an editor, you should use a formal style. Include the following information:

– The New German Media Makers (NdM) are a collective of journalists, some of whom are from an immigrant background, who are trying to make journalism more diverse. (cf. ll. 11–13)

– While around 25 % of the German population come from an immigrant background, this is only true for 5–10 % of the editorial staff. (cf. ll. 19–22)

– In 2021, the collective acquired the sponsorship of several high and low pressure areas in Germany for January. (cf. ll. 8–11, 46)

– In Germany it is possible to give names to high and low pressure areas if you sponsor them. (cf. ll. 32/33)

– The names were usually very traditional German names. (cf. ll. 14/15)

– The organisation gave them names from the largest groups of minorities found in Germany. (cf. ll. 4–6)

– By using this light-hearted topic, the organisation is trying to raise awareness regarding a more serious topic: Germany is an immigration country and this should be represented in the media. (cf. ll. 14–17, 28/29)

Subject: Diversity initiatives in Germany — *subject*

Dear Catherine, — *form of address*

Thank you very much for this task. I immediately thought of a project I read about on Instagram recently. — *introduction*

There is an interesting initiative among journalists in Germany to name weather fronts according to the population groups that most represent immigrants. Instead of assigning only German names, as has been the practice since the trend was adopted from the USA, the New German Media Makers are calling for better representation of the current German population. This group of journalists from diverse backgrounds has created a system that, this year, will assign low pressure systems male and high pressure systems female immigrant names. With this initiative, they want to point out that while around 25 % of the German population are from immigrant backgrounds, only 5–10 % of the editorial staff come from minority groups. This will symbolically emphasise the serious problems in achieving inclusive journalism, and will continue throughout the month of January. The #WeatherCorrection campaign is co-operating with similar organisations in Austria and Switzerland, and is financed by donations. — *information on the campaign*

I hope you can use some of the information for your article.   closing phrase

Best wishes,   sign off

Elena   *(193 words)*

Assignment

You are going to take part in an international youth conference about sustainable business ideas. To prepare for the discussions, participants share an example from their own country on the conference website.
Write an article for this website in which you present "Lieferrad DA".

Der Spargel kommt per Lastenrad
Von Astrid Ludwig

1 Lange schon hegte das Professoren-Trio die Idee für einen Lieferservice der anderen Art. Einen, der die Umwelt schont, den örtlichen Handel stärkt, Mitarbeiter fair bezahlt und trotzdem rentabel ist. Doch die Wirtschafts- und Logistikexperten Johanna Bucerius und Axel Wolfermann von der Hochschule Darmstadt und Kai-Oliver Schocke
5 von der Frankfurt University of Applied Sciences fanden niemanden, der bereit war, das auch auszuprobieren. Dann aber kam Corona. „Als wir gesehen haben, wie schlecht es dem Einzelhandel geht, haben wir den Lieferservice selbst gestartet", berichtet Bucerius. Beim hessischen Wirtschaftsministerium beantragten die drei Forscher Fördergeld. Sie bekamen rund 100 000 Euro, mit denen E-Lastenräder ange-
10 schafft und Gehälter für das studentische Team aus Hilfskräften und Kurierfahrern gezahlt werden konnten.

Seit dem Sommer rollen die schwarzen Lasten-Bikes mit dem gelbblauen Aufdruck „Lieferrad DA" durch Darmstadt. Sie bringen Blumen, Bücher, Wein, Lebensmittel, die nicht gekühlt werden müssen, Kleidung, Kosmetik oder auch Medikamen-
15 te von den Einzelhändlern direkt nach Hause zu den Kunden. „Es lief gut an", sagt Axel Wolfermann – dank Werbung über soziale Medien sowie Kontakten zur Stadt und örtlichen Wirtschaft. Ein Spargelbauer im Stadtteil Arheilgen machte den Anfang. Bei manchem Geschäft fragten die Studenten auch persönlich an.

Mittlerweile nutzen rund 50 Einzelhändler in Darmstadt den unentgeltlichen Lie-
20 ferservice. Darunter auch große Händler wie das Modekaufhaus Henschel und die Buchladen-Kette Thalia. Armin Pourhosseini, Mitbegründer des Naturkosmetik-Shops „Woodberg", hat sich nach eigenen Worten bewusst für den klimaschonenden Raddienst entschieden. […] Umweltschutz gehört für ihn zum Geschäftsmodell. Für seine Naturprodukte nutzt er recyceltes Verpackungsmaterial, bei Versand und Be-
25 zahlung bietet er Kunden Modelle an, die Ökoprojekte unterstützen. Rund vier von zehn Bestellungen aus Darmstadt lässt er von „Lieferrad DA" zustellen.

Die studentischen Radkuriere haben gut zu tun. Wöchentlich fahren sie zwischen 100 und 150 Pakete aus. „Weihnachten ging es deutlich nach oben, da waren es rund 300 Pakete pro Woche. Das war Rekord", so Wolfermann Am Valentinstag nahmen
30 die Ausfahrten ebenfalls zu, und Ostern werde sicherlich eine weitere Herausforde-

132

rung, vermutet Bucerius. Bis Ende 2020 brachte „Lieferrad DA" montags bis freitags insgesamt 1 068 Pakete an die Haustüren. Die zwei studentischen Kuriere radelten mehr als 3 000 Kilometer durch die Straßen Darmstadts.

Die Kunden bestellen bei den Händlern, die die Aufträge an das Studententeam
35 weiterleiten. „Wird bis 12 Uhr bestellt, liefern wir am selben Tag aus", sagt Florian Treiber. Der Dreiundzwanzigjährige, der Logistikmanagement an der Hochschule Darmstadt studiert, ist für die Tourenplanung zuständig. Er pflegt die Bestellungen in die Tourensoftware ein, prüft, ob Händler wegen vieler oder schwerer Pakete mehr-fach angefahren werden müssen, checkt Öffnungszeiten, rechnet Pufferzeiten ein und
40 übernimmt die Datenanalyse. Weil Kundendaten sensibel sind, stellt die Hochschule dafür einen gesicherten Laptop zur Verfügung. Treiber ist für die Kuriere erreichbar, „falls ein Kunde nicht da, die Adresse falsch oder der Akku leer ist". Vor Weihnach-ten ist er sogar selbst als Fahrer eingesprungen – ein lehrreicher Blick auf die andere Seite. „Das Projekt ist ohnehin eine super Einstiegsmöglichkeit in die Logistik-
45 branche", findet der Student. Und das ohne Druck und schlechte Bezahlung, über die Paketzusteller immer wieder klagen. Die Lieferrad-Kuriere und <u>Hiwis</u> werden pro Stunde honoriert, nach den Sätzen der Hochschule. Studenten mit Bachelorabschluss erhalten rund 15 Euro. „Sie werden zudem in das Forschungsprojekt einbezogen, bringen ihre Erfahrungen ein", ergänzt Bucerius. Der Lieferdienst ist auch Gegen-
50 stand mehrerer Bachelorarbeiten.

Das Professoren-Trio ist zufrieden mit dem Projekt. Zum Jahresende ist zwar die Förderung ausgelaufen, doch eine Fortsetzung ist in Sicht. Noch ist die Hochschule Darmstadt Betreiberin und der Lieferdienst gebührenfrei. Doch es soll eine neue Rechtsform gefunden werden, damit „Lieferrad DA" als Verein oder GmbH Gewin-
55 ne generieren kann. Denn die Forscher wollen auch herausfinden, unter welchen Be-dingungen ein derartiger Lieferservice rentabel bestehen kann. Bei voller Auslastung betragen die Kosten je Lieferung derzeit rund vier Euro. Der Einzelhandel, sagt Wol-fermann, habe Interesse an dem Lieferdienst, aber angewiesen ist das Projekt auf zu-sätzliche Kunden wie die Stadt, kommunale Betriebe, Unternehmen oder Wochen-
60 markt-Beschicker. Andere Kommunen haben schon Interesse am Aufbau eines ähnli-chen Lieferdienstes bekundet. *(640 Wörter)*

Astrid Ludwig, „Der Spargel kommt per Lastenrad", in: https://www.faz.net/aktuell/rhein-main/
hochschule-darmstadt-der-spargel-kommt-per-lastenrad-17258331.html

Anmerkungen
Z. 13 DA: Autokennzeichen Darmstadts
Z. 46 Hiwi: studentische wissenschaftliche Hilfskraft

Lösungsvorschläge

Your task is to write an article for a project website. The project in question is an international youth project, so those being addressed are mainly young people. Focusing on this group of addressees and your purpose, your article should be written in a rather formal and neutral language, but some informal or colloquial language is also allowed. Often the assignments for mediation tasks tell you to which part(s) of the original text your mediation should be limited. In this case, however, there are no additional questions narrowing down the content needed for your article, so the whole text should be summarised with a special focus on the project's sustainability. The following points should come up in your solution:

– *headline (fitting to text form)*
– *introductory paragraph: what makes "Lieferrad DA" (a delivery company that delivers products via bike) a perfect example of sustainable entrepreneurship?*
  - *protects the environment (cf. l. 2)*
  - *good for local business (cf. l. 2)*
  - *fair salaries for employees (cf. l. 2)*
  - *profitability (cf. l. 3)*
– *characteristics of the project:*
  - *founded by three university professors (business, logistics, applied sciences) (cf. ll. 1, 3–5)*
  - *Covid pandemic as the perfect opportunity to start a delivery service by bike (cf. l. 6)*
  - *ministry provided funds (cf. ll. 8/9)*
  - *marketing via social media and through personal contacts (cf. ll. 16/17)*
  - *staff (both administrative and drivers) made up of students (cf. ll. 27, 32, 34, 35–37)*
  - *customers order directly from retailers, who inform "Lieferrad DA", who are responsible for the delivery (cf. ll. 34–40)*
– *success of "Lieferrad DA":*
  - *in high demand (among bigger and smaller retailers); sustainability is an important value for many businesses (cf. ll. 19–23)*
  - *peak times around holidays (cf. ll. 28–31)*
  - *very employee-friendly: students are paid quite well and can gain experience in their field of business (e. g. logistics) (cf. ll. 43–50)*
– *future outlook:*
  - *new subsidies in sight (cf. ll. 51/52)*
  - *so far, the delivery service does not generate money, but new and profitable business models are planned (cf. ll. 52–56)*
  - *hope to gain new clients (cf. ll. 58–60)*
  - *expansion to other cities (cf. ll. 60/61)*

A green idea with a bright future

headline

Sustainable entrepreneurship combines protecting the environment with supporting local business, paying fair salaries and still being profitable. This is what "Lieferrad DA", a bike delivery service founded in Darmstadt, a town near Frankfurt, is all about.

introductory
paragraph

Inspired by the Corona pandemic and with the help of a government grant, three university professors working in the fields of business, logistics and applied sciences set up the company in the summer of 2020 and started delivering all sorts of goods to people's doorsteps. From the start, they advertised on social media and made use of their good relationships with the town's administration as well as with local businesses to succeed. Customers can directly order from the participating retailers. These are in touch with "Lieferrad DA" who then handle the rest of the delivery process.

characteristics of
the project

The service is in high demand with both big and small businesses using it. Particularly during peak times, such as Christmas or other holidays, the students, who make up most of the workforce, deliver several hundreds of parcels per week. Still, working conditions at "Lieferrad DA" are better than with most other delivery services. The employees are not only paid university's standard hourly wages, but are also given the chance to work behind the scenes and incorporate their work experience into their academic studies and future careers.

success of
"Lieferrad DA"

So far, the company's services are free of charge. For the future, profitable business models are planned although new subsidies are also in sight. With a hopefully growing client base and a planned expansion to other cities, the project will continue to set a good example of sustainable entrepreneurship.   *(275 words)*

future outlook

Um Ihnen die Prüfungsaufgaben 2024 schnellstmöglich zur Verfügung stellen zu können, bringen wir sie in digitaler Form heraus.

Sobald die Original-Prüfungsaufgaben 2024 freigegeben sind, können sie als PDF auf der Plattform **MySTARK** heruntergeladen werden. Ihren persönlichen Zugangscode finden Sie auf der Umschlaginnenseite, vorne im Buch.

Aktuelle Prüfung

www.stark-verlag.de/mystark